BY VADIM PETROV, IGOR LYSENKO, AND GEORGY EGOROV

With Never-Before-Published Personal Reminiscences by the Family of Vasily Filatov

Translated from the Russian by Marian Schwartz and Antonina W. Bouis

THE ESCAPE OF ALEXEI

son of Tsar Nicholas II

What Happened the Night the Romanov Family Was Executed

HARRY N. ABRAMS, INC., PUBLISHERS

Editor, English-language edition: Ellen Nidy
Designer, English-language edition: Ana Rogers

PAGE 2: The family of Nicholas II, 1913. Left to right: Grand Duchesses Olga and Marie, Tsar Nicholas II, Tsarina Alexandra Fyodorovna, Grand Duchess Anastasia, Tsarevich Alexei, and Grand Duchess Tatiana.
PAGE 3: Tsarevich Alexei with Tsarina Alexandra Fyodorovna.

Library of Congress Cataloging-in-Publication Data

Petrov, Vadim
The escape of Alexei, son of Tsar Nicholas II : what happened the night the Romanov family was executed / by Vadim Petrov, Igor Lysenko, and Georgy Egorov ; with personal reminiscences by the family of Vasily Filatov ; translated from the Russian by Marian Schwartz and Antonina W. Bouis
p. cm.
ISBN 0-8109-3277-6
1. Aleksei Nikolaevich, Czarevitch, son of Nicholas II, Emperor of Russia, 1904–1918. 2. Filatov, Vasily Ksenofontovich, 1904?–1988. 3. Princes—Russia—Biography. 4. Pretenders to the throne—Russia. 5. Nicholas II, Emperor of Russia, 1868–1918—Assassination. 6. Nicholas II, Emperor of Russia, 1868–1918—Family. 7. Romanov, House of. 8. Russia—Kings and rulers—Biography. 9. Russia—History—Nicholas II, 1894–1917. I. Lysenko, Igor. II. Egorov, Georgy. III. Title.
DK254.A496P48 1998
947.08'3'092—dc21 98-34122
[B]

Published in 1998 by Harry N. Abrams, Incorporated, New York

Printed and bound in the United States of America

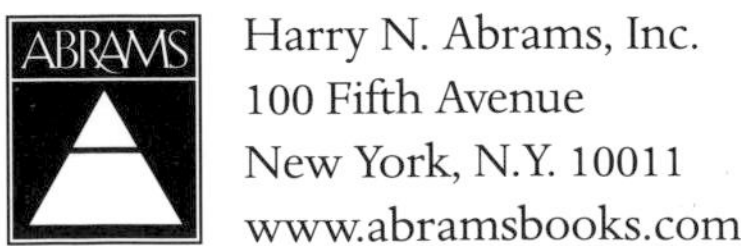

Harry N. Abrams, Inc.
100 Fifth Avenue
New York, N.Y. 10011
www.abramsbooks.com

Contents

The suppression of the bourgeois state by the proletarian state
is impossible without a violent revolution.

Vladimir Ilich Lenin

I cannot forecast to you the action of Russia.
It is a riddle wrapped in a mystery inside an enigma.

Sir Winston Spencer Churchill

The old-style Julian calendar was in use in Russia until February 1918. The dates used in this book follow the Julian calendar until February 1918 and from this date onward follow the Gregorian calendar used in the West. In the twentieth century the Julian calendar ran twelve days behind the Gregorian calendar.

Hammerfest
Vardo
Varanger Fd
Alexandro
Lofoden Is
Tromsö
LAPLAND
Kola
Peninsu
NORWAY
Narvik
R. Tornea
Bodö
Tornea
Lulea
White
Sea
Uleaborg
SWEDEN
Umea
Gulf of Bothnia
FINLAND
Onega
Trondhjem
Nikolaistadt
Lake
Ladoga
Lake
Onega
Gefle
Abo
Helsingfors
Bergen
Christiania
PETROGRAD
Gulf of Finland
Orkney Is
Stockholm
Revel
Stavanger
The Naze
Skager Rak
Kattegat
Gothenburg
Pskoff
Aberdeen
North
Riga
Tver
Edinburgh
DENMARK
Copenhagen
Baltic Sea
Libau
RU
Dvinsk
R. Dwina
MOSCOW
Sea
Malmö
Vilna
Vitebsk
Heligoland
Kiel
Hamburg
Königsberg
GERMANY
Danzig
Minsk
Tula
Bremen
Orel
HOLLAND
Hague
Berlin
Warsaw
Bobruisk
Calais
Brussels
R. Vistula
Kha
Cologne
Dresden
Channel
Lille
R. Rhine
Kief
Carpathian Mts
Lemberg
R. Dnieper
Yekaterinos
Paris
R. Seine
AUSTRIA
Vienna
R. Dniester
Munich
ODESSA
Rosto
Berne
Budapest
FRANCE
SWITZ
HUNGARY
RUMANIA
Azof
Sea
Milan
Trieste
Danube
Venice
Crimea
Bucharest
Belgrade
Sebastopol
Marseilles
Genoa
ITALY
Adriatic Sea
Black Sea
SERBIA
Sofia
R. Ebro
BULGARIA
Constantinople
Corsica
Salonica
TURKEY
Barcelona
Rome
Scutari
Trebizond
Sardinia
GREECE
Aegean
Brussa
Angora
Naples
Brindisi
MEDIT
Palermo
Ionian
Sea
ASIA MINOR
Smyrna
Konia

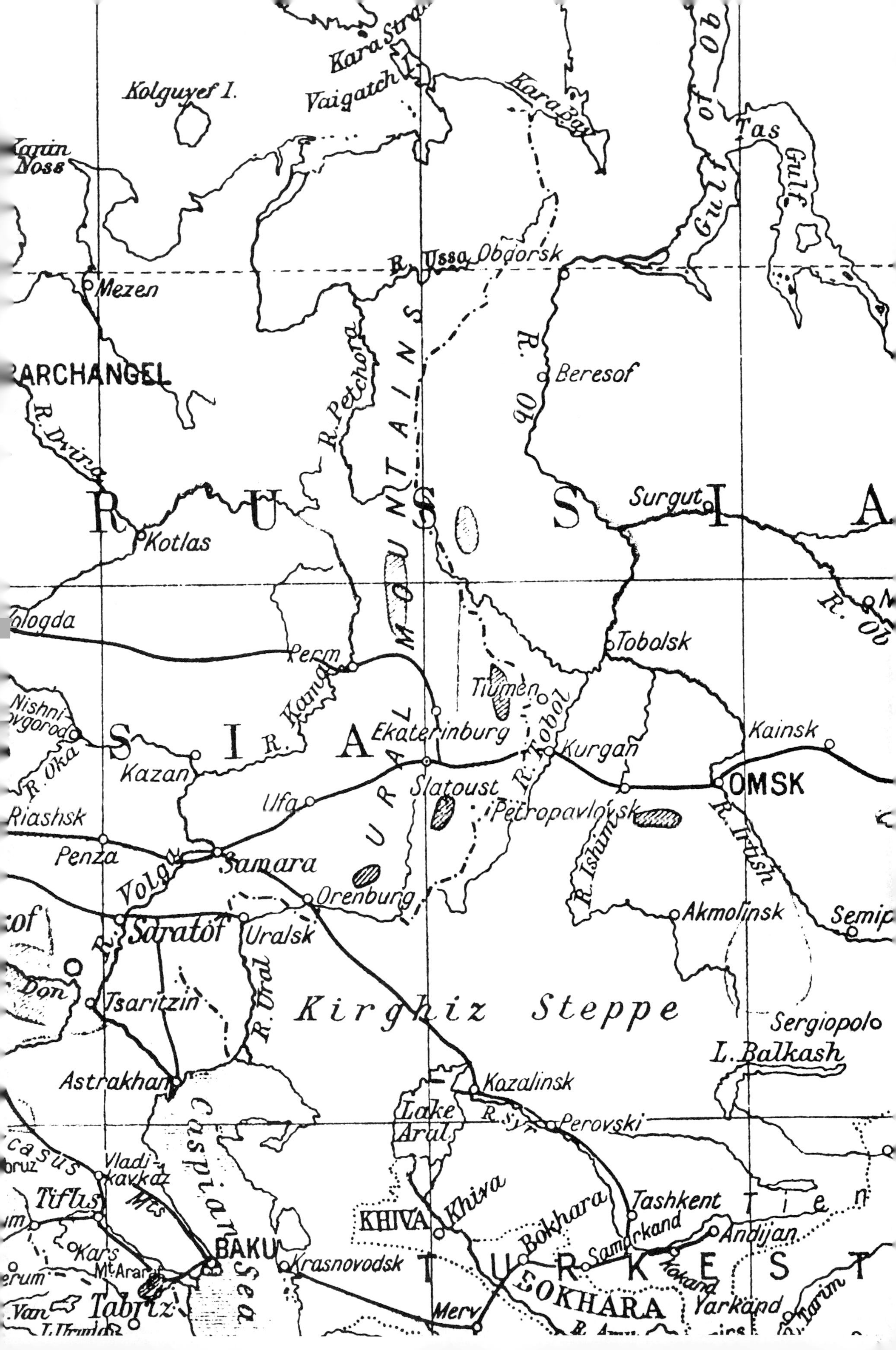

Kara Strait
Kolguyef I.
Vaigatch I.
Kara Bay
Gulf of Ob
Tas Gulf
Kanin Noss
R. Ussa
Obdorsk
Mezen
ARCHANGEL
R. Petchora
R. Ob
Beresof
R. Dvina
R U S S I A
Surgut
Kotlas
URAL MOUNTAINS
Vologda
R. Ob
Perm
Tobolsk
Tiumen
R. Kama
Nishni-Novgorod
Ekaterinburg
R. Tobol
Kainsk
S I A
Kurgan
R. Oka
Kazan
R.
Slatoust
OMSK
Ufa
Riashsk
Petropavlovsk
R. Ishim
R. Irtish
Penza
Samara
R. Volga
Orenburg
Akmolinsk
Saratof
Uralsk
Semip
R.
Don
R. Ural
Tsaritzin
Kirghiz Steppe
Sergiopolo
L. Balkash
Astrakhan
Kazalinsk
Caspian Sea
Lake Aral
R. Syr
Perovski
Vladi-kavkaz
Caucasus
Tiflis
Khiva
KHIVA
Tashkent
Bokhara
Samarkand
Andijan
Kars
BAKU
Krasnovodsk
T U R K E S T
Kokand
Mt. Ararat
Erzerum
Tabriz
BOKHARA
Yarkand
Van
Merv
Tarim
R. Amu

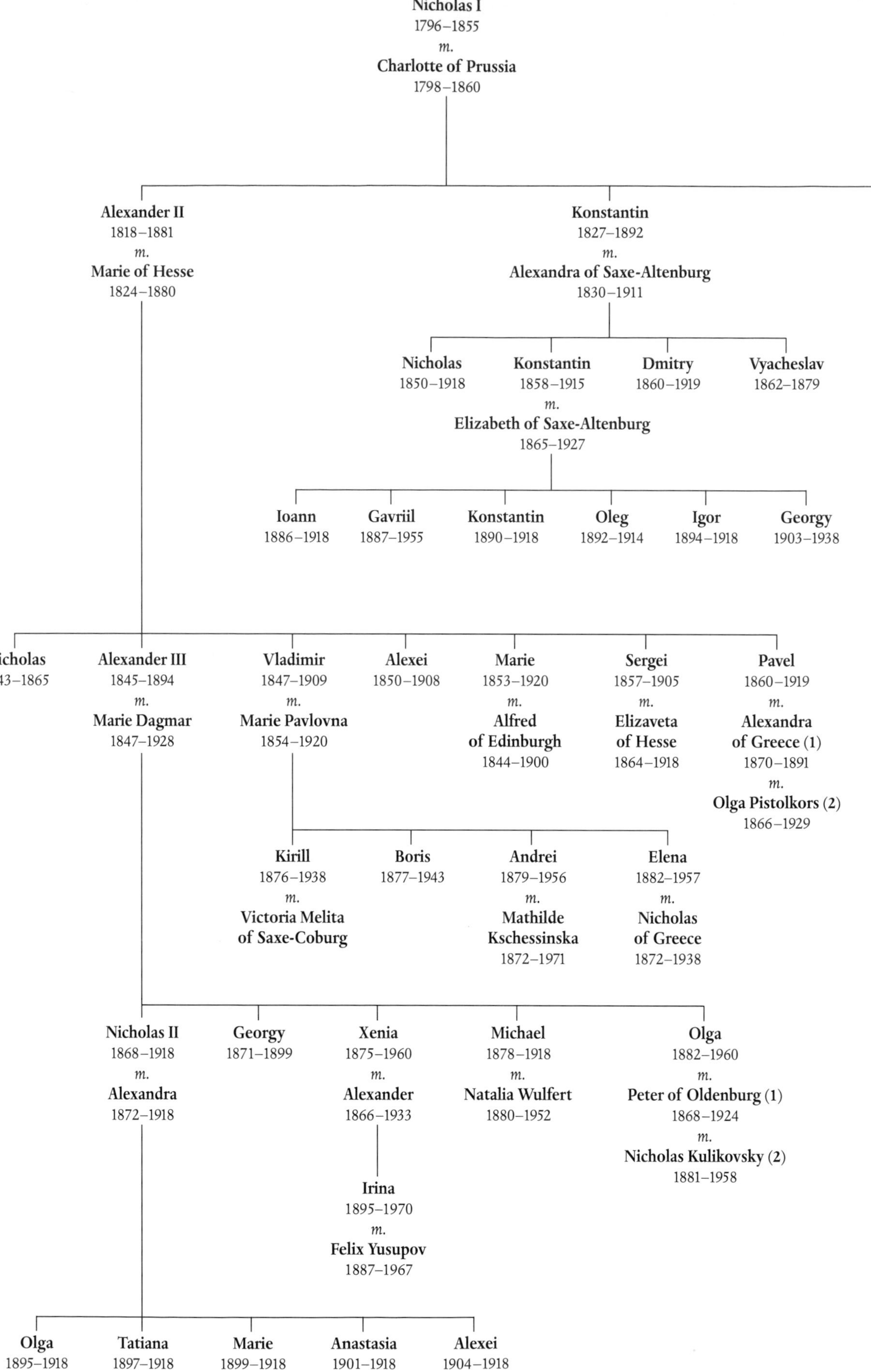
Nicholas I
1796–1855
m.
Charlotte of Prussia
1798–1860
Alexander II
1818–1881
m.
Marie of Hesse
1824–1880
Konstantin
1827–1892
m.
Alexandra of Saxe-Altenburg
1830–1911
Nicholas
1850–1918
Konstantin
1858–1915
m.
Elizabeth of Saxe-Altenburg
1865–1927
Dmitry
1860–1919
Vyacheslav
1862–1879
Ioann
1886–1918
Gavriil
1887–1955
Konstantin
1890–1918
Oleg
1892–1914
Igor
1894–1918
Georgy
1903–1938
Nicholas
1843–1865
Alexander III
1845–1894
m.
Marie Dagmar
1847–1928
Vladimir
1847–1909
m.
Marie Pavlovna
1854–1920
Alexei
1850–1908
Marie
1853–1920
m.
Alfred
of Edinburgh
1844–1900
Sergei
1857–1905
m.
Elizaveta
of Hesse
1864–1918
Pavel
1860–1919
m.
Alexandra
of Greece (1)
1870–1891
m.
Olga Pistolkors (2)
1866–1929
Kirill
1876–1938
m.
Victoria Melita
of Saxe-Coburg
Boris
1877–1943
Andrei
1879–1956
m.
Mathilde
Kschessinska
1872–1971
Elena
1882–1957
m.
Nicholas
of Greece
1872–1938
Nicholas II
1868–1918
m.
Alexandra
1872–1918
Georgy
1871–1899
Xenia
1875–1960
m.
Alexander
1866–1933
Irina
1895–1970
m.
Felix Yusupov
1887–1967
Michael
1878–1918
m.
Natalia Wulfert
1880–1952
Olga
1882–1960
m.
Peter of Oldenburg (1)
1868–1924
m.
Nicholas Kulikovsky (2)
1881–1958
Olga
1895–1918
Tatiana
1897–1918
Marie
1899–1918
Anastasia
1901–1918
Alexei
1904–1918

Romanov Family Tree

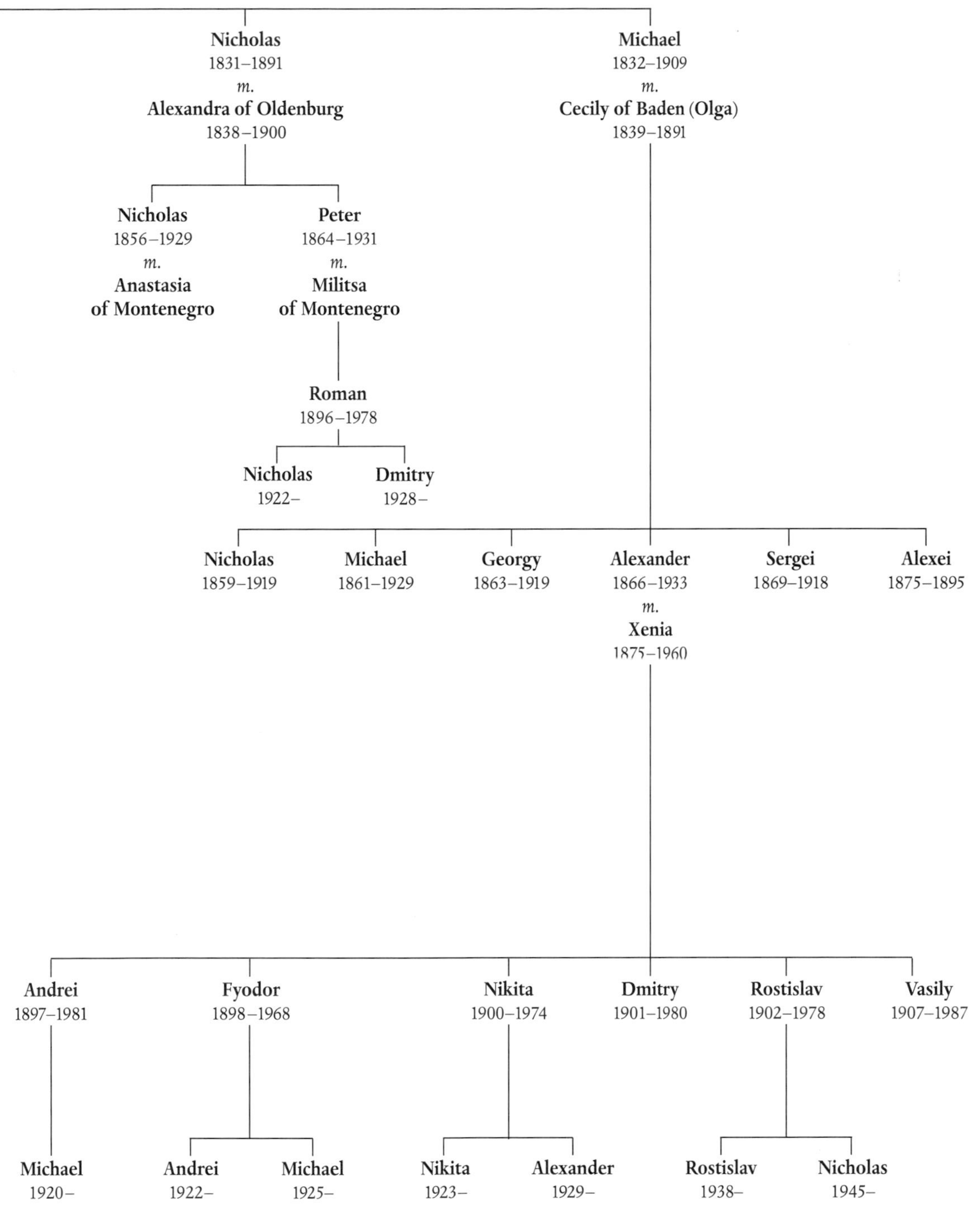

from the Russian publisher

In 1988, in a district center outside Astrakhan, a village geography teacher by the name of Vasily Ksenofontovich Filatov died. Shortly before his death, he began telling his wife and children—a son and three daughters—the fantastic story of his life. From his stories they learned that Vasily Filatov was not his real name, that in reality he was Alexei Romanov, son of Nicholas Romanov, the last Russian tsar, and that he had been rescued by soldiers when the rest of his family was executed in 1918. At the time Vasily told his story, the remains of the tsar's family had not yet been discovered on the old Koptyaki Road on the outskirts of Ekaterinburg. The fact of the tragedy had not become a hot topic among historians and had not yet attracted worldwide attention. When all that did happen, the astonished members of his family were convinced that many of the stories told by Vasily Filatov, down to trivial details, coincided with facts that had just become known. The eightieth anniversary of the execution served as impetus for identifying the Ekaterinburg remains and for new research utilizing modern methods.

As Nikolai Alexeyevich Sokolov, Special Judicial Investigator for the Whites under Admiral Alexander Kolchak, put it from the very beginning, the case of the execution of the tsar's family had "the peculiarity of not having what one almost always does have in murder cases and what most often serves to prove the actual fact of murder: corpses. As a result, in this case, the very fact that there was a murder had to be verified by alternate routes."[1] The lack of objective proof has inevitably given rise to various versions of the story.

During the Soviet period, the commonly accepted official version of the execution was based on the myth that the decision to execute the tsar's family "was taken consciously, in recognition of the objective situation at the time, and carried out with purely proletarian, steely decisiveness."[2] Hence the misleading idea that the execution had been thoroughly thought out and precisely organized. The official version was that the victims' bodies were burned, so it was inconceivable that a member of the tsar's family could have survived and reached freedom.

Today we know that the decision was made and the execution readied and implemented in less than three days and that the "fiery revolutionaries" were the same uneducated young adventurers who executed Grand Duke Michael Alexandrovich Romanov (Nicholas II's brother), Archbishop Hermogen of Tobolsk, and many others on their own authority, without waiting for orders from Moscow. For the rest of their lives, the revolutionaries who survived fought each other for the right to be considered the principal murderer and to enjoy the advantages awarded to such a figure. But that was later. At the time of the execution, in 1918, when the Whites were approaching the city and no one knew which side would win, when the Bolsheviks were not yet the only ruling party and the revolution was still a coup, the matter of sorting out who had what power still lay ahead. At the time, killing "God's Anointed" and his children might have seemed a terrifying task, and it is very likely that the executioners may not have been of one mind. Among them there could easily have been men who sympathized with the victims and attempted to rescue some of them.

As soon as one becomes acquainted with the depositions of the participants in the execution, the legend of the meticulous organization of the execution and burial crumbles. They all talk about the chaotic shooting and about the bungling and disorganization during the burial, but they differ on the details. One gets the impression that they agreed on the outline of the story but that each man filled in the gaps with details of his own. This is what they would have had to do if a member of the Romanov family had survived the execution and was unaccounted for during the burial. An attempt to reconstruct the execution—chaotic firing in a smoke-filled room—leads to the conclusion that such an outcome was entirely possible. And if this was the case, then it unquestionably had to be concealed and kept secret all their lives.

When one looks at the sources from this point of view, discrepancies in the depositions of the executioners become obvious. For example, in their reminiscences of the execution and burial, they all talk about the "corsets" or "brassieres" with diamonds sewn into them that were discovered on the victims' bodies. Only in Yurovsky's depositions is it specifically stated that only three of the children—Tatiana, Olga, and Anastasia—were wearing "some kind of special corsets." Of course, these were not ordinary corsets but special corsets made by Alexandra herself, or on her orders.

The purpose is clear. She could hardly have supposed they would shoot her children, but she did think the precious jewels would provide for her children's support if the family were split up. So, Marie should have been wearing one of the corsets as well. Not only that, but it would seem perfectly natural for the mother to be concerned above all about her only son, her youngest child, who was ill and thus the most helpless of all. Not one statement contains any testimony about precious jewels found on Alexei's body. Or about an amulet holding Rasputin's portrait and the text of a prayer, which was discovered "around the neck of each of the young ladies." The tsarevich wore one just like it. Nonetheless, there is not a word about it. Either for unexplained reasons they didn't undress the body of Alexei or . . . he wasn't there. Note that in 1998, a government commission established that the remains of Alexei and Marie were missing from the burial site.

What if they were saved after all? Could they have survived, and what would their fate have been if they had? The simplest way to deal with this question is the way it was dealt with by officials in the St. Petersburg Central District Registrar's Office in 1997: they issued a certificate (to whom we don't know) stating that Alexei and Marie Romanov died in 1918. The authors of this book take a different view. They cite their own, absolutely independent investigation. The originality of the approach is explained by the professions of the authors, which are rather unusual for a case involving historical research.

One of them, Vadim Vadimovich Petrov, is a candidate of medical sciences whose dissertation was on optimizing the establishment of identity of unidentified bodies. A forensic medical expert, he participated in several of the forensic analyses included in this book; he also comments on the forensic analyses done by others. Igor Vladimirovich Lysenko is a nuclear physicist and a graduate from the Theological Academy. He worked with Vasily Filatov and the Commission for the Canonization of Saints of the Holy Synod of the Russian Orthodox Church. Georgy Borisovich Egorov is a professor with a Ph.D. in engineering, a systems analyst in various technical and humanitarian spheres, and an expert on the chemistry of high temperatures (including the combustion of powders) and on measurement precision and content. A prize-winning skier, he has competed in international skiing competitions for the disabled in Ekaterinburg, where he runs a ski center for disabled children. Knowledgeable with sports prostheses and nonconventional medicine, Egorov is well qualified to answer the question of how the tsarevich, an adolescent suffering from hemophilia, may have survived the execution to live another seventy years. The authors believe that he could have done so if someone had helped him—especially someone who had mastered the methods of nonconventional medicine and who knew the healing properties of local plants (one is instantly reminded that Rasputin, who treated Alexei with herbs and nonconventional medicine during his childhood, was from the area around Ekaterinburg).

One of the documents in this book is a statement from the Center for the Treatment of Hemophilia confirming that many hemophiliacs live long lives. According to the center, hemophiliacs can have children, but they usually do so at an older age. Vasily Filatov had his first child, Oleg Vasilievich Filatov, in 1953, when he was forty-nine years old. Oleg Filatov and one of his sisters have blond hair, which can also be a consequence of hemophilia in one of the parents. According to his wife's testimony, Vasily Filatov never went to the doctor, but his draft card indicated that he was permanently discharged from military service under the article that includes diseases of the blood. Scientific analysis of the medical information found in Vasily Filatov's archives is not yet complete. One of the diagnoses there has been erased and then removed with acid.

That the authors are scientists determines the unusual genre of this book: it takes a historical-forensic approach. The authors are not professional historians; their approach to historical facts and archival sources is not bound by persistent official stereotypes. They examine even well-known historical facts from new angles. In this book they come to the conclusion that, after abdicating, Nicholas II and his family represented no threat to the new government. The Romanov family could have been used more advantageously, like a trump card in the game of politics. It made no sense to execute them mindlessly and then fabricate legends about the threat of the "banner of monarchy" to the armed forces of a Siberian republic run by a right-wing Socialist Revolutionary government.

The authors reconstruct a detailed picture of the chaotic execution in the cellar of the Ipatiev house, and with detailed maps of Ekaterinburg and its surroundings, they establish the probable route of the truck that transported the bodies to the burial site. They analyze the poor condition of the rural Koptyaki Road, which the truck traveled on, and the places along the way where the truck stopped. As a result, the authors argue the likelihood that some of the people loaded onto that improvised hearse were not dead and may have escaped from the truck on the way to the burial site. Then, after painstakingly reconstructing the execution and burial, the authors prove that it would have been impossible to burn the corpses.

After reaching this conclusion, the authors study the story of Vasily Filatov's life, revealing the discrepancies in his official biography. Registered on his birth certificate as a shoemaker's son who received a far from brilliant education and worked as a geography teacher in a village school all his life, Filatov nonetheless knew several European languages, played several musical instruments, and taught his children music according to the numerical method—the same method by which the children of

Tsar Nicholas II were taught music. While walking through the halls of the tsar's summer home, Tsarskoe Selo, Vasily Filatov suddenly said: "All of this here has changed, even the handle on this door was different."

History has known quite a few pretenders, but it is highly unlikely that an entire family would lie about this and painstakingly fabricate a legend.

We have taken an interest in Oleg Filatov's story about his father's life and are stunned by the resemblance between Vasily Filatov's four children and many representatives of the Romanov dynasty. The book's authors, with the help of other criminologists, legal scholars, and medical experts, have studied the documents presented by the Filatovs and conducted comparative scientific analysis on the handwriting samples, photographic portraits, and medical depositions. The results of their initial analysis are so convincing that there is no doubt of the need to continue the research with the help of an even broader group of scientists.

By publishing this book, regardless of whether the reader shares the authors' conclusions or whether the version they are setting forth will be confirmed, the publisher is confident of the scientific, moral, and political relevance of the problem under examination. We feel we must use every opportunity to clarify in as much detail as possible the circumstances and consequences surrounding the Ekaterinburg tragedy.

Tsarevich Alexei, 1916.

Emperor Alexander III with his family.

OPPOSITE: **Tsarevich Nicholas Alexandrovich in an army infantry uniform, 1887.**

the funeral, greeted the new year of 1917 with his family, and on February 22 left to return to Headquarters.

During this time there was increasing unrest in the capital over the shortage of bread, and on February 23 nearly 100,000 workers went on strike. On February 24, students joined the workers, and the number of strikers ballooned to 200,000. The next day a general strike began, and unrest infiltrated the heart of the city. Although the movement had developed spontaneously, it quickly became political. Demonstrations were held at the factories and on Znamenskaya Square in front of Nikolaevsky Station, with people shouting "Down with the war!" and "Down with autocracy!"

The tsar arrived at Headquarters on the evening of February 23 and did not receive news of the strikes and demonstrations in Petrograd until February 25. Although his Council of Ministers did not attach too much significance to the demonstrations, Nicholas II immediately telegraphed the commander of the Petrograd Military District, General Sergei Semyonovich Khabalov: "I hereby enjoin you to stop the disorders in the capital tomorrow. They cannot be allowed during this difficult time of war against Germany and Austria."[2]

On February 26, General Khabalov and Alexander Dmitrievich Protopopov, the minister of internal affairs, carried out the imperial injunction. The police took up positions on bell towers, fire towers, attics, and the roofs of tall buildings and fired on the demonstrators. Machine guns fired from the bridges and all along Nevsky Prospekt, and mounted cavalry attacked the demonstrators. That evening, an event occurred that seemed to justify an open attack by the police: more than fifteen hundred soldiers from the Fourth Company of the Reserve Battalion of the Pavlovsky Regiment emerged from their barracks and suddenly opened fire on a detachment of mounted policemen.

On February 27, a rebellious crowd took the main arsenal by storm. One after another, the garrison's military units crossed over to the side of the insurgents. The soldiers of the Volynsky Regiment brought the Litovsky, Preobrazhensky, and Moskovsky Regiments out on the street to join the rebellion. The next morning, the entire city was in the hands of the insurrection. Mikhail Vladimirovich Rodzianko, chairman of the State Duma, informed Nicholas at Headquarters: "Situation grave. Anarchy in the capital. Government paralyzed. Transportation, food, and fuel supplies completely disrupted. Scattered shooting in the streets . . . immediate measures must be taken, for tomorrow will be too late. The decisive hour has come for the fate of the Homeland and the dynasty."[3]

At the news of the uprising of the Petrograd garrison, Nicholas II sent a new military district commander, General Ivanov, to Petrograd with the elite St. George Battalion, which numbered seven hundred men, as well as a machine-gun squad, with an order to "institute order in the capital and its environs."[4] At the same time, Grand Duke Michael Alexandrovich telephoned the chief of staff, Supreme Commander Adjutant General Mikhail Vasilievich Alexeyev, asking him to inform the tsar that in order to reinstate peace he would have to dismiss the Council of Ministers and appoint a new premier, for which capacity he was recommending Prince Vladimir Nikolaevich Lvov. Nicholas II replied only that he had sent troops to Petrograd and that he would make further decisions upon his arrival at Tsarskoe Selo. However, he did not make it that far.

On February 28, the revolutionary movement spilled over into the surrounding areas of the capital. In Tsarskoe Selo, the units guarding the Alexander Palace "declared their neutrality" and thus abandoned the imperial family. In Kronstadt, a naval bastion in the Gulf of Finland, power passed into the hands of the revolutionaries, and the insurgent sailors killed Admiral Viren, their commanding officer, and numerous other officers.

Having given instructions to send the most reliable, loyal units from the fronts to Petrograd to quell the insurgency, the tsar himself decided to depart Headquarters for Tsarskoe Selo to be with his family. The imperial train left Mogilev following a route through Orsha, Vyazma, and Likhoslavl. Nicholas expected to arrive at Tsarskoe Selo on March 1 at three-thirty in the afternoon, but en route, at Malaya Vishera Station, it was discovered that the next large station, Lyuban, had already been occupied by revolutionary troops and that further passage by the imperial train would be dangerous. Subsequently, Nicholas ordered the train to proceed via Pskov to the headquarters of General Nikolai Vladimirovich Ruzsky, commander of the northern front.

Many memoirists and historians have criticized this decision, as well as Nicholas's decision to depart from Headquarters in the first place. John Hanbury-Williams, former head of the British mission in Mogilev, assessed the tsar's departure from Mogilev as his "first imprudent and almost insane step toward his own doom and his family's."[5] The historian Viktor Alexandrov, a contemporary of these events, believed that as long as Nicholas II was in the middle of his army, which numbered many millions of men, he was personally invulnerable and possessed the essential means of governing, but that "by leaving his most secure refuge, he simply set off on a senseless adventure."[6] Many other contemporaries also considered Nicholas's departure from Mogilev foolhardy. We believe that the situation did not yet seem threatening to Nicholas and that he was leaving to join his family of his own free will.

However, let us return to the events of the last night of February 1917. War Minister Mikhail Alexeyevich Belyaev in Petrograd reported to Headquarters that General Khabalov had been put under arrest. Mass demonstrations were beginning in Moscow as well. On March 1, the Moscow garrison went over to the side of the insurgents, and the commanding general, Mrozovsky, was arrested. The same scenario was taking place in the cities of Kharkov, Nizhny Novgorod, and Tver. Admiral Alexander Vasilievich Kolchak, the commander of the Black Sea fleet, after receiving information on the events in Petrograd, ordered the commandant of Sevastopol Fortress to cut postal and telegraph communications between the Crimean peninsula and Russia. Worried that they would lose control of their troops, the commanders-in-chief on other fronts issued similar orders.

In Petrograd, the Provisional Committee of the State Duma issued an appeal:

> A provisional committee of the State Duma, considering the difficult conditions of domestic collapse provoked by measures of the old government, finds itself forced to take the restoration of state and public order into its own hands. Conscious of the full responsibility of the decision it has taken, the committee expresses confidence that the population and the army will help it in its difficult task of creating a new government that corresponds to the desires of the population and that can enjoy its trust.
>
> Chairman of the State Duma, Mikhail Rodzianko.[7]

On March 1, General Ivanov arrived at Tsarskoe Selo from Mogilev to meet the troops that he was going to take to Petrograd to restore order—only to find that the 68th Infantry Regiment in Luga and the 67th Tarutinsky Regiment at Alexandrovskaya Station had gone over the side of the insurgents. Colonels Domanevsky and Tille delivered the following report to him from the chief of the general staff, Mikhail Ilich Zankevich:

> All reserve units quartered in the capital have gradually gone over to the side of the Provisional Government composed of members of the State Duma. Since twelve o'clock in the afternoon on February 28, the legitimate military authorities have not had a single unit at their disposal, and the insurgent population has ceased its fighting. The officers of the units that refused to obey orders set out for the Duma with the aim of retaking power. Lower ranks showed up there as well. The Provisional Government put the officers back in their places, and order began to be instituted in the units. However, the reserve battalions supported order only within the framework of the provisional government and not the permanent government. They cannot be relied upon in the fight against the revolution. Some of the police have been removed, and some have hidden. A few ministers have been arrested. The ministries, including the war ministry, could continue their work only once they had obtained the consent of the Provisional Government, i.e., by essentially recognizing it. The same situation is being played out in the outlying garrisons. It is difficult to count on instituting order by force or on an armed struggle with the insurgents and the Provisional Government. This would require many troops, and, moreover, the troops that are newly arrived have fallen on hard conditions with respect to their quarters and food. All the surrounding areas of Petrograd and even the entire Petrograd District are crammed with reservists and refugees. We must obtain supplies from deep in Russia, but proper supplies cannot be provided without the knowledge of the Provisional Government. Given these conditions, a procedure for suppressing the uprising so that it reflects as well as possible on the course of the war is probably attainable only by agreement with the Provisional Government rather than by means of armed struggle. . . . At the present moment, an armed struggle would make a bad situation more complicated and worse. Each hour is precious. Order and a normal course can be restored most easily by way of agreement with the Provisional Government.[8]

Grand Duke Kirill Vladimirovich.

General Ivanov had no choice but to turn back to Mogilev. The tsar's attempt to crush the revolution by force had ended in failure.

Meanwhile, under the command of Grand Duke Kirill Vladimirovich, the tsar's cousin, the Marine of the Guard, the most loyal and elite troops of the Alexander Palace, had marched to the Taurides Palace to declare their allegiance to the Duma. At the Taurides Palace, two revolutionary organs had formed under one roof in a single day: the Provisional Committee of the State Duma and the Executive Committee of the Petrograd Soviet of Workers Deputies. Vladimir Nikolaevich Voeikov, the Commandant of the Court of Nicholas II, writes in his memoirs:

> The sailors in the Marine of the Guard, which at that time formed part of the security troops [for the imperial residence], began to evaporate. In the end, only officers remained, and the deserting sailors headed off to Petrograd to their barracks, where on the morning of March 2 they held a meeting to which they invited their commander, who at that time was Grand Duke Kirill Vladimirovich.
>
> The grand duke explained to the sailors the import of the events taking place. The result of his explanation was not the return of the deserting sailors to fulfill their duty but a decision to replace their highly esteemed banner with a red rag, under which the Marine of the Guard followed their commander into the State Duma.
>
> Grand Duke Kirill Vladimirovich, with his tsarist monogram on his epaulettes and a red ribbon on his shoulders, appeared on March 1, at four-fifteen in the afternoon, at the State Duma, where he reported to Duma Chairman M. V. Rodzianko: "I have the honor of appearing before Your Excellency. I am at your disposal, as is the entire nation. I wish Russia only good." Then he stated that the Marine of the Guard was at the complete disposal of the State Duma. . . . In reply, M. V. Rodzianko expressed confidence that the Marine of the Guard would help them deal with their enemy (but he didn't explain which one).
>
> Inside the State Duma, the grand duke was received quite graciously, since even before his arrival at the commandant's office in the Taurides Palace it was generally known that he had sent notes to the heads of the units of the Tsarskoe Selo garrison announcing:
>
> "I and the Marine of the Guard entrusted to me have fully allied ourselves with the new government. I am certain that you, too, and the unit entrusted to you will also ally yourselves with us.
>
> "Commander of the Marine of the Guard, His Highness, Rear Admiral Kirill."[9]

Of course, Grand Duke Kirill Vladimirovich describes this event somewhat differently:

> One of my battalions was responsible for the security of the imperial family at Tsarskoe Selo, but the situation in the capital had become extremely dangerous, and I ordered them to return to the capital. These were nearly the only loyal troops whom one could trust to restore order if the situation continued to deteriorate. . . .
>
> One time a very agitated officer from the Marine of the Guard approached me and reported that my sailors had locked up the officers and that serious disruptions were about to break out in the barracks. I rushed over there immediately to speak with the sailors. They were in a truculent mood, and although I was able to restore calm, it was all most unpleasant. I was convinced, however, that despite the revolution and anarchy, my men remained loyal to me. They themselves volunteered to take turns guarding me and my family, and despite the general chaos, no one ever inflicted any unpleasantness on us. . . .
>
> In the last days of February, anarchy had reached such heights in the capital that the government [Provisional] appealed to the soldiers and commanders, suggesting that they come to the Duma and thus demonstrate their loyalty. . . . The government's instruction put me in a decidedly awkward position. Since I commanded the Marine of the Guard, the government's order . . . applied to my subordinates and . . . affected me personally as commander. I had to decide whether to obey the government order and bring my sailors to the Duma or withdraw, casting them on the tyranny of fate in the whirlpool of revolution. . . . The only thing that concerned me was how, by what means, even at the price of my own honor, to restore order in the capital and do everything in my power to allow the Sovereign to return to the capital. . . .
>
> With these thoughts in mind, I set out for the barracks of the Marine of the Guard, still hoping that I would not be forced to drink that bitter cup. When I arrived, though, it turned out that I did not need to make any choice at all; the men themselves wanted to go to the Duma.
>
> And so I set out for the Duma at the head of a battalion from the Marine of the Guard. En route we were fired upon by foot soldiers so I transferred to an automobile.
>
> It was Babel in the Duma. Soldiers in unbuttoned tunics and caps pushed back on their heads were trying to outshout one another. Deputies were hoarse from screaming. Something unimaginable had come to pass. . . . Soldiers were driving the officers out onto the stairs with the butts of their rifles and a rain of curses. I knew many of the officers well. . . . In this grievous atmosphere I spent the remainder of the day guarded by my own sailors. Late that night a student from the Institute of Mines stopped by my room to tell me a car was waiting and I could go.[10]

On the evening of March 1, the imperial train arrived at Pskov Station. The commander-in-chief of the northern front, Adjutant General Ruzsky, handed Nicholas II a telegram from the chief of staff, Supreme

Commander Adjutant General Alexeyev, requesting in the name of Rodzianko that he consent to the formation of a government responsible not to the emperor but to the State Duma. A few hours later, Nicholas II agreed to the formation of a new government, while retaining for the emperor responsibility for the ministers of war, the navy, and foreign affairs.

One circumstance played a fateful role in further events. It seems that Headquarters received telegrams containing disinformation to the effect that total calm had ensued in the capital and that the troops had joined the Provisional Government as a body. There was no mention that a revolution was in progress calling for the overthrow of Nicholas II, not merely limiting his power.[11]

That same night, Ruzsky contacted Duma Chairman Rodzianko by telephone to convey the imperial injunction for the new government, which at this point sounded like bitter irony. This was already not going to be enough. "Hatred for the dynasty has reached such extremes," Rodzianko replied, "that ominous demands are being heard for abdication in favor of his son under a regency of Michael Alexandrovich."[12] Although by now even that was not going to be enough.

General Ruzsky informed Alexeyev at Headquarters about this conversation, and Alexeyev in turn circulated a telegram to all the commanders at the fronts, conveying what Rodzianko had said about the need for the sovereign to abdicate. Alexeyev personally added that "the situation evidently allows for no other solution."[13] Alexeyev then conveyed the replies from the front commanders to Ruzsky.

Alexeyev's telegram to the commanders at the front:

> His Highness is in Pskov, where he has given his consent to publishing a proclamation, granting the desire to institute a ministry responsible to the chambers and instructing the State Duma chairman to form a cabinet. When the commander-in-chief of the Northern Front informed the State Duma chairman of this decision, the latter in a conversation at the state apparatus at three-thirty on March 2 replied that the appearance of such a proclamation might have been timely on February 27. At present, though, this act is belated because one of the most terrible of all revolutions has begun. The masses are nearly impossible to restrain, and the troops are demoralized. For the time being they still believe the State Duma chairman, but he fears that it is going to be impossible to contain popular passions, that now the dynastic issue has been put point-blank, and the war can be prosecuted only by meeting the demands that he abdicate the throne in favor of his son under a regency of Michael Alexandrovich.
>
> The situation evidently allows for no other resolution, and every minute of further hesitation only raises the claims since the army's existence and the operation of the railroads are for all intents and purposes in the hands of the Petrograd Provisional Government. The active army has to be saved from collapse, the war with the external foe prosecuted to the end, and Russia's independence and the dynasty's fate saved. This has to be moved to the forefront, even if it means costly concessions. If you share this opinion, then would you be so good as to telegraph with all haste our most loyal request to His Highness through the Northern Front's commander-in-chief [Ruzsky] and inform me that you have done so.

I repeat. Every minute lost could be fateful for the existence of Russia. We must have unified thinking and goals among the top chiefs of the active army and save the army from hesitation and any possible instances of betrayal of duty. The army must do everything in its power to fight the external foe, and the decision regarding domestic affairs shall free it from the temptation of taking part in the overthrow, which will come about more painlessly on a decision from above.

March 2, 1917.
Alexeyev[14]

After receiving responses to his telegram, Alexeyev dispatched the following telegram to the tsar:

To our Sovereign Emperor
I humbly present to Your Imperial Highness the following telegrams received in the name of Your Imperial Highness:

1. From Grand Duke Nicholas Nikolaevich.

"Adjutant General Alexeyev informs me of the unprecedented and fateful situation that has come about and asks me to support his opinion that a victorious conclusion to the war, so necessary for the good and future of Russia and the salvation of the dynasty, calls for taking extraordinary measures.

"As a loyal subject, I feel that the duty and spirit of my oath require me to pray in all humility to Your Imperial Highness to save Russia and your heir, knowing full well your sacred love for Russia and for him.

"Make the sign of the cross and transmit to him your legacy. There is no other solution.

"As never before in my life, with especially bitter prayer, I pray to God to strengthen and guide you.

"Adjutant General Nicholas."

2. From Adjutant General Brusilov:

"I beg you to inform the Sovereign Emperor of my most loyal request, based on my devotion and love for my homeland and the tsar's throne, that at the given moment the sole outcome that can save the situation and give us an opportunity to continue fighting our external foe, without which Russia will be lost, is to renounce the throne in favor of the sovereign heir tsarevich under a regency of Grand Duke Michael Alexandrovich. There is no other possible solution. Speed is of the utmost importance if the popular conflagration that has broken out and spread is to be put out quickly. Otherwise it will bring with it incalculable and catastrophic consequences. This act will save the very dynasty itself in the person of the lawful heir.

"Adjutant General Brusilov."

3. From Adjutant General Evert:

"Your Imperial Highness, Your Highness's chief of staff has explained to me the situation that has come about in Petrograd, Tsarskoe Selo, the Baltic Sea, and Moscow, and the result of the negotiations between Adjutant General Ruzsky and the State Duma chairman.

"Your Highness, as long as they are quelling domestic disorders, the army cannot be relied upon in its present composition. It can be restrained only in the name of Russia's salvation from inevitable enslavement by the country's most evil enemy should it prove impossible to prosecute the struggle further. I am taking all measures to see that news of the actual state of affairs in the capital does not penetrate to the army, in order to protect it from inevitable agitation. There are no means whatsoever for stopping the revolution in the capital.

"An immediate decision is necessary that can bring the disorders to a halt and preserve the army for the struggle against our enemy.

"Given the situation as it now stands, and finding no other possible solution, this boundlessly devoted and loyal subject of Your Highness begs Your Highness in the name of the salvation of our homeland and dynasty to take a decision that is in accord with the statement of the State Duma chairman, as he expressed it to Adjutant General Ruzsky, as the sole solution evidently capable of halting the revolution and saving Russia from the horrors of anarchy.

"Adjutant General Evert."

I most loyally submit these telegrams to Your Imperial Highness and implore you to take a decision without delay as the Lord God inspires you. Delay threatens Russia with ruin. For the time being the army has managed to fend off the disease that has gripped Petrograd, Moscow, Kronstadt, and other cities, but one cannot vouch for further preservation of military discipline. If the army gets involved in domestic politics, that will mean the inevitable end of the war, Russia's disgrace, and its collapse.

Your Imperial Highness, love your homeland fervently and for the sake of its integrity and independence, for the sake of achieving victory, be pleased to take a decision that can provide a peaceful and auspicious outcome from the exceedingly grave situation that has come to pass. I await your injunctions.

March 2, 1917.
Adjutant General Alexeyev[15]

There was one more telegram from General Sakharov, addressed to Ruzsky:

Adjutant General Alexeyev has conveyed to me the criminal and outrageous reply from the State Duma chairman to you regarding the Sovereign Emperor's most gracious decision to grant the country a responsible ministry, and has invited the commanders-in-chief to report to His Highness through you regarding the resolution of this issue, depending on the situation.

My ardent love for His Highness will not permit my soul to reconcile itself to the possible implementation of the vile suggestion conveyed to you by the State Duma chairman. I am certain that it was not the Russian people, who have never laid a hand on their tsar, that contemplated this evil deed but a handful of insurgents known as the State Duma, who treacherously exploited an opportune moment to carry out their criminal intentions. I am certain that the army at the front would be standing unwaveringly behind their supreme leader if they were not called upon to defend the homeland from the external foe and if they were not in the hands of those same state criminals who have seized the very fount of the army's life.

Such are the stirrings of my heart and soul. Moving on to the logic of reason, and taking into consideration the hopelessness of the situation that has come about, I, unwaveringly devoted to His Highness, sobbing, am forced to admit that, yes, the most painless solution for the country and for maintaining the possibility of fighting our external foe is the decision to meet the conditions already stated so that procrastination does not provide food for further, even more vile claims.

Jassy, March 2, 1917, General Sakharov[16]

Late that evening the commander of the Baltic fleet sent a telegram addressed to the emperor:

With immense difficulty, I am keeping the fleet and the troops in my charge in obedience. In Revel, the situation is critical, but I have not lost hope of restraining it. I am most loyally joining the petitions of the commanders-in-chief of the fronts for the immediate passage of the decision formulated by the chairman of the State Duma. If the decision is not taken in the next few hours, there will be a catastrophe entailing innumerable calamities for our homeland.

March 2, 1917, No. 260. Vice Admiral Nepenin[17]

The commander of the Black Sea fleet, Admiral Kolchak, refrained from sending a personal telegram to the emperor, but he "unequivocally endorsed Rodzianko's notification about the seizure of power."[18]

On the afternoon of March 2, 1917, Ruzsky reported to Nicholas II on telegrams from the commanders of the fronts and fleets, as well as on the arrest of some of the ministers. He also notified the tsar that State Duma deputies Alexander Ivanovich Guchkov and Vasily Vitalievich Shulgin were on their way to Pskov to meet with him. After the report, Nicholas II handed Ruzsky telegrams he had signed addressed to State Duma Chairman Rodzianko, the chief of staff, Supreme Commander Alexeyev, and the Grand Duke Nicholas Nikolaevich, as well as the texts of two edicts for the Senate. But they were never sent. On the advice of Voeikov, Nicholas II decided first to hear out Guchkov and Shulgin.

Voeikov cites the texts of these unsent documents:

To the Chairman of the State Duma:

There is no sacrifice I would not make in the name of the genuine good and for the salvation of my dear Mother Russia. For this reason I am prepared to abdicate the throne in favor of my son so that he remains with me until he reaches his majority under the regency of my brother, Grand Duke Michael Alexandrovich.

Nicholas.

General Staff Headquarters

In the name of the good, the tranquility, and the salvation of my ardently loved Russia, I am prepared to abdicate the throne in favor of my son. I beg everyone to serve him faithfully and without dissimulation.

Nicholas.

To our Governor-General in the Caucasus, His Imperial Highness Grand Duke Nicholas Nikolaevich, I enjoin you to be Supreme Commander-in-Chief.

Nicholas.[19]

When he took back the unsent telegrams, Nicholas II sent for Dr. Fyodorov, with whom he had long consulted on the health of the heir. Georgy Shavelsky, archpresbyter of the Russian army and navy, describes their conversation:

"Tell me, Sergei Petrovich, candidly. Can Alexei Nikolaevich ever recover completely?" the sovereign asked Dr. Fyodorov.

"If Your Highness believes in miracles, then there are no limits to a miracle. If you want to know what science says, then I have to say that as yet science knows no instance of full recovery from this illness. It may be merely a matter of the length of the illness. Some of these patients have died in infancy, others at age seven, some at twenty, and Duke Abrutsky lived to the age of forty-two. No one has lived longer than that," replied Dr. Fyodorov.

"So you consider the illness incurable?"

"Yes, Your Highness!"

"What can we do then! Alexei Nikolaevich and I will settle in Livadia. The Crimean climate has a very propitious effect on him, and there, God willing, he will grow stronger."

"Your Highness is mistaken if you think that after your abdication you will be allowed to live with Alexei Nikolaevich when he becomes Sovereign."

"What do you mean they won't let me? That is impossible!"

"That's right, they won't let you, Your Highness!"

"I cannot live without him. Then I will abdicate for him as well. This matter must be clarified!"[20]

After this he invited in Count Fredericks, and Colonel Naryshkin, the head of the Imperial Chancellery, and Voeikov as well, who together had apparently come to the same conclusion as Dr. Fyodorov.

Grand Duke Nicholas Nikolaevich.

That evening, when Guchkov and Shulgin arrived in Pskov, Nicholas decided against entering into a discussion with them but listened impassively to Guchkov's speech and then reservedly declared his decision to abdicate the throne. Voeikov recalls:

> A short while later the manifesto was typed. The sovereign signed it in his office and said to me, "Why don't you come in?" I replied: "There is nothing there for me to do." "No, come in," said the sovereign.
>
> Thus, entering the salon car behind the sovereign, I was present in that trying moment when Emperor Nicholas II handed his manifesto of abdication from the throne to the commissars of the State Duma, whom he mistakenly believed to be representatives of the Russian people. Then and there the sovereign asked the minister of his court to affix his seal. The manifesto proclaimed the following:
>
> "In these times of great struggle against a foreign enemy who for nearly three years has been trying to enslave our Homeland, the Lord God has seen fit to send down upon Russia yet another difficult trial.
>
> "Popular domestic upheavals threaten to reflect calamitously on the further conduct of a sustained war.
>
> "The fate of Russia, the honor of her heroic army, the good of her people, the entire future of our dear Fatherland demand that this war be waged to a victorious conclusion no matter what.
>
> "Our cruel enemy is harnessing his last forces and the moment is nigh when our valorous army, together with our glorious allies, will break our enemy decisively. During these decisive days in the life of Russia, we have deemed it a matter of conscience to facil-

itate for our people the close unity and serried ranks of all our popular forces for the speedy attainment of victory and, in agreement with the State Duma, have recognized it as a good to abdicate the Throne of the Russian State and disencumber ourselves of supreme power.

"Not wishing to part with our beloved son, we transfer our legacy to our brother, Grand Duke Michael Alexandrovich, and bless him on his ascension to the Throne of the Russian State.

"We command our brother to rule state affairs in full and inviolable unity with the representatives of the people in the institutions of legislation on the basis of those principles which they shall establish, and in doing so swearing an inviolable oath to our ardently beloved Homeland.

"We call on all loyal sons of the fatherland to carry out their sacred duty to it in obedience to the tsar in this trying moment of national tribulations and to help him and the representatives of the people lead the Russian state onto the path of victory, well-being, and glory. May the Lord God help Russia.

"Nicholas.

"March 2, 15:00 hours, 1917, Pskov.

"Sealed: Minister of the Imperial Court Adjutant General Count Fredericks."[21]

That night, Nicholas II set out for Headquarters in Mogilev. From Sirotino Station he sent his brother Michael Alexandrovich the following telegram:

To his Imperial Highness Michael. Petrograd.

Events of recent days have forced me to decide irrevocably on this extreme step. Forgive me if I have grieved you and because I was unable to forewarn you. I shall remain your faithful and devoted brother forever. I am returning to headquarters and from there in a few days I must go to Tsarskoe Selo. I fervently pray to God to help you and your Homeland. Nicky.[22]

When Guchkov and Shulgin delivered Nicholas II's act of abdication to the Provisional Government, they joined Rodzianko, Alexander Kerensky, Pavel Nikolaevich Milyukov, Georgy Evgenievich Lvov, Nikolai Vissarionovich Nekrasov, and others for a meeting—at ten o'clock in the morning at 12 Millionnaya Street, in the apartment of Prince Mikhail Sergeyevich Putyatin, where Grand Duke Michael Alexandrovich was staying. Opinions about how to proceed diverged: Milyukov and Guchkov tried to convince Michael Alexandrovich to accept the throne; Kerensky, Lvov, Rodzianko, and Nekrasov tried to talk him out of it—and they insisted on having their way. After consulting with Rodzianko and Lvov, Michael Alexandrovich declared that he did not feel he could accept the throne without the people's approval, signed an act of abdication, and handed it to Rodzianko.

The text of the manifesto, accepted at six o'clock in the evening, proclaimed:

A heavy burden has been placed on me by the will of my brother, who has transferred to me the imperial throne of all Russia in a year of unexampled warfare and upheavals among the people.

Inspired by a thought shared with the entire people, that the good of the Homeland comes before all else, I have firmly resolved to accept supreme power only if such is the will of our great people, on whom falls a universal election through our representatives in the Constituent Assembly to establish a form of governance and new laws for the Russian state.

For this reason I call upon the Divine blessing and beg all citizens of the Russian power to submit to the Provisional Government, which at the initiative of the State Duma arose and has been invested with all the fullness of power up until such time as a universal, direct, equal, and secret election can be held, in the briefest possible time. By its decision on the form of governance, the Constituent Assembly shall express the will of the people.

March 3, 1917.
Michael[23]

We will continue to trace the fate of the two brothers, who signed abdications one after the other, in the following chapters. Here, however, let us note that Nicholas II's abdication in favor of Michael Alexandrovich and Michael II's in favor of the Constituent Assembly were both immediately taken by Russian society as a fait accompli. On September 1, by decree of the head of the Provisional Government, Kerensky—himself a participant in the March 2 gathering at 12 Millionnaya Street, where he was the most active supporter of abdication—declared Russia a republic, and the monarchy was dissolved without the will of the Russian people ever being expressed at the Constituent Assembly. The Romanovs, now merely citizens of the new Russia, represented no political threat to the new power. No one, least of all Nicholas II, was demanding the restoration of the monarchy, and the new government had no interest in its immediate destruction.

This new government itself, however, was anything but stable or monolithic. The public's sympathies were growing increasingly radical, and by fall 1917 the liberal democratic Provisional Government had become right-wing socialist, with the local organs of power, the Soviets, held firmly by a bloc of Bolsheviks and Left Socialist Revolutionaries. In the absence of any sort of democratic tradition, the establishment of a dictatorship in the new Russia moved from the sphere of the probable to the inevitable.

In this ever-changing and volatile struggle for political power, a given party's attitude toward the fate of the former tsar's family became one of the measures of its commitment to the revolution, which meant that the newly overthrown Romanovs were now gravely endangered.

Empress Marie Feodorovna with her son Nicholas, 1871.

chapter 2.

In Captivity

Reader, stop!
Here is the guard booth.
Here the bayonet and scream.
And the slogan. And the password.
But mostly—
here is the blue forget-me-not
like a gleeful boyish season.

—Nikolai Aseyev

■ At Tsarskoe Selo ■

On March 3, 1917, Colonel Nicholas Romanov (now no longer Tsar Nicholas II) returned to Mogilev from Pskov. He met with his mother, Empress Marie Feodorovna, for what turned out to be the last time—although neither of them knew it. He listened to General Alexeyev's report on the situation at the front. And on the morning of March 8, he bid an emotional farewell to all the officers of his staff and prepared to depart for Tsarskoe Selo. As Nicholas was boarding the train, four members of the State Duma—Alexander Bublikov, Semyon Gribunin, Kalinin, and Vasily Vershinin—arrived at Headquarters to accompany him. General Alexeyev now made a very different report to Nicholas: he announced the resolution of the Provisional Government to "deprive the abdicated emperor Nicholas II and his spouse of their freedom."

Empress Alexandra Fyodorovna was informed of the Provisional Government's decision that same day by General Kornilov, whom Nicholas himself had appointed commander of the Petrograd Military District. On March 9, the new revolutionary guards replaced the imperial guards at the Alexander Palace. The Romanov family was now officially "deprived of liberty." Many in the imperial retinue, however, remained with the family voluntarily, including Major General Vasily Alexandrovich Dolgorukov, Marshal of the Imperial Court Pavel Konstantinovich Benckendorff, Colonel Evgeny Stepanovich Kobylinsky, the ladies-in-waiting Baroness Sofia Karlovna Buxhoeveden, Countess Anastasia Gendrikova, Yulia Alexandrovna Dehn, and Anna Stefanovna Demidova, the court reader Ekaterina Adolfovna

Тоб. Город. Продов. Ком.

Продовольственная карточка

№ 54.

Фамилія Романовъ

Имя Николай

Отчество Александровичъ

Званіе Экс-Императоръ

Улица „Свобода"

№ дома

Составъ семьи семь

Подпись выдавшаго карточку

The food ration card of Nicholas II.

Schneider, Drs. Evgeny Sergeyevich Botkin and Vladimir Nikolaevich Derevenko, the teacher Pierre Gilliard, the parlor maids Tutelberg and Ersberg, the servant Aloizy Egorovich Trupp, the cook Ivan Mikhailovich Kharitonov, and the kitchen boy, Leonid Sednev. The terms of the arrest were not harsh. The family was served by 150 people; they received all newspapers without exception, and they were allowed to take walks of unlimited duration in the park. The head of the family shoveled snow in the park, sawed wood, and spent time with his son.

According to Quartermaster General Alexander Sergeyevich Lukomsky, as early as March 2 the new war minister, Guchkov, had informed Nicholas that he "would need to go abroad immediately." On March 8, the Provisional Government, in a telegram signed by Kerensky and Prince Lvov, also promised "the Sovereign and his family unimpeded exit abroad"—through Murmansk to England. On March 10, the British ambassador, Sir George Buchanan, replied to an inquiry from the minister of foreign affairs, Milyukov, that King George, by consent of his ministers, had offered the tsar and tsaritsa hospitality on British soil. Buchanan informed Milyukov that one of the British ships cruising in the North Sea had been ordered to take the Romanov family out of Russia. Kerensky was in charge of organizing the transit of the imperial family from Tsarskoe Selo to the port of Murmansk. The arrangements seemed to be going smoothly. The German command had even replied to a preliminary inquiry that "not one military unit of the German fleet would attack any vessel transporting the Sovereign and his family."[1]

But, suddenly, to Milyukov's inquiry about when the cruiser would arrive in Murmansk, Buchanan "reported with embarrassment that his government 'was no longer insisting' on its invitation."[2] Buchanan's daughter, Mariel, later wrote:

> The embassy courier brought a decoded London dispatch to my father. As he read it, his face changed.
>
> "The cabinet no longer wishes the tsar to come to Great Britain," he said.
>
> "Why?"
>
> "They're afraid. . . . They're afraid of riots in the country. They're afraid strikes will break out. . . . There is a danger of disorders if the Romanovs even land in England. So I have to inform the Russian government that our agreement with them no longer stands."[3]

As long as there were rumors that the imperial family was fleeing abroad, noisy demands for their imprisonment were heard on all sides in Russia: the revolutionaries wanted them thrown into the Sts. Peter and Paul Fortress; sailors at Kronstadt wanted to transfer them there. Let us take a longer look at this particular issue.

More than enough has been already been written about the prison conditions under the Bolshevik Chekists. To quote the testimony of Petirim Sorokin, Kerensky's secretary, about his arrival at the Sts. Peter and Paul Fortress in January 1918:

> Number sixty-three in this famous bastion of the fortress [the Trubetskoy] was a small cell with a tiny, covered window. It was dirty and cold inside, and half-frozen rivulets of water ran down the walls. There were no cots or chairs. Instead, there was simply a tattered straw mattress on the floor. . . . It was forbidden to receive food, clothing, books, or linens from family members. . . . we slept together on the damp and torn straw mat. Suddenly my cell mate started laughing:
>
> "Would either one of us, as we were planning and welcoming the revolution, ever have guessed that the revolutionary government would arrest us?"
>
> We laughed, and I asked Argunov:
>
> "What do this cell and the tsarist prison you were in have in common?"
>
> "Nothing! They're as different as the courtyard of an inn and a first-class hotel. . . ."

> "Constituent Assembly disbanded," we read that afternoon in the paper. Utterly dispirited, after dinner we and the other prisoners gathered in the prison yard to say goodbye to Kokoshkin and Shingarev [former ministers in Kerensky's government] who were supposed to be moved to the hospital that evening. That afternoon one of the guards who had passed out the meal said:
>
> "Heard anything about your [other] friends?"
>
> "No. What happened?"
>
> "Last night Communists broke into the hospital and killed them. They might try to kill you, too. We're doing what we can to prevent it, but if a lot of them come, all we can do is open your cell doors and the gates in this sector of the yard. Not that there's any way out of the prison yard."
>
> "At the very least just do that," we begged. "Better to die in the yard than in our cells, like rats in traps."[4]

We quote this excerpt here to let the reader compare it with the reminiscences by Voeikov, who was in a neighboring cell the year before, when Sorokin was still secretary to the minister of justice:

> We drove through several of the fortress gates and finally reached . . . the Trubetskoy bastion, and they led me up the stone stairs to the second story—to cell number seventy-two, which was a room with a painted asphalt floor and plastered walls covered with sizing paint. The ceiling was vaulted. Under it was one small window that let in very little light due to two thick iron grates, as well as the ice that had formed on the inside 2–3 vershoks [5–7 inches] deep. Two walls of the cell were damp, the temperature felt close to two degrees [35° F]. . . . There was a canvas mattress on the cot stuffed with hay or straw, one or one and a half fingers thick. The pillow was a slender, filthy, and very smelly object, square in shape, about three fingers thick. . . . There was no bedding or toilet articles. We were allowed to wear outer clothing only if we were summoned to reception or taken out on walks; the rest of the time we were supposed to wear prison underwear and robes. . . .
>
> A few days later . . . steps of a large number of people could be heard quickly approaching my cell. The door opened noisily and in burst a crowd preceded by men in soldier's uniforms, their guns held horizontal, in a very aggressive mood. I felt a critical moment had arrived. The thought occurred to me to grab the icon near my cot, which I had been allowed as an exception. . . . The day I surrendered my squadron, the Horse Guardsmen had blessed me with this hinged icon. On the back of the icon (which by some miracle I still have) was engraved: "To our dear and ardently loved father and squadron commander, Captain Voeikov, from the lower ranks of the squadron of His Highness's Horse Guards 19th Regiment, 15/7 1902 15/8 1905." I grabbed the icon and took

> a few steps forward, saying, "Read this," and I showed them the inscription. . . . There was some confusion, the guns were turned bayonet down, and everyone came to a halt. The soldiers' procession was joined by the fortress commandant, Staff-Captain Krivtsov, who had been waiting to see how the visit to my cell by this stirred-up horde would end. When they saw the icon, though, the soldiers started walking out one by one, and the last three or four even bowed to me as they left.[5]

The contrasts between these two stories speak for themselves. While the latter shows that prison conditions under the Provisional Government were not good, they were not yet as squalid and brutal as they became under the Bolsheviks. The angry mobs could still be placated by their fear of God and were not yet killing the prisoners.

But it was Kerensky, the head of the Provisional Government, who actually instituted many of the policies that have been attributed to the Bolsheviks. He was the one who decreed the infamous policies of *prodotriad* (food detachment), whereby armed detachments bought excesses of bread and other foodstuffs from the peasants at very low prices fixed by the state, and *zagradotriad* (barrage detachment), whereby certain detachments followed the Red Army into battle and started firing so that the soldiers could not turn back. And it was Kerensky who signed the law regarding "extrajudicial arrests," that is, the extrajudicial retributions just described. It was also Kerensky who paralyzed the courts by introducing the institution of public accusers, which was intended not to ensure that laws were obeyed, but rather to ensure "revolutionary expediency." It is no surprise that under Kerensky the following episode occurred.

In April 1917, a detachment of machine gunners from the Petrograd Soviet under the command of Maslovsky (also known as Mstislavsky) and Vasily Vasilievich Yakovlev (also known as Konstantin Alexeyevich Myachin) showed up at the Alexander Palace demanding that the guards hand over the prisoners. The guards refused, and a compromise was agreed upon. Nicholas took Maslovsky and Yakovlev from room to room throughout the palace, and they reported to the Soviet on their "viewings." According to the testimony of Milyukov and Sorokin, Kerensky plotted this "raid" as an attempt to seize the Romanovs and put them in that same Trubetskoy bastion of the Sts. Peter and Paul Fortress.[6]

In the following months at Tsarskoe Selo, nothing untoward happened to the Romanov family. All was calm until August 9 when Kerensky informed the Romanovs of their impending departure. Let us turn to Sorokin:

> A few days before exiling Tsar Nicholas and his family to Tobolsk, my old friend and comrade-in-arms, Mr. V. S. Pankratov, stopped by the editorial offices of *The People's Will* and informed me that he had been put in charge of the emperor's guard and was going to take him into exile. V. S. Pankratov was an old revolutionary who had spent twenty years in the Shlisselburg Fortress. Despite this, he was an extremely humane man, without a hint of personal animosity toward the tsar or the old regime as a whole. So I was

> glad that they had chosen him for this mission, and I was confident he would be able to provide the imperial family with whatever comforts proved feasible. In no way were the motives for the exile ill-intentioned. On the contrary, I knew that Kerensky had wanted to send the family to England but the Soviet had not agreed to this. . . . The family absolutely had to be sent away somewhere where their lives would be out of danger and where the extremists could not say that the tsar represented a threat to the revolution. In Tobolsk at that time there were few revolutionary feelings and absolutely none of the fanaticism, and under V. S. Pankratov's protection, the tsar would not be in danger of assassination. "Be that as it may," said Pankratov, "if the Bolsheviks ever take the upper hand, God only knows what might happen."[7]

On the eve of departure, August 13, Kerensky inspected the convoy and addressed the soldiers in parting: "Remember, soldiers: you don't hit a man when he's down. Behave politely, not crudely. Don't forget, this is a former emperor. Neither he nor his family should experience hardship."[8] He also arranged a meeting—the final farewell meeting, as it turned out—for the brothers Nicholas and Michael Romanov, who had not seen each other since the abdications. Although there is evidence to support the theory that Kerensky attempted to imprison the tsar and his family, he did not endorse the brutality for which the Bolsheviks later became known.

On the morning of August 14, escorted by a military guard, the Romanov family was sent to Tobolsk, a provincial seat east of the Ural Mountains in Siberia. They were still allowed to keep some of their retinue, and traveling with them were aide-de-camp General Ilya Leonidovich Tatishchev, Dolgorukov, Dr. Botkin, Gilliard, Countess Gendrikova—in all, including servants, thirty-nine people. Dr. Derevenko, Alexei's doctor, the children's English teacher Charles Gibbes, and Baroness Buxhoeveden would come later. At Tyumen, in the Urals, the family transferred to a steamer, the *Russia,* and sailed down the river Tur, then the Tobol, arriving in Tobolsk on August 19. The Governor's House had been set aside for them, but it was not yet ready, so the family spent seven days aboard the ship, taking boat trips to the Abalaksky monastery. On August 26, they finally moved into the two-story, stone Governor's House with its balcony and palisade, its electricity and running water—all surrounded by an iron fence.

In Tobolsk

Founded in 1587, Tobolsk was one of the centers of Russian colonization in Siberia and a common place to send political exiles. In 1917, the town had 22,000 residents, 2,332 houses (including 50 made of stone), numerous trade establishments, and several small enterprises. For the most part, the population was employed as tradesmen, artisans, and fishermen: the town had a pier, a bank, and a museum. The nearest rail station was 190 miles away in Tyumen. Archbishop Hermogen headed the bishopric. At one time he had been Rasputin's associate, then his enemy. Hermogen had been granted his position as archbishop of Tobolsk by Prince Lvov, the chief procurator of the Holy Synod, after the February Revolution. Hermo-

Tsarevich Alexei, 1917.

gen was one of the authors of the idea to send the tsar's family to Tobolsk, and he had personally made a trip to Petrograd to present his proposal to Kerensky.

The imperial family was fairly comfortable in the Governor's House. The town's population was sympathetic toward the prisoners. Commissar Vasily Semyonovich Pankratov arrived in Tobolsk on September 1. The Romanovs were prohibited from leaving the enclosed yard and small garden and were even escorted to church under guard. With them in attendance, the local residents did not miss a service. The daily routine was monotonous: lessons for the children, walks in the garden, home theatricals, in which Commissar Pankratov occasionally participated, a home cinema arranged by Alexei. All in all, the Romanovs experienced no privations—except boredom. They were allowed their personal correspondence, and they received the newspapers. When money stopped coming from Petrograd to support the prisoners, food was bought in town on credit.

The situation changed after the October Revolution when the Bolsheviks came to power, but not as quickly as one might think. It was not until February 23, 1918, that Colonel Kobylinsky, who had led the Romanovs' guard since March 1917, received a telegram from Petrograd saying that "the people do not have the funds to support the tsar's family." It was signed by the people's commissar of state property, Vladimir Alexandrovich Karelin (a Left Socialist Revolutionary who, along with Maria Spiridonova, Shteinberg, and other Socialist Revolutionary leaders, had joined Lenin's Bolshevik government).

At this point, let us pause and consider what might have been.

As soon as the news of the tsar's abdication reached the public, plots were hatched to declare it "coerced and therefore subject to annulment" and to rescue the imperial family from their fallen position. Viktor Alexandrov, Robert Vilton, Nikolai Sokolov, and Alexander Mosolov have written about the popularity of this idea in certain circles, but not about the specific attempts that were actually made to free the tsar's family by force.[9] For example, Staff Captain Sokolov traveled to Tobolsk from Moscow for the purpose of freeing the tsar. Upon arriving in Tobolsk, he and two other officers, utterly unprepared, suffered several misadventures including arrest and were forced to leave without undertaking anything concrete.[10] Mark Konstantinovich Kasvinov reported on a group led by Archbishop Hermogen and Staff Captain Lepilin, the head of the local Union of Front-line Soldiers, that was planning a rescue attempt and about a group led by Colonel Solovyov,[11] but in the final analysis nothing serious was undertaken. Actual events unfolded in the following manner.

In February 1918, the Special Commissar of the Dutsman was sent to Tobolsk from the Red Army in Omsk, and in late March a detachment of one hundred Red Army soldiers from Omsk arrived under the command of Demyanov. Soon, another Red Army detachment arrived from the provincial Soviet in Ekaterinburg, led by commanders Alexander Dimitrievich Avdeyev and Zaslavsky. Commissar Pankratov was dismissed from his post. On April 6, the Tobolsk Soviet held new elections, and Bolshevik Pavel Dmitrievich Khokhryakov became its chairman. The Soviet's Executive Committee disbanded the Tobolsk Duma and the local assemblies, barred the clergy from political activity, and seized control of the guard at the Governor's House.

On April 22, an extraordinary commissar of the VTsIK (All-Russian Central Executive Committee) arrived in Tobolsk to transfer the imperial family to Ekaterinburg, the Red capital of the Urals. This was Yakovlev, whom the Romanovs already knew from the machine gunners' "raid" of the Alexander Palace. The military commissar of the Ural province, Filipp Goloshchekin, placed the armed detachments of commanders Chudinov, Avdeyev, and Busyatsky under Yakovlev's command. The Bolsheviks were consolidating their power, which meant that things were going to change for the tsar and his family.

On the morning of April 26, Nicholas and Alexandra, accompanied only by their daughter Marie and twelve servants and guarded by Yakovlev's attachment, left Tobolsk in carriages. Forty-eight hours later, they transferred to a train in Tyumen. Alexei, who was too ill to travel, Olga, Tatiana, Anastasia, and the remaining servants were detained in Tobolsk.

In Ekaterinburg

By 1918, the Ural organization of the RSDRP(b) (Russian Social Democratic Workers Party [Bolshevik]) had 35,000 members, including 3,000 in Ekaterinburg and 2,400 in Perm. The nucleus of the organization consisted of the armed workers' detachments that had been formed back in the years 1905–7 and that, unlike their Moscow counterparts, had not suffered serious loss before 1917. During this time, the armed Uralites of the RSDRP(b) may have been the strongest armed organization in Russia. It is no surprise that their commander, Yakov Sverdlov, occupied the post of chairman of the VTsIK Presidium.

In February 1918, the Soviet government for the first time "remembered" the tsar's family, which had been arrested by the Provisional Government. In March, the Soviets had sent detachments of Red Guards from Omsk and Ekaterinburg (both Bolshevik strongholds by this time) to Tobolsk, and in April they decided to remove the imperial family from Tobolsk. Evidently, by this time Moscow was counting on using the Romanovs, in the context of intensifying civil war, as hostages—a unique instrument of pressure against its political opponents, both domestic (the Whites) and foreign (Russia's enemies in World War I).

VTsIK Extraordinary Commissar Yakovlev was in charge of taking the tsar from Tobolsk. When and where he was taking the tsar and part of his family was unknown. Where he was trying to take them and at whose initiative is unclear to this day.

Vasily Yakovlev (Konstantin Myachin).

Konstantin Alexeyevich Myachin (the Party pseudonym of Vasily Vasilievich Yakovlev), who was born in 1885 in Ufa, south of Perm, had joined the revolutionary movement at age eighteen. In 1905, he participated in the Bolshevik armed workers' detachment fighting the Black Hundreds, throwing bombs at Cossacks and police. He directed an armed workers' detachment in Zlatoust (in the Urals, south of Ekaterinburg), led an attack on a mail train in Miass where much gold was seized, and ran security for illegal meetings, assemblies, and private gatherings. From 1909 to 1911, he lived in emigration in Switzerland and Belgium, where he collaborated with Maxim Gorky and Leonid Krasin, and met with exiled revolutionaries including Trotsky, Kollontai, and Lenin. In 1917, he returned to Petrograd and collaborated with the Socialist Revolutionaries Mstislavsky (Maslovsky), Mikhail Artemevich Muravyov (who later raised a rebellion in the Volga region), and Boris Viktorovich Savinkov. During the October Revolution in Petrograd, Yakovlev led the seizure of the telephone station and participated in the disbanding of the Constituent Assembly. His mandate as plenipotentiary for the Romanovs' transit from Tobolsk to Ekaterinburg had been signed by Sverdlov, Varlaam Alexandrovich Avanesov, and Shteinberg, who was the people's commissar of justice, a Left Socialist Revolutionary.

Not surprising then are the contradictory opinions of researchers on Yakovlev: a Bolshevik and subsequently the head of one of the Gulag camps;[12] a Socialist Revolutionary;[13] an agent of the kaiser's secret service;[14] and even a double agent in the British service.[15] Yakovlev's biography is dramatic. While serving as commander-in-chief of the Ufa-Orenburg front under Socialist Revolutionary Muravyov, the commander-in-chief of the eastern front, fighting the White Czechs, Yakovlev betrayed Soviet power. Muravyov mutinied against the Bolsheviks, and Yakovlev retreated with White Admiral Kolchak's troops to Omsk.

When the civil war ended, Yakovlev ended up in China—Harbin and Shanghai. In 1928, he returned to the Soviet Union, gave himself up, and was sentenced to the firing squad. However, his death sentence was commuted to brief imprisonment in the Solovetski Islands in the White Sea (home to the Bolshevik concentration camps). He was subsequently released and his conviction expunged. In 1938 he was arrested again and executed. He was rehabilitated in 1969, but two years later his rehabilitation was rescinded in light of accusations from the Communist Party that he had been a provocateur.

Yakovlev's arrival in Tobolsk in April 1918 had been preceded by definite preparation. In March 1918, at a session of the VTsIK Presidium, Goloshchekin, the military commissar of the Ural province, had made a special trip to Moscow to request that the Romanovs be moved to a safer place. At the suggestion of VTsIK Chairman Sverdlov, a decision was made to prepare to put the former tsar on trial for crimes against the country and the people and therefore to transfer the Romanovs from Tobolsk to Ekaterinburg under the supervision of a VTsIK plenipotentiary.

So, on April 28, at five o'clock in the morning, with the Romanovs in car number 42 of the Samara-Zlatoust Railway and an armed detachment of "as many as 100 men,"[16] Yakovlev set out from Tyumen. However, he did not turn west, toward Ekaterinburg, but east, toward Omsk. He informed Avdeyev, who was traveling with him, that he had received an order to travel not to Ekaterinburg but to Moscow via a circular route through Omsk, Chelyabinsk, and Samara. As Yakovlev's subordinate, Avdeyev could not object, but Busyatsky, who stayed behind in Tyumen, wired Ekaterinburg that the train had gone in the direction of Omsk. By ten o'clock that morning, Alexander Georgievich Beloborodov, the chairman of the Ural Soviet Presidium, had sent a telegram to "everyone, everyone, everyone," branding Yakovlev a traitor to the cause of the revolution and declaring him outside the law. At Beloborodov's request, Kosarev, the chairman of the Western Siberian Provincial Soviet Presidium, sent "significant forces" to the junction at Kulomzino to arrest Yakovlev.[17]

When Yakovlev learned of this at Lyubinskaya Station, he uncoupled the locomotive and raced to Omsk with the one car. Fortunately for Yakovlev, he and Kosarev were old friends, so he was not arrested. He convinced Kosarev that he needed to contact Sverdlov, and the two of them went to the telegraph office together. There Yakovlev received an order from Sverdlov to return to Ekaterinburg. He turned back and at nine o'clock in the morning on April 30 arrived at his destination. At the Ekaterinburg II (Shartash) station, he handed over the three Romanovs, obtained a receipt, responded to the rather harsh accusations in the Soviet, and departed for Moscow.

These are the facts, which have been interpreted by almost all the investigators to mean the following: Yakovlev was carrying out an attempt to free Nicholas and take him beyond the reach of the Ural Soviet.[18] Recently published documents have introduced some clarity into what was behind Yakovlev's unsuccessful attempt.[19]

Let us compare the texts of the documents with Yakovlev's actions.

On April 9, VTsIK Chairman Sverdlov informed the Ural Provincial Soviet that Yakovlev had been instructed to transfer Nicholas from Tobolsk to Ekaterinburg alive and to surrender him to Beloborodov or Goloshchekin. Sverdlov demanded total confidence for Yakovlev. Evidently, in carrying out Sverdlov's order, Goloshchekin put all Ural armed detachments in the Tyumen–Tobolsk region at Yakovlev's disposal.

Yakovlev picked up Nicholas in Tobolsk, brought him to Tyumen on April 26, and wired

Sverdlov: "Is the route the same or have you changed it? Inform Tyumen immediately. Am following the old route. Reply needed immediately. Yakovlev." Less than three hours later, Sverdlov replied: "The old route. Report: Are you taking the Cargo or not? Sverdlov."

According to Yakovlev's memoirs, on the morning of April 27 he wired Sverdlov from Tyumen: "Only some of the baggage has been brought. . . . Ekaterinburg, except for Goloshchekin, has just one desire, to put an end to it, no matter what happens to the baggage. . . . Reply: should I go to Ekaterinburg or through Omsk. . . . Waiting for an answer, standing at the station with the baggage. Yakovlev." Sverdlov replied: "Go to Omsk, go to Kosarev, Sovdep [Soviet of Workers', Peasants', and Soldiers' Deputies] Chairman Kosarev, proceed conspiratorially, will give further instructions in Omsk." This means that Yakovlev was taking the Romanovs to Omsk on direct order from Sverdlov, with whom he was in operational communication, and that they had warned Goloshchekin, as well as the military units along the route, of their journey.

On the morning of April 28, Ural Provincial Soviet Presidium Chairman Beloborodov wired Sverdlov and sent a circular letter down the Omsk Railway: "The Provincial Soviet, having discussed the conduct of Commissar Yakovlev [who was a special commissar not subordinate to the Ural Provincial Soviet], . . . sees in it a direct betrayal of the revolution, a desire for some unknown purpose to take the former tsar out of the revolutionary Urals despite precise written instructions from the VTsIK chairman. . . . Commissar Yakovlev must be arrested."

On April 29, after receiving Beloborodov's telegram, Sverdlov responded harshly to Ekaterinburg: "Everything Yakovlev does is in direct implementation of an order I have given. . . . Give Yakovlev your complete confidence, no interference. Sverdlov."[20]

On April 28, in Omsk, in his telegraph conversation with Sverdlov, Yakovlev received a new order: "Return immediately to Tyumen. Have reached an agreement with the Uralites . . . received guarantees of personal responsibility from the regional leaders. Hand over the entire cargo to the representative of the Ural Provincial Committee, travel with him . . . take along reinforcements from Kosarev in Omsk. The task remains as before, you have done what is most important. . . . Greetings. Sverdlov."[21]

What happened? What events forced Sverdlov to give in to the Uralites and to order Nicholas's train turned around? We don't know, and there are no documents to enlighten us. However, Yakovlev implemented this new decree impeccably; he brought the "cargo" to Ekaterinburg, had Beloborodov sign a receipt for them, responded to all the Soviet's questions, and was released to go to Moscow.

A day before Yakovlev's arrival in Omsk, Kosarev sent a telegram to Ekaterinburg, harshly condemning the Uralites for "separatist acts" (meaning violations of executive and Party discipline, at the time a very serious accusation) and "extremely hasty decisions."[22] What kind of decisions we don't know, for no other documents have been preserved. However, the telegrams and actions we've just seen lead us to conclude that the Uralites thwarted Moscow's plans to send Nicholas II abroad.

In addition, when Yakovlev handed the Romanovs over to Beloborodov in Ekaterinburg on April 30, nothing had been readied for their reception, which makes it all the more clear that originally Yakovlev had not been planning to take the tsar and his family there.

Let us look at the response of Reinhold Berzin, the commander-in-chief of the North Urals front, to a query from Lenin into the status of the Romanovs in Ekaterinburg. It sheds some light on Moscow's perspective:

> Three addresses: Moscow, the Soviet of People's Commissars; the press office of the People's Commissariat of War; and the TsIK.
>
> Moscow newspapers I have received have printed an item about the murder of Nicholas Romanov by Red Army soldiers at a station near Ekaterinburg. I hereby report officially that on 21 June, I, together with members of the military inspection and the military commissar of the Ural Military District [Goloshchekin] and members of the All-Russian Investigative Commission, conducted a survey of the buildings where Nicholas Romanov and his family are being held and an inspection of the guards and security. All the members of the family and Nicholas himself are alive, and all information about their murder and so forth are provocations. June 27, 1918, 0:05 A.M. Commander-in-chief of the Northern Urals Front, Berzin.[23]

It is noteworthy that Lenin assigned responsibility for the safety of the former tsar to an army commander, Berzin, and not to the chairman of the Ural Provincial Soviet, Beloborodov. Moscow was obviously afraid that the Ural Soviet in Ekaterinburg might take excessive initiative.

A look at Lenin's concern regarding the Ural Soviet and Kosarev's criticism of "separatist acts by the Ural Soviet" helps to explain what fears of this kind meant at the time.

The term *partizanshchina* filtered through all the ruling circles of the RKKA (the Worker–Peasant Red Army) and into the military historical literature devoted to the civil war period as a term for those who committed "separatist acts." It was used almost as a swear word to criticize commanders who had followed the path either of partisan fighters or of local Cossack leaders and who were not noted for a high degree of discipline.

The "partisan" actions of Ural Soviet Chairman Beloborodov apparently did not enjoy Moscow's support. And although Beloborodov attempted to vindicate himself to Lenin, the latter obviously lost faith in him and relied on the more disciplined Berzin. The Ural Provincial Soviet may well have intended to destroy the tsar and his family independently, but these intentions were kept in strict check for the time being on the orders of Moscow through its representatives in the Ural Soviet: Military Commissar Goloshchekin (Sverdlov's proxy) and Mebius, the head of the Military–Revolutionary Committee (Trotsky's proxy). However, as soon as these checks weakened, for one reason or another, the situation spiraled out of control. For example, evidence that Moscow ordered the shooting of Grand Duke Michael Alexandrovich may never be found, although at the time of his execution the direct line of communication between Ekaterinburg and Moscow was still functioning.

For now, we can say that on April 30, 1918, Nicholas, Alexandra, and Marie were hastily settled in a two-story building on the corner of Ascension Boulevard and Ascension Lane that had been requisitioned on April 29 from Ipatiev, a mining engineer. The commander Avdeyev, whom the Romanovs knew from Tobolsk, was appointed house commandant. After almost a month on their own in Tobolsk, Alexei, Tatiana, Olga, and Anastasia arrived in Ekaterinburg on May 23. The number of servants allowed the tsar's family decreased markedly. Some fell away in Tobolsk, others were separated in Ekaterinburg, and a third group were sent to prison "for provocational outbursts." Baroness Buxhoeveden, Colonel Kobylinsky, the parlor maids Tutelberg and Ersberg, and the foreigners Gilliard and Gibbes were ordered to leave the Urals.

By the end of May only five people remained with the tsar's family: Dr. Botkin, lady-in-waiting Demidova, the servant Trupp, the cook Kharitonov, and the cook's apprentice Sednev. The heir's doctor, Derevenko, lived in a private apartment and had the right to enter the Ipatiev house at any time. Although living conditions for the Romanov family were more modest than in Tobolsk, the house was in perfect order, and "the food was excellent and abundant and served on time."[24]

By this time, other representatives of the tsarist dynasty were also under arrest in the Urals. Grand Duke Michael Alexandrovich had been moved to Perm in February 1918, and Grand Duchess Elizaveta Fyodorovna (the empress's older sister), Grand Duke Sergei Mikhailovich, the sons of Grand Duke Konstantine—Ioann, Konstantin, and Igor—and the young Prince Vladimir Pavlovich Paley had been moved to the small town of Alapaevsk (ninety-three miles north of Ekaterinburg) in May. The Grand Dukes Nicholas Mikhailovich, Pavel Alexandrovich, Dmitry Konstantinovich, and Georgy Mikhailovich remained in Petrograd.

In Perm, Grand Duke Michael Alexandrovich lived at liberty on the second floor of the royal rooms on Siberia Street with his wife, the Countess Brasova; Colonel Znamenovsky; his personal secretary, the Englishman Brian Johnson; and his valet, his driver, and his cook. In Alapaevsk, the Romanovs took up quarters in the Napolnaya School (located at the edge of town by a field) under guard, but their movements were not restricted. They could go to church, to the stores, and for walks through the town. This continued until the situation in the Urals underwent a cardinal change.

On May 25, 1918, the Czechoslovak Legion—tens of thousands of Austro-Hungarian prisoners of war, Czechs and Slovaks by nationality, who were traveling east by train, intending to sail to France from Vladivostok—mutinied against the Bolsheviks. They were joined by units of Cossacks, and by the following day they had captured Chelyabinsk (in the Urals, south of Ekaterinburg). They developed a three-pronged attack: east to Omsk and Kurgan, west to Zlatoust, and north to Ekaterinburg. The situation stabilized when the White Czechs halted at Argayash (in the direction of Ekaterinburg) on May 28. But the relative calm lasted less than two weeks. The attack was renewed, and the White Czechs, together with the Russian Whites, and local rebels managed to seize city after city. By July 11, Ekaterinburg was half encircled and had lost its direct connection with Moscow.

In Moscow, the Fifth Congress of Soviets opened on July 4. Originally, the congress was going to discuss whether to put the ex-tsar on trial, but now there were far more pressing matters. On July 5, the Left Socialist Revolutionary Maria Spiridonova gave her famous speech railing against the Bolsheviks for concluding the Treaty of Brest in March and thus losing huge amounts of Russian territory.

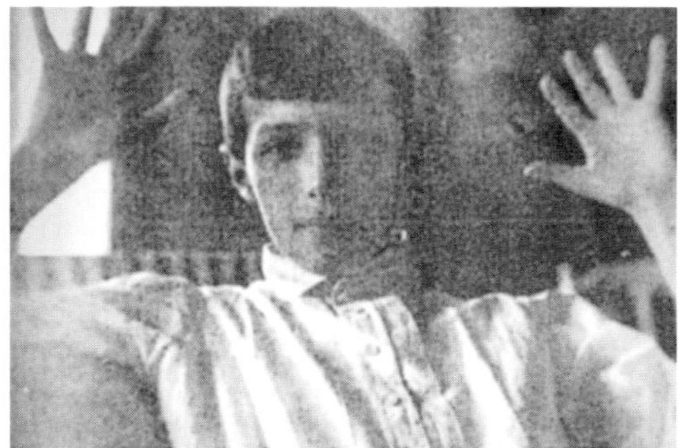

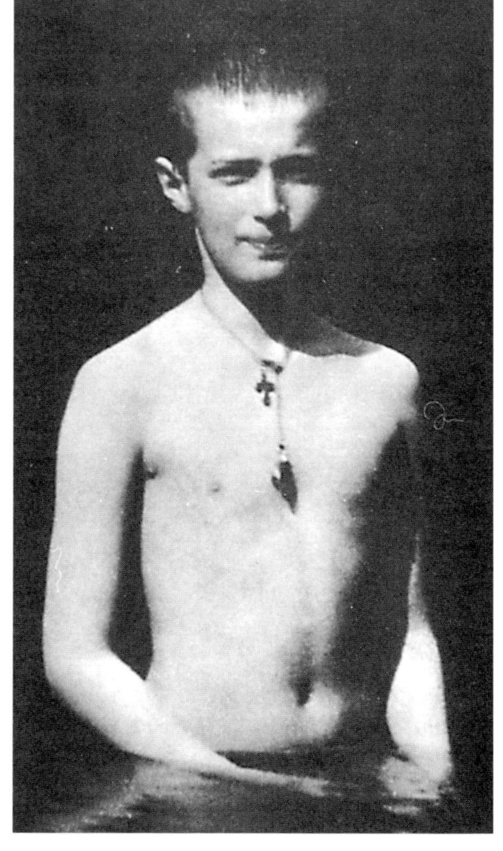

TOP: The Ipatiev house in Ekaterinburg as viewed from Ascension Avenue.

ABOVE: Tsarevich Alexei, 1918.

RIGHT: Tsarevich Alexei wearing an amulet containing a portrait of Rasputin and the text of a prayer.

On July 6, the Left Socialist Revolutionary Blyumkin killed the German ambassador Count Wilhelm Mirbach. On July 6 and 7, the Socialist Revolutionaries rebelled against the Bolsheviks, taking control of communications in the capital.

The situation throughout Russia was becoming critical, and there were now serious reasons for panicking on all sides. As we consider the subsequent events in Ekaterinburg, we must remember that they developed in the confusion of the retreat of the Red Army, when time was running out, and in the absence of any direct communications with Moscow.

Letter of Dr. Botkin to the Ekaterinburg Executive Committee

[Undated]
To the Provincial Executive Committee
Mr. Chairman,

As a physician who for the last ten years has treated the Romanov family, now under the jurisdiction of the Executive Committee, and in particular Alexei Nikolaevich, I appeal to you, Mr. Chairman, with the following entreaty. Alexei Nikolaevich is subject to pains in the joints from bumps that are completely unavoidable in a boy of his age and that are accompanied by seepage of fluids and resultant excruciating pains. In these events the boy suffers day and night with inexpressible pain, so that none of his closest relatives, not to mention his mother with chronic heart ailments who does not spare herself for him, can stand taking care of him for long. My fading strength is not enough, either. The patient's attendant Klim Grigoriev Nagorny, after several sleepless night filled with torment, can barely stand on his feet and would not be able to stand at all if it were not for the appearance of Alexei Nikolaevich's English teacher Mr. Gibbes and in particular, his tutor Mr. Gilliard. Calm and balanced, they help each other, and by reading and a change of impressions distract the patient from his suffering during the day, relaxing him, and at the same time giving his family and Nagorny the chance to sleep and gather strength for their shifts. Mr. Gilliard, to whom Alexei Nikolaevich is particularly attached after the seven years that he has been with him constantly, spends entire nights with him during his illness, giving the exhausted Nagorny a chance to sleep. Both teachers, and in particular, I repeat, Mr. Gilliard, are totally irreplaceable for Alexei Nikolaevich, and I, as a physician, must admit that they often bring more relief to the patient than medical methods, which in these situations is unfortunately extremely limited. In view of the above, I am, in addition to the request of the parents of the patient, earnestly asking the Executive Committee to allow Messrs. Gilliard and Gibbes to continue their selfless service to Alexei Nikolaevich Romanov, and because the boy is right now in one of the most acute attacks of his suffering, especially difficult to bear as a consequence of overtiredness caused by travel, to not refuse them—or, at least Mr. Gilliard alone—access to him tomorrow.

Evgeny Botkin

Grand Duchesses Olga, Tatiana, and Marie.

chapter 3.

The Execution

The twentieth century. Men wandering down roads,
Between the fires, making us think:
Being a beast is easy, so is being a god,
But being a man—now that is hard.

—Evgeny Vinokurov

Until the last few days of June 1918, the conditions in which the Romanovs were held at the Ipatiev house remained relatively normal. The situation seemed calm. However, on July 4, on the basis of fabricated accusations of drinking and theft, Commandant Avdeyev was removed from his post, his assistant, Alexander Mikhailovich Moshkin, was put under arrest, and some of the house guards were replaced.

At the time a flurry of rumors circulated in Moscow and abroad that Nicholas II had been executed. On June 20, Vladimir Dmitrievich Bonch-Bruevich, the administrator of the Soviet of People's Commissars, sent an inquiry to the chairman of the Ekaterinburg Soviet asking if the rumors were true, and four days later the Soviet ambassador in Berlin, Adolf Ioffe, sent a similar inquiry to Lenin, who in turn queried Commander Berzin in the Urals.

Months later, the White Army General Mikhail Konstantinovich Diterikhs, who together with Admiral Alexander Kolchak was investigating the murders of the imperial family, linked the rumors to the actual murder of the ex-tsar's brother, Grand Duke Michael Alexandrovich.

Indeed, late on the evening of June 11, 1918, associates of the Perm Cheka staged the abduction of Michael Alexandrovich and his secretary, the Englishman Brian Johnson, drove them out to the forest beyond Motovilikha, and executed them that night. On June 13, the Perm Cheka sent a telegram to Moscow reporting the prisoners' abduction and the Cheka's—apparently unsuccessful—search for them. We know that after this the provincial Cheka staged another abduction, following the same scenario as the real one, using two of the grand duke's servants made up to look like Michael Alexandrovich and Johnson.[1] These zigzags attest that neither discipline nor planning was involved in the execution of the grand duke and his secretary; it was clearly the consequence of the confusion following in the wake of the Red Army's retreat from the blows of the White Army.

Moscow was obviously losing control over its local organs in districts along the front. By sending this inquiry to Ekaterinburg, Moscow clearly had by no means excluded the possibility that the provincial Soviet may have executed Nicholas II without its sanction. As in Perm, confusion reigned in Ekaterinburg's organs of power. The changing of the guard at the Ipatiev house was probably no coincidence, but rather a link in a hastily made plan by the Ekaterinburg Soviet.

On July 4, the commandant of the Ipatiev house, Yakov Yurovsky, was appointed deputy chairman of the provincial Cheka, with Grigory Petrovich Nikulin as his assistant. The first thing they did was completely replace the inside guards; there were also outside guards stationed between the two high, solid fences that surrounded the house. Now the house guard consisted of ten men: the chief, Pavel Spiridonovich Medvedev, and the guards Starkov, Labushev, Kolotov, Letyomin, Netrebin, the brothers Andrei and Alexander Strekotin, and two other men whose names are still unknown.

Back in Moscow, events were unfolding quickly, and not at all as had been foreseen before the Fifth Congress of Soviets.

A political crisis had broken out—the Left Socialist Revolutionaries had quit the government, the German Ambassador Mirbach had been murdered, the Socialist Revolutionaries had mutinied, and the situation on the domestic fronts was deteriorating catastrophically. All this served to push the "open trial on the crimes of the former tsar against his country and people" to the back burner. Given this urgent situation, the VTsIK Presidium decided to hand the trial over to its counterparts in the Urals.

The situation was not much calmer in Ekaterinburg. On July 14, an extraordinary session of the Ural Soviet's Presidium was called, and it was announced that General Gaida's shock troops were advancing on the city, the Red Army soldiers were retreating, and it could well be a matter of days before Ekaterinburg fell. The Ural Soviet immediately sent a telegram to the Kremlin:

> Moscow, the Kremlin. To Sverdlov. Copy to Lenin. Ekaterinburg transmits the following: Inform Moscow that due to military circumstances we cannot wait for the trial date set by Filipov [the party pseudonym for Goloshchekin]. If your opinion is contrary, inform us right now without delay. Goloshchekin, Safarov. Contact Ekaterinburg yourself about this. Zinoviev[2]

However, direct connection to Moscow had been cut, and the telegram took a circuitous route through Perm, Vyatka, Vologda, and Petrograd, not reaching its destination until July 16. Moscow's response to the telegram is unknown, but it is known that the Ural Soviet did not wait for a response. On the same day, the Soviet took matters into its own hands and decided to destroy the tsar's family:

> [On the letterhead:] Worker–Peasant Government of the Russian Federative Republic of Soviets, Ural Provincial Soviet of Workers', Peasants', and Soldiers' Deputies, Presidium. [Stamp:] Top Secret.
>
> Minutes of the meeting of the Provincial Executive Committee of the Communist Party of the Urals and the Military Revolutionary Committee.

All members participating.

Issue of liquidating the former tsar's family, the Romanovs, discussed.

At the suggestion of the military commissar, as well as the chairman of the Military-Revolutionary Committee, the meeting unanimously resolved to liquidate the former tsar Nicholas Romanov and his family, as well as the servants remaining with them.

Furthermore it was resolved to carry out this decision before July 18, 1918, and responsibility for implementation was assigned to Comrade Yurovsky [handwritten insertion over the typed text], a member of the Extraordinary Commission [the Cheka].

Executive Committee Chairman: Beloborodov
Military Commissar: Goloshchekin
Head of Revolutionary Headquarters: Mebius

[Seal:] Ekaterinburg Executive Committee of the Soviet of Workers', Peasants', and Soldiers' Deputies; Military–Revolutionary Committee.

Ekaterinburg, July 14, 1918, 2 A.M.[3]

To execute the resolution, the Executive Committee created a commission composed of Fyodor Nikolaevich Lukoyanov (chairman of the Ural provincial Cheka), Beloborodov, Goloshchekin, Georgy Safarov, Peter Voikov, Nikolai Sosnovsky, Pavel Bykov, and possibly others.

Yurovsky and Peter Zakharovich Ermakov were to search for a burial site, and Voikov was to prepare the kerosene, alcohol, and sulfuric acid (which Yurovsky did after lunch on July 17) as well as organize the disinformation. There is no need to cite here the history of the correspondence between Nicholas II and certain "loyal officers" who were purportedly plotting the escape of the tsar and his family. These letters have already been reprinted numerous times by a wide range of authors. Supposedly conveyed to the tsar through Dr. Derevenko, who had free access to the Ipatiev house, as well as by other routes, the letters served to justify the urgent execution of the Romanovs and were more than likely prepared by the Ural Soviet expressly for the impending trial. Diterikhs was the first to prove that this correspondence was an out-and-out falsification.[4] The Romanov execution in Ekaterinburg—just like the execution of the grand duke and his secretary a month earlier in Perm—was cloaked in disinformation.

On the morning of July 16, on orders from Yurovsky, the chef's young assistant, Sednev, was taken from the house and put in the guard booth outside. At half past eleven that night, representatives of the Ural Soviet handed Yurovsky the sentence. They waited a while for Ermakov and Mikhail Medvedev, who had gone for a truck and been detained. When they returned it was well after midnight. The driver, Sergei Ivanovich Lyukhanov, left the truck in the courtyard with the motor running so that the noise of the engine would drown out the shots and screams. We know exactly who the executioners were from the following document:

First body of the Ekaterinburg Soviet. Sitting: second from the left, Alexander Beloborodov; third, Pavel Bykov; last, Filipp Goloshchekin.

[On the letterhead:] Revolutionary Committee under the Ekaterinburg Soviet of Workers' and Soldiers' Deputies, the Revolutionary Headquarters of the Ural District, Extraordinary Commission [Cheka].

List of the special team for the Ipatiev house (1st Kamishl Rifle Regiment)

Commandant: Laois [Laslo] Gorvat
Anzelm Fisher
Izidor Edelshtein
Emil Fekete
Imre Nagy
Viktor Grinfeld
Andreas Vergazi
Provincial Commissar Sergei Vaganov
Pav Medvedev
Nikulin
Ekaterinburg, July 18, 1918, Head of the Extraordinary Comm: Yurovsky[5]

Add Ermakov, Mikhail Medvedev, and Yurovsky himself, and the list is complete. No doctor or clergyman participated in the execution.

Let us now turn to Yurovsky:

> I went to wake the prisoners.
>
> Botkin slept in the room closest to the entrance. He came out and asked what was going on. I told him that everyone had to be awakened since there was trouble in the city and it was dangerous for them to remain here and that I would move them to another place. Getting ready took a long time, around forty minutes. When the family was dressed I led them to a selected room at the bottom of the house. This is the plan that Comrade Nikulin and I had worked out (I must say here that we had not considered the fact that the windows would let the noise out, second that the wall against which they would be shot was stone, and third, which could not have been foreseen, that the shooting would take on a disorderly character). The last should not have happened, since every man would be shooting one person and therefore everything would be orderly. The reasons for the disorderly shooting became clear later. Even though I had warned them through Botkin not to take anything with them, they nevertheless had collected all kinds of trifles, pillows, purses, and so on, and, I think, a small dog.
>
> Down in the room (at the entrance to the right there was a very wide window, almost the width of the wall), I suggested they stand along the wall. Obviously, at that moment they still did not suspect what awaited them. Alexandra Fyodorovna said, "There aren't even any chairs here." Nicholas was carrying Alexei in his arms. And he stood in the room, holding him. Then I had two chairs brought in, and Alexandra Fyodorovna sat on one to the right of the door toward the window almost in the corner. Next to her, moving left from the entrance, stood the daughters and Demidova. Then they put Alexei next to them in an armchair, behind him came Dr. Botkin, the chef, and others, while Nicholas remained standing opposite Alexei. At the same time I had given orders for the men to come down and told them to be ready and for each man, when the command came, to be in his place. Nicholas seated Alexei and stood so that he blocked him. Alexei sat in the corner to the left of the door and I said, as far as I remember, to Nicholas that his royal relatives and friends both in the country and abroad were trying to free him and that the Soviet of Workers' Deputies had resolved to have them executed. He asked, "What?" and turned his face to Alexei, and at that moment I shot at him and killed him on the spot. He did not even have time to turn back to us to get an answer.[6]

Many have written about what happened next—participants in the events, historians, and experts.

The eleven to be executed stood or sat close together in two or three rows. Judging by the diagrams and photographs, the section of wall behind their backs was no more than thirteen feet wide.[7] Opposite them, shoulder to shoulder, stood the twelve members of the firing squad and behind them the guards who did not fire (five to seven men, of whom two had rifles). In a room approximately 90 feet square and 220 cubic feet in volume, then, there were as many as thirty people. It is these cramped conditions that inevitably determined the choice of weapon for the execution and the unexpected circumstances that arose, with all their consequences.

We can assert that the shooting was done with sawed-off rifles of the following types:[8]

Three types of revolvers: the .30-caliber Nagan (7.62 mm), the .35-caliber Nagan (9 mm), and the .42-caliber (10.66 mm) Smith & Wesson.[9]

Four types of pistols: the .28-caliber (6.43 mm) Browning, the .32-caliber (7.63 mm) Browning,[10] the .32-caliber (7.63 mm) Mauser,[11] and the .45-caliber (11.43 mm) Colt.[12]

Yurovsky, Ermakov, and Mikhail Medvedev wrote about their Mausers in their memoirs, but only one 7.63 mm bullet was found, and the bullet head was sufficiently misshapen that it cannot be definitively proved a Mauser.[13] There is also only one mark from an 11.43 mm Colt bullet, on the floor.[14] There are three marks from 6.43 mm Browning bullets and six from the 7.63 mm Browning (one in the wall, one on the floor,[15] and four bullets found at the burial site),[16] as well as three or four (two on the floor) from 10.66 mm Smith & Wesson bullets. Most of the firing clearly was done with Nagans: eight or nine marks from 9 mm bullets and seven from 7.62 mm bullets[17] found in the room and nine (7.62 mm) bullets also found at the burial site.[18]

Thus, if we count the bullets that ricocheted, which would have fallen on the floor and been removed during the cleanup, we can assume that in the course of the execution forty to fifty shots were fired. This is very curious because, altogether, the twelve men had eighty-five to ninety cartridges. And half of them had a second revolver or pistol! Something must have happened to impede the execution—something that forced them to stop shooting.

What happened becomes clear when we consider the following question: What kind of gunpowder was used for the execution?

The cartridges of the .42-caliber Smith & Wesson revolver issued by the Russian army before 1895 and used by police units up until 1917 were equipped only with black (smoking) powder.[19] The cartridges from the .30-caliber Nagan revolver, the 1895 model, were designed for smokeless powder.[20] However, until 1910, some of these cartridges were still equipped with black powder. They were stored away in rear arsenals and issued last, when reserves were scraping bottom—and by 1918 that was probably the case. The cartridges from the .35-caliber Nagan revolver (with transitional modification) were equipped with only black powder.[21] Pistol cartridges, as a rule, were equipped with smokeless powder.

By the time the first few rounds (more than thirty shots) were fired, the small room would have become filled with gunpowder gases. It would have been too smoky for anyone to see the gun in his own hand, let alone his targets. The mixture of gases from the burnt smokeless gunpowder and the black (smoking) gunpowder is unusually caustic, causing tearing eyes, coughing, and nausea. The firing squad would have been forced to exit the room quickly, leaving half their cartridges unspent, with no opportunity to verify who was dead and who was still alive among the victims. Mikhail Medvedev writes about this very vividly: "You can't see anything in the room because of all the smoke—now we are firing at barely visible silhouettes in the right corner who are falling. . . . One of the soldiers is wounded in the finger and the neck—either by ricochet or he was creased by bullets from the rifles of the Latvians in the second row, who could not see in the gun smoke. . . . In the passage I saw Pavel Medvedev—he was deathly pale and vomiting."

We know that gunpowder smoke can induce vomiting, especially in someone who is drunk. We also know that drinking was one of the so-called reasons for replacing the previous guard. While this was probably a trumped-up charge that enabled Yurovsky to replace the old guard with his men, we also know that drinking among the soldiers was far from uncommon. It is certainly true that the habits of the new guard were no better than the supposed habits of the old.[22]

Strekotin writes about the complications caused by the gunpowder as well: "The smoke blocked out the electric light and made breathing difficult."[23] Even without the smoke, the only lightbulb did not provide a lot of illumination.

Filipp Proskuryakov recalls that "even an hour (or two) later, the smokiness was like a fog."[24] There was no doctor present at the execution. Can we really believe that unqualified men competently took the pulse of the victims in that heap of bloody bodies? One thing we can say with confidence: the execution squad ended up firing only at those victims who were moving, either falling down or standing up. According to the testimony of many of the witnesses, this is what happened with the lady-in-waiting. According to Medvedev: "A white pillow moved from the door to the right corner of the room. In the gunsmoke a woman's figure dashes from the screaming women's group to the closed door and immediately falls, put down by Ermakov's shots."

Judging from the distribution of bullet marks on the walls, it is obvious that most of the shots were fired at the lower portion of the wall rather than at the upper portion.[25] The executioners were firing at whoever was falling. On the floor itself, only six bullet marks were found[26] and this with fifty shots fired!

The victims were quickly dragged to the waiting truck, which was standing with its motor running right in Ascension Lane, and thrown in the back of it. It was strictly forbidden to make noise, to say nothing of firing a gun, in the street—Ural Military Commissar Goloshchekin had seen to that. According to Yurovsky, "When the execution was done, we had to move the bodies, and the distance was relatively far—how to do it? Someone suggested stretchers (we hadn't thought about it beforehand). . . . the whole procedure took twenty minutes." Due to the small dimensions of the winding exit, it would have been difficult to carry the eleven bodies out to the truck in less than seven or eight minutes.

Here we need to touch on two murky questions. The first concerns the use of bayonets. A great deal has been written about how the victims were bayoneted, in addition to being shot.[27] The scientist Kryukov talks about finding evidence on the remains of injuries from a sharp instrument.[28] However, in the cellar room, bayonet traces were found only on the wall of the arch,[29] not on the floor.

The second question is even more curious. Bullet wounds have been found in the femurs and tibias of four of the nine skeletons.[30] The angle of the bullets shows that the victims were in a vertical position when they were shot. Yet the executioners were firing at almost point-blank range! Why were

The half-cellar room of the Ipatiev house where the execution took place. The excisions made by the investigator Sergeyev are visible on the walls.

RIGHT: Yakov Yurovsky.

they not aiming at the victims' chests or heads? Apparently, as the room filled with smoke, the men began shooting at the victims' legs because that was all that was visible.

Judging from the evidence of gun smoke and the lack of evidence of bayonet marks, the likelihood is high that there were living interspersed with dead in the back of the truck.

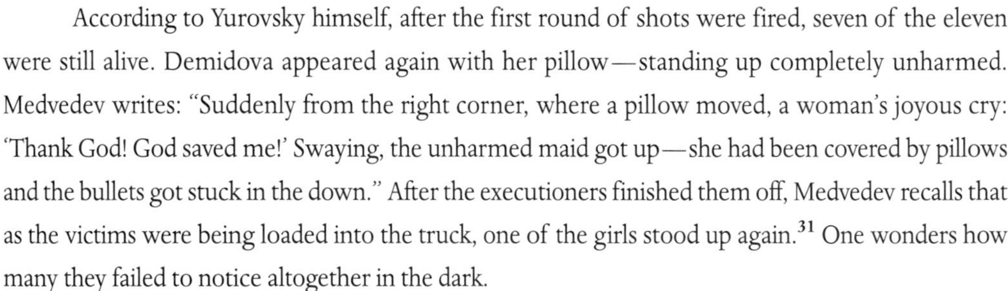

According to Yurovsky himself, after the first round of shots were fired, seven of the eleven were still alive. Demidova appeared again with her pillow—standing up completely unharmed. Medvedev writes: "Suddenly from the right corner, where a pillow moved, a woman's joyous cry: 'Thank God! God saved me!' Swaying, the unharmed maid got up—she had been covered by pillows and the bullets got stuck in the down." After the executioners finished them off, Medvedev recalls that as the victims were being loaded into the truck, one of the girls stood up again.[31] One wonders how many they failed to notice altogether in the dark.

The truck was driven by Lyukhanov. There is some disagreement on the exact size of the truck.

Historians say the truck was a Fiat but disagree on the size. But we know that there was room for three men, in addition to the driver, in the cab. With Lyukhanov sat Yurovsky, Ermakov, and Vaganov.

What happened in the back would have been hard to see from the cab at night, and the truck moved slowly down the miserable road, rocking and jolting over the numerous ruts and bumps. It was moving slowly enough that anyone still alive could have crawled out while the truck was moving. Which is exactly what happened: the execution team set out to bury eleven bodies and reached the burial site with only nine.

Documents published in recent years confirm this theory.[32] We cite the execution protocol:

> [On the letterhead:] Worker–Peasant Government of the Russian Federative Republic of Soviets, Ural Provincial Soviet of Workers', Peasants', and Soldiers' Deputies, Presidium.
>
> Ekaterinburg, July 19, 1918, 2200
>
> [Stamp:] Top secret.
>
> Minutes of the special session of the Provincial Executive Committee, the members of the Extraordinary Commission [Cheka], and Revolutionary Headquarters.
>
> At this session, those present heard a report confirming the liquidation of the Romanov family by the organs of the Extraordinary Commission in accordance with the resolution of July 7, 1918. This resolution was implemented on July 17, 1918 at 1:15 A.M.
>
> Executed were:
>
> Nicholas Romanov
> Alexandra Fyodorovna Romanova
> Alexei Nikolaevich Romanov
> Olga Nikolaevna Romanova
> Anastasia Nikolaevna Romanova
> Tatiana Nikolaevna Romanova
> Marie Nikolaevna Romanova
> Evgeny Sergeyevich Botkin
> Alexei Egorovich Trupp
> Anna Demidova St. [epanovna]
> Ivan Mikhailovich Kharitonov
>
> Provincial Soviet Chairman: Beloborodov
> Head of Revolutionary Headquarters: Mebius
> Ural Provincial Military Commissar: Goloshchekin
>
> [Stamp:] Ekaterinburg Executive Committee of the Soviet of Workers', Peasants', and Soldiers' Deputies; the Military–Revolutionary Committee.

Now let us compare this with an excerpt from another document that was published in 1992, after the remains of the Romanovs had been found:

> Conclusions. Manifest evidence allows us to assume that this is the burial site for the imperial family and their courtiers:
>
> Skeleton No. 1 conforms to Demidova.
> Skeleton No. 2 conforms to Dr. Botkin.
> Skeleton No. 3 conforms in age to Olga.
> Skeleton No. 4 conforms to Tsar Nicholas II.
> Skeleton No. 5 conforms in age and size to Marie.
> Skeleton No. 6 in age and size conforms to Tatiana.
> Skeleton No. 7 conforms to Alexandra.
> Skeleton No. 8 may have been a servant.
> Skeleton No. 9 was probably another servant.
> The remains of the Tsarevich Alexei and Anastasia were not found."[33]

For a more complete picture of the bloodshed, we will now move to Alapaevsk, where on the following night, July 17–18, 1918, still more members of the imperial family were executed. Grand Duchess Elizaveta Fyodorovna, Grand Duke Sergei Mikhailovich, Princes Ioann Konstantinovich, Konstantin Konstantinovich, and Igor Konstantinovich, and Prince Vladimir Pavlovich Paley were executed and thrown down an old mine shaft—a different mine shaft, but a remarkably parallel fate to that of the tsar's family. This execution was supervised by Safarov, a member of the Executive Committee of the Ural Soviet, and Govyrin, the Cheka chairman in Alapaevsk, who had made a special trip from Ekaterinburg.

After the execution, on the morning of July 18, the Alapaevsk Executive Committee sent a telegram to Ekaterinburg reporting that the prisoners had escaped with the help of unknown armed men and that searches to find them had been unsuccessful. The Ural provincial Soviet sent an analogous telegram to Moscow. This disinformation was revealed in September, when Alapaevsk fell to the Whites. The committee of inquiry quickly discovered the mine shaft with its corpses—the site had been well known to the local population all along.

In October, the victims' bodies were dug up and buried in a crypt in the Alapaevsk church. Later, when the White Army retreated, they took the bodies with them. The corpses eventually found their resting places in the Church of St. Serafim at the Russian theological mission in Beijing, China.

Let us return, however, to the execution in Ekaterinburg. At about three o'clock in the morning, according to Yurovsky's reminiscences, or before two, according to other sources,[34] the truck laden with the bodies of the executed prisoners drove away from the Ipatiev house down Ascension Lane, the Tarasovsky embankment, and Mechanics Street (see map of Ekaterinburg). They crossed the Iset River by a small bridge on Pokrovsky Boulevard. They would not have gone by way of the dam—a strategic site at this time, immediately before the evacuation of Ekaterinburg—as it would have certainly been guarded, and subjecting the truck to inspection was obviously not part of the Chekists' plans. They then followed the route down Uktusskaya Street and Main Boulevard and, at the fork with the Moscow road, at the right past the racetrack and toward the Upper Iset plant, crossed the Iset below Upper Iset Pond. Three railway crossings later, the truck came out on the Koptyaki dirt road (see map, pages 90–91). The truck traveled about four miles down the Koptyaki road to the railroad crossing at Nizhny Tagil (booth number 184), and then another one and a half to two miles to the tract known as the Four Brothers.

It had been a rainy week (see document, page 218), and the roads in and outside of town had suffered. According to Sokolov and Edvard Radzinsky,[35] the vehicle was continuously getting stuck in the holes and ruts and had to keep stopping. The first such stop, most likely, was on Pokrovsky Boulevard before the bridge over the Iset at the crossing of the railway tracks leading to a machine plant.

It took the truck an hour and a half to get to the burial site, and by then it was growing light. The executioners met up with a brigade of about twenty-five Red Army soldiers who had been summoned there beforehand by Ermakov. Yurovsky: "I asked Ermakov who they were and why they were there. . . . Why he needed so many I still don't know. I did hear shouts of 'We thought we'd get them here alive, but they're dead!'"

When the truck could not make it any farther, they transferred the bodies to sleds and made their way through the forest to the designated burial site, an abandoned mine in the Four Brothers tract. The tract took its name from four giant pines that marked the spot of a gold mine that had been abandoned before the burial team arrived. Ermakov had previously selected one of the mine shafts, which was about ten feet deep and partially filled with water, for the burial. The corpses were taken off the sleds and undressed so their clothing could be burned. The men lit bonfires "to destroy the clothing without any remains so that there would be no clues if the corpses were found for some reason."

It was in the process of undressing the corpses and destroying the clothing that the executioners discovered the jewels. The matter of tsarist jewels does not enter into our investigation—we touch upon it only to the extent that it sheds light on one detail that is important to us: on which bodies, exactly, these jewels were found. According to Yurovsky's note,[36] precious stones and jewelry were found sewn into the corsets of Tatiana, Olga, and Anastasia and into the girdle of Alexandra. Mikhail Medvedev also talks about diamonds in three of the girls' brassieres.[37] But there were four daughters. Apparently they did not undress the fourth. That two independent sources would make a mistake in counting the bodies with jewels is doubtful—all the imperial valuables were strictly accounted for. Even though the corsets were destroyed, the participants in the burial would have been careful about counting how many had contained the precious jewels.

One more detail. "Around the neck of each of the young girls hung an amulet into which a portrait of Rasputin and the text of his prayer had been sewn."[38] We can be very certain that exactly the same kind of amulet hung around the neck of Alexei, the "baby" and the heir whom the tsar and tsaritsa loved so much and took such pains to protect. Nonetheless, neither Yurovsky nor Medvedev says a word about it. Why not? Didn't they undress Alexei?

Undressing the corpses, throwing them down the mine shaft, and burning their clothing took

A section of the Koptyaki road covered with crossties. In the bottom photograph is Pavel Ermakov.

eight hours, until two o'clock in the afternoon. After that, roadblocks were set up to the north and south of the Four Brothers, and Yurovsky and Ermakov left precipitately for town. Why?

Ermakov does not say a word in his memoirs about this.[39] Yurovsky does so only very vaguely: "I went to the regional executive committee and reported to the authorities that things were not good." In what way were things not good? Was it because there had been witnesses to the burial? Because people had seen them and "knew that something was up"? Were they worried that when the Whites took Ekaterinburg, they would find the corpses? This had not bothered the executioners in Alapaevsk. Or were Yurovsky's worries still more significant? Could he have come up two dead bodies short?

If so, the delay of half a day at the burial site becomes understandable. Yurovsky must have sent some of the Red Army soldiers out on a search—"I sent another group of men to the city, because they were not needed," he says—and waited for the results. The search party would have come back empty-handed: Alexei and one of the grand duchesses had been lost and not found.

The affair had now taken a very dangerous turn. Yurovsky immediately set up roadblocks and he and Ermakov went to town to report to "the regional executive committee." In town, a decision must have been made: burn the remaining corpses to conceal the fact of the two missing bodies from the Soviet leadership. Commissar Goloshchekin "soundly berated Ermakov and sent him to get the bodies." Why was Ermakov "soundly berated"? Was it because he had not chosen a reliable burial spot? Was it because two bodies were missing?

Ermakov returned to the burial site and had the bodies removed from the mine shaft—out of the water! Mikhail Medvedev writes: "When all the bodies were hauled up by the feet with ropes from the water . . . before them lay . . . 'miracle-working relics': the icy water in the mine had not only washed away the blood but had frozen the bodies so that they looked as if they were alive—the faces of the tsar, the girls, and the women even had rosy cheeks." What about the face of Alexei?

Yurovsky got the kerosene and sulfuric acid in Ekaterinburg and arranged for several carts and brought a truck to be sent back to the mine shaft, where he was going to do the burning. In his memoirs, he writes honestly: "We had never done anything like that before [and hadn't prepared for it], and no one knew how to go about it. Polushin, I think, said he knew, so that was all right since no one had the slightest idea how it would work out."[40] It didn't. The corpses didn't burn—they smoked and sizzled, but they just wouldn't burn.

Nor could they have burned in those conditions. Today we know, for example, that in the open air the bodies of Hitler and Eva Braun burned for two full days. Soldiers burned all the gasoline in the garage of the imperial chancellery and even furniture, but all to no avail: the bodies still wouldn't burn. From a forensic standpoint, the likelihood of burning the two corpses (for example, Alexei and Marie Romanov), in haste, without a store of previously prepared dry wood, is minuscule.

So they decided to bury the Romanovs' remains somewhere. Yurovsky and his men put the bodies, four of them now partially burned, into the truck, drove back out onto the Koptyaki road, and turned toward Upper Isetsk. According to Mikhail Medvedev: "Not far from the crossing . . . in a swampy hollow the truck got stuck in the mud—wouldn't budge forward or back. No matter how hard they tried, it wouldn't move. They brought boards from the house of the railroad guard at the crossing and finally managed to push the truck out of the swampy hole that had formed." And suddenly . . . they had an idea! "The hole right in the road is the ideal secret fraternal grave for the last Romanovs."

We will be discussing the memoirs of the participants in more detail in Chapter 4. For now, let us limit ourselves to one question: How can so many varying accounts of the same event exist? Several men, direct participants in what was anything but a mundane event, describe it in completely different ways.

Let us keep in mind that only the execution protocol cited earlier was written immediately after the events took place. The memoirs of the participants did not emerge for several years, even decades, after the fact. Thus we need to begin the "search for the legend" with this protocol. It is short and simple: eleven people were executed. It doesn't say how many were buried or where. Only after the White

Army, which was never able to find the burial site, retreated from the Urals in 1920 did Yurovsky come forward with the first official report of this historic event. He created the legend in what has become known as the "Yurovsky Note": eleven people executed, eleven corpses transported to the site, two burned, nine secretly buried, burial site not specified—if anyone had found the site, the whole story would have come together.

There is a handwritten addendum to the Note that has given rise to many disputes. It reads: "Koptyaki [is] 18 v[ersts] [12 miles] from Ekaterinburg. To the northwest, the RR line crosses at the ninth verst, between Koptyaki and the Upper Isetsk plant."[41] Its authorship has been ascribed to the famous Soviet historian Pokrovsky.[42] The Romanovs' remains were found by researchers in 1979 in precisely this spot. However, in Chapter 4 we illustrate that, even without this disputed addendum, the burial site by the Koptyaki road is precisely designated in Yurovsky's reminiscences of 1934 and in Mikhail Medvedev's of 1963.

Following Yurovsky's lead, the remaining "legend spreaders" wrote their memoirs: Ermakov, Sukhorukov, Nikulin, Mikhail Medvedev, and Isai Rodzinsky—all Chekists, men of proven worth to the Soviet regime. Their reminiscences diverge in many respects but are united in the basic story line: they executed eleven people, they transported eleven bodies, they burned some of them (either two or four), and they buried the rest secretly.

This is the legend in its most general form. However, certain details take some sorting out. While extracting the undressed corpses from the water, Sukhorukov claims, he specifically recognized Alexei and Anastasia, whom he had never seen in person before. Every one of them recalled personally finishing off the "strangely living" Alexei. Neither Yurovsky nor Ermakov nor Nikulin mentions a word about the gunpowder smoke, as if there had never been any. They simply fired until the barrels and cartridges of their weapons were completely spent, felt for pulses in the victims, and finished off those still alive on the spot. True, they left no traces. But that doesn't matter.

Every one of these reports was written for internal consumption, in full confidence that no outsider would ever read it. What was most important in writing these reports was to prove beyond a shadow of a doubt that the order had been carried out. All eleven people had been executed and all the bodies had been either destroyed or buried. No one had been left alive.

As for describing the location of the burial site, it had quickly become clear that the local inhabitants knew all about it; so there was no use in trying to keep it a secret any longer.

In 1928, the poet Vladimir Mayakovsky was in Ekaterinburg, and the chairman of the Ural Soviet Executive Committee, Paramonov, showed him the burial site.

Past Iset—
the mines and cliffs
Past Iset—
the whistling wind,
at verst number nine
the ispolkom driver

> stopped, stood,
> silent . . .
> Here is a cedar,
> axed over and over,
> Notches straight through the bark
> By the root of the cedar
> a highway
> and in it an emperor—
> buried.
>
> —Vladimir Mayakovsky, 1928

On July 17, Yurovsky announced the execution to the Ekaterinburg Provincial Executive Committee. A telegram was immediately sent to Moscow, to the chairman of the Soviet of People's Commissars, Lenin, and to VTsIK Chairman Sverdlov:

> From the Provincial Soviet Presidium of the worker–peasant government. In view of the enemy's advance on Ekaterinburg and the Cheka's discovery of a significant White Guard plot having as its purpose the abduction of the former tsar and his family. The documents are in our hands. By resolution of the Provincial Soviet Presidium, Nicholas Romanov was shot on the night of sixteen July [sic]. The family has been evacuated to a safe place. Because of this we have issued the following announcement: "In view of the advance of counterrevolutionary bands on the Red capital of the Urals and the possibility of the crowned hangman eluding popular justice (a plot has been uncovered involving White guards attempting to abduct him and his family and compromising documents have been found and will be published), the Provincial Soviet Presidium, by the revolution's will, resolved to execute the former Tsar Nicholas Romanov on the night of July 16, 1918. This sentence has been carried out. Romanov's family, held with him under guard, has been evacuated from Ekaterinburg in the interest of public safety. The Provincial Soviet Presidium." [This was the announcement that the White guards discovered pasted up all over Ekaterinburg when they entered the city on July 25, 1918.] Documents of the plot are being sent immediately by courier to the Soviet of People's Commissars and the Central Executive Committee. We await news at the apparatus. We urgently request a reply. We are waiting at the apparatus.[43]

The text is very odd, as it gives the impression that there was a direct conversation. But we know that direct contact between Ekaterinburg and Moscow had been interrupted since July 10 or 11 and would remain that way for several months. The earlier telegram sent by the Ural Soviet to the Kremlin that arrived in Moscow on July 16 had traveled for about twenty-four hours by a circuitous route and bore the appropriate number and Zinoviev's signature. This telegram under consideration, however, lacked either a number or a signature. All the previous telegrams sent from Ekaterinburg had been addressed directly to Sverdlov. It was standard to send Lenin a copy, but in this case we have a telegram addressed directly to Lenin, with a copy to Sverdlov.

It is difficult to shake the suspicion that this telegram was fabricated significantly later, when the scheme for further disinformation had been efficiently (not in the usual Ural manner!) elaborated and after it had become clear that no one had found the burial site of the Romanovs. To keep anything from being verified, the "telegram" bears no numbers or signatures.

Moscow's reaction to this information is obvious from the following protocols:

Excerpt from protocol no. 1 of the session of the VTsIK Presidium on the execution of Nicholas II.

> July 18, 1918.
> Heard: the report of the execution of Nicholas Romanov. (Telegram from Ekaterinburg.)
> Resolved: the following resolution is passed with regard to the discussion: The VTsIK, in the person of its Presidium, recognizes the decision of the Ural Provincial Soviet as correct. Instruct Comrades Sverdlov, Sosnovsky, and Avanesov to compose the appropriate news report for the press. Publish information about the documents (diaries, letters, etc.) of the former Tsar Nicholas Romanov in the possession of the TsIK. Instruct Comrade Sverdlov to create a special commission to sort through these papers and their publication.
> VTsIK Secretary V. Avanesov.[44]

From protocol no. 159 of the session of the Soviet of People's Commissars on the execution of the tsar's family.

> July 18, 1918.
> Chairing: Vladimir Ilich Ulianov (Lenin).
> Present: Gukovsky, V. M. Bonch-Bruevich, Petrovsky, Semashko, Vinokurov, Soloviev, Kozlovsky . . . Trotsky . . . [thirty-two names total].
> Heard: 3. Extraordinary statement by TsIK Chairman Comrade Sverdlov on the execution of the former Tsar Nicholas II under the sentence of the Ekaterinburg Soviet and on the approval of this sentence by the TsIK Presidium. . . .
> Resolved: To take into consideration . . .
> [No signatures.][45]

These protocols need no comment.

On January 27, 1919, in the courtyard of Sts. Peter and Paul Fortress, Grand Dukes Nicholas Mikhailovich, Pavel Alexandrovich, Dmitry Konstantinovich, and Georgy Mikhailovich were executed without charges ever having been brought against them—in retribution for the execution of Karl Liebknecht and Rosa Luxemburg in Germany. Their graves have never been found.

The Accounts of the Executioners

From Yakov Yurovsky's account at a conference of old Bolsheviks in Sverdlovsk [Ekaterinburg] about the execution of the royal family [written in February 1934]

February 1, 1934.
. . . It was assumed that if time allowed, they [Nicholas and Alexandra] would have been tried. But as was previously noted, the front was moving ever closer from the beginning of July and, finally, was within 35–40 versts [23–26 miles], which inevitably brought the ending closer.

Since it was a question then of great political significance that could not be resolved without permission from the center [Moscow], and since the situation of the front did not depend only on the Urals but on the capabilities of the center (for by that time the centralization of the Red Army was becoming more and more concentrated), communications and conversation on this issue with the center were continual. Around July 10, there was a decision in case leaving Ekaterinburg became inevitable. That was the only explanation for why execution without trial was put off until July 16, and Ekaterinburg was finally left on July 15–16, and the evacuation of Ekaterinburg was done in complete, so to say, order and timeliness. It was also around the 10th or 11th that Filipp [Goloshchekin] told me that Nicholas would have to be liquidated and that we had to be prepared for that.

We did not have experience in methods of liquidation then, since we did not deal with such things, and therefore it is understandable why there was much that was hurried about the business, especially also because of the danger and nearness of the front making it worse. He [Goloshchekin] told me: certain comrades feel that in order to do this reliably and quietly, it should be done at night, right in their beds while they sleep. It seemed inconvenient to me and I said that we would think about how to do it and get ready.

On the morning of July 15 Filipp arrived and said that the business had to be liquidated tomorrow. The cook Sednev (a boy of thirteen) was to be sent back home or somewhere in the middle of the country. It was also said that we would execute Nicholas and officially announce it, whereas for the family, here it might be announced, but how, when, and in what order no one knew yet. That meant everything demanded profound caution, as few people as possible, and absolutely reliable ones.

On the fifteenth I began getting ready, since it had to be done quickly. I decided to use as many men as there were people to be shot, gathered them together, told them what it was about and that they had to prepare themselves and as soon as we got final orders they would have to act swiftly. I must say here that executing people is not as easy as some might think. This isn't at the front but in what we call "peacetime" circumstances. These were not simply bloodthirsty people, but people fulfilling the heavy duty of revolution. That is why the circumstance occurred at the last moment; when two of the Latvians refused, they lacked character.

On the morning of July 16 I sent away the boy cook, Sednev, on the excuse of meeting with his uncle who had come to Sverdlovsk. The usual intermediary Botkin, and then one of the daughters, asked why and where and how long Sednev would be away. Seems Alexei missed him. Receiving an explanation, they seemed satisfied. I prepared 12 Nagan pistols and assigned whom to shoot to each man. Comrade Filipp warned me that a truck would arrive at midnight, they would say the password, they would be allowed in, and we were to give them the corpses to take away and bury. Around eleven that night I got everyone together again and announced that we would have to liquidate the prisoners soon. I warned Pavel Medvedev about being thorough in checking the guards outside and inside, and that he and the corporal of the guard keep an eye themselves around the house and the house where the outside guards lived and that they keep in communication with me. And, at the very last moment, when everything was ready for the execution, to warn the guards and the rest of the team that if they heard shots from the house, not to worry and not come outside and if something really worried them to let me know through established communications.

The truck did not arrive until half past one, and the extra waiting time added to the anxiety, the waiting in general, and, most importantly, the nights were short. It was only after the arrival, or the telephone calls [saying] that they had left, that I went to wake the prisoners.

Botkin slept in the room closest to the entrance. He came out and asked what was going on. I told him that everyone had to be awakened since there was trouble in the city and it was dangerous for them to remain here and that I would move them to another place. Getting ready took a long time, around forty minutes. When the family was dressed I led them to a selected room at the bottom of the house. This is the plan that Comrade Nikulin and I had worked out (I must say here that we had not considered the fact that the windows would let the noise out, second that the wall against which they would be shot was stone, and third—which could not have been foreseen—that the shooting would take on a disorderly character.) The last should not have happened, since every man would be shooting one person and therefore everything would be orderly. The reasons for the disorderly shooting became clear later. Even though I had warned them through Botkin not to take anything with them, they nevertheless had collected all kinds of trifles, pillows, purses, and so on, and, I think, a small dog.

Down in the room (at the entrance to the right there was a very wide window, almost the width of the wall), I suggested they stand along the wall. Obviously, at that moment they still did not suspect what awaited them. Alexandra Fyodorovna said, "There aren't even any chairs here." Nicholas was carrying Alexei in his arms. And he stood in the room, holding him. Then I had two chairs brought in, and Alexandra Fyodorovna sat on one to the right of the door toward the window almost in the corner. Next to her, moving left from the entrance, stood the daughters and Demidova. Then they put Alexei next to them in an armchair, behind him came Dr. Botkin, the chef, and others, while Nicholas remained standing opposite Alexei. At the same time I had given orders for the men to come down and told them to be ready and for each man, when the command came, to be in his place. Nicholas seated Alexei and stood so that he blocked him. Alexei sat in the corner to the left of the door and I said, as far as I remember, to Nicholas that his royal relatives and friends both in the country and abroad were trying to free him and that the Soviet of Workers' Deputies had resolved to have them executed. He asked, "What?" and turned his face to Alexei, and at that moment I shot at him and killed him on the spot. He did not even have time to turn back to us to get an answer.

And here instead of order, disorderly firing began. The room, even though very small, was big enough for everyone to enter and do the execution properly. But many apparently shot from the doorway, and since the wall was stone, the bullets began ricocheting around, and the firing increased when the executees started screaming. With great difficulty I managed to stop the shooting. The bullet of one of the executioners behind me whizzed past my head, and one man was shot in the hand, either the palm or the finger. When the shooting stopped, the daughters, Alexandra Fyodorovna, and I think, the lady-in-waiting Demidova, as well as Alexei were still alive. I thought that they had fallen down in fear or maybe intentionally and that's why they were still alive. We started finishing them off (to keep down on the blood, I had suggested earlier that they shoot in the heart area). Alexei was just sitting stunned, and I finished him off. They shot at the daughters, but nothing worked, and then Ermakov used the bayonet, and that did not help, and then they were shot in the head. The reason why the execution by shooting of the daughters and Alexandra Fyodorovna was difficult I learned only in the woods.

When the execution was done, we had to move the bodies, and the distance was relatively far—how to do it? Someone suggested stretchers (we hadn't thought about it beforehand), so we removed the traces from a sleigh and stretched a sheet, I think, on them. Checking that all were dead, we started moving them. Then we noticed that there was blood everywhere. I immediately ordered them to get the soldier's cloth, and we put a piece in the stretcher and then spread the cloth inside the truck. I had Mikhail Medvedev receive the bodies. He is a former Chekist and presently working for the GPU [a precursor of the KGB]. He and Ermakov Peter Zakharovich were supposed to get and take away the corpses. When the first few bodies were taken away, someone told me—I don't remember who—that someone else was pocketing valuables. Then I realized that apparently there were valuables in the things they had brought with them. I immediately stopped the removal, gathered the men, and demanded they turn in the valuables. After some resistance, two men returned the valuables. Threatening to shoot any marauders, I pulled those two out and put, as I remember, Comrade Nikulin in charge of the transport of the bodies, warning him that the executed had valuables. We collected everything that was in their things that they had taken with them, as well as the things themselves, and sent them to headquarters. Comrade Filipp, apparently to spare me (since I was not very healthy), told me not to go to "the funeral," but I was very concerned about hiding the bodies well. Therefore I decided to go myself, and a good thing, otherwise the bodies would have fallen into the hands of the Whites. You can imagine what a campaign they would have raised over the business.

Leaving orders to wash and clean up, we left around three, or maybe a bit later. I took along several people from the indoor guards. I did not know where the bodies were supposed to be buried, that had been assigned to Comrade Ermakov by Filipp. (By the way, Pavel Medvedev told me that night that he saw Comrade Filipp running to headquarters, walking around the house, probably quite worried how it would take place.) Ermakov took us somewhere in the Upper Isetsk plant. I had not been in that area and did not know it. Approximately 2–3 versts [1½–2 miles], or maybe more, from the Upper Isetsk plant we were met by a whole escort on horseback and in carts. I asked Ermakov who they were and why they were there, and he told me that he had prepared for them to be there. Why he needed so many I still don't know. I did hear shouts of "We thought we'd get them here alive, but they're dead!" Another 3–4 versts [2–2½ miles] along the truck got stuck between two trees. Here some of Ermakov's men started pulling on the girls' blouses and it turned out that they had valuables on them and men were stealing them. I gave orders to stop the men and not let anyone near the truck.

The truck was stuck and not moving. I asked Ermakov, "Are we far from the spot?"

He said, "Not far, beyond the railroad track."

Besides being stuck in the trees, we were in a swampy place. Whichever way we turned, it was boggy. I thought, he got so many men and horses here, too bad there isn't a single wagon, only these traps.

There was nothing for it but to unload the truck to lighten the weight, but even that did not help. Then I had them [the bodies] loaded in the traps, since we could not wait any more, it was getting light. At dawn we drove up to the famous landmark.

Several dozen steps away from the mine shaft intended for the burial there were peasants around a campfire, probably having spent the night after mowing hay. On the way we had run into individuals and it was becoming impossible to continue our work with people around. I must say that things were becoming difficult and everything could have been ruined. At the time I did not yet know that the shaft was no good for our purposes. And then there were the damned valuables. I did not know then that there were so many of them, and Ermakov's people were wrong for this work and there were too many of them. I decided to dissolve the men. I had learned that we had traveled approximately 15–16 versts [10–10½ miles] from the city and were within 2–3 versts of the village of Koptyaki. We had to surround the area, which I did. I sent some men to encircle the region and also sent some into the village to keep people from leaving, with the explanation that the Czechoslovaks were in the area. And that our units were moving this way and that it was too dangerous to go outside. And also they were to make everyone they met turn around and go back to the village and to shoot the stubborn and disobedient ones.

I sent another group of men to the city, because they were not needed. After that, I ordered them to load [sic] the corpses, undress them to burn the clothing, to destroy the clothing without any remains so that there would be no clues if the corpses were found for some reason. I had them light bonfires. When they started undressing them we found that the daughters and Alexandra Fyodorovna, although I don't remember if she wore what the daughters wore or whether she wore just the protective garments. The daughters, however, had brassieres made of solid diamonds and other valuable stones, that were not only a way to hold valuables but also protective armor. That was why neither bullets nor bayonet gave results when they were shot and bayoneted. By the way, their suffering before death was their own fault and no one else's.

There was about half a pood [17 pounds] of these valuables. Their greed was so great that Alexandra Fyodorovna, by the way, had a huge piece of round gold wire, bent into the form of bracelet, weighing around a pound. The jewels were ripped out of the clothes on the spot so we would not have to drag around bloodied rags with us. The jewels that the Whites discovered when they were digging had to be, undoubtedly, those that were sewn into the clothes separately and which remained in the ashes after they were burned. The comrades who found some diamonds the next day turned them in to me. How did they miss the other remaining jewels? They had enough time. Most likely, they simply didn't think. We must assume, by the way, that some of the valuables are being returned to us through Torgsin [a Soviet store that accepted hard currency, gold, and jewelry], since, probably, the peasants from Koptyaki village picked them up after we left. We picked up the jewels, burned the clothing, and threw the corpses, completely naked, into the mine shaft. And this is where the new headache began. The water barely covered the bodies; what could we do? We decided to blow up the shaft with bombs to make it collapse. But that did not work naturally. I saw that we were not having any success with the burial, we couldn't leave it that way, and we had to start all over. What should we do? Where could we stick them?

At around two that day, I decided to go into town, since it was clear that the corpses had to be removed from the mine shaft and moved to another place, since besides the fact that even a blind man could find them, the spot was given away, people had seen us and knew that something was up. I left the guards in place, took the valuables, and left. I went to the regional executive committee and reported to the authorities that things were not good. Comrade Safarov and I don't remember who else heard me out, but said nothing.

Then I found Filipp, explaining to him the necessity for moving the corpses to another place. When he agreed, I suggested that he send people right away to haul out the corpses. I would look for a new spot. Filipp called in Ermakov, soundly berated him, and sent him to get the bodies. At the same time I had him bring bread, lunch, since the men there had not slept in almost twenty-four hours, were hungry and exhausted. They were supposed to wait for me to return. Getting and hauling out the corpses was not very simple, and they spent a lot of time on it. Apparently, they spent all night, since they left late.

I went to the city executive committee to see Sergei Egorovich Chutskaev, then chairman of the city executive committee, to get his advice; maybe he knew of a good place. He suggested some very deep and abandoned mines on the Moscow road. I got a car, took a few men from the regional Cheka, I think Polushin and someone else, and we set off, but about a verst or so from the spot, the car broke down, we left the driver to repair it and went off on foot, examined the place and found that it was good—the whole point was not to have anyone see us. There were people living nearby, so we decided that we would come, pick them up and send them to the city and when the operation was over, we would release them. That's what we decided. We got back to the car, but it needed to be hauled [towed]. I decided to wait for a passing vehicle. In a short while someone was coming in a cart with a pair of horses. I stopped them, it turned out the fellows knew me and were hurrying to their plant. It was with great reluctance, but they had to give me the horses.

While we were traveling, another plan came up: burn the corpses, but no one knew how to do it. Polushin, I think, said that he knew, fine and good, since no one knew how it would turn out. I still had my mind set on the mine on the Moscow road, and therefore, transporting the bodies, and I decided to get wagons and besides which, I had a plan, in case of any problems, to bury them in groups in various spots along the road. The road leading to Koptyaki, near the landmark, is full of clay, so that if we could bury them without anyone watching, no way in hell would anyone guess, just bury and drive over it with a cart, nothing but a muddy mess. So, three plans. But we had no transport, no car. I went to the garage of the chief of military transport, to see if they had a car. There was a car, but only for the chief. I've forgotten his name, but he turned out to be a scoundrel and he was executed in Perm, I think. The chief of the garage or deputy chief of military transport, I don't remember exactly, was Comrade Pavel Petrovich Gorbunov, at present deputy of Gosbank, and I told him I urgently needed a car. He said, "Ah, I know what for." And he gave me the chief's car. I went to the chief of supplies for the Urals, Voikov, to get gasoline or kerosene as well as sulfuric acid, in case we had to disfigure the faces, and also shovels. I got all that. As comrade commissar of justice of the Urals Oblast [Province], I gave orders to take ten carts without drivers from the prison. They loaded everything up and left. I had a truck sent there, too. I stayed to wait for Polushin, the "specialist" in burning, who was late somewhere. I waited at Voikov's for him. But by eleven o'clock, he still wasn't there. Later I was told that he had started out on horseback to get to me and he fell off the horse hurting his leg and that he could not come. Bearing in mind that a car could get stuck again, I left with some comrade I don't remember on horseback around midnight to the place where the corpses were. I had an accident, too. The horse tripped, fell to its knees, and then on its side, squashing my leg. I lay on the ground for over an hour until I could get back on the horse. We got there late at night, and the work on hauling [the corpses] was under way. I decided to bury a few bodies on the road. They started digging a hole. It was almost ready at dawn, when a comrade came up to me and announced that despite the orders not to let anyone near, a man appeared, an acquaintance of Ermakov, whom he allowed close enough to see that they were digging, since there were mounds of clay. Even though Ermakov insisted that the man could not have seen, other comrades, besides the one who had told me, started to illustrate, that is, to show where he had been and that he had to have seen.

So that plan was foiled. It was decided to restore the pit. Waiting until evening, we loaded up the wagon. The truck was waiting in a spot where it was allegedly guaranteed not to get stuck (the driver was the laborer Lyukhanov). We headed for the Siberian road. Crossing the railroad tracks, we loaded the corpses back in the truck and soon got bogged down again. We struggled for two hours, and it was close to midnight, when I decided that we had to bury them right there, since at this late hour no one could see us there, there were only a few people who could see us—the railroad signalman, since I had sent people to get pieces of wood to cover the spot where the corpses would be, so that the only guess people would make if they found the sleepers was that they had been placed on the ground to let a truck drive over. I forgot to mention that that evening, or rather that night, we got stuck twice. We unloaded everything, got out, and the second time we were hopelessly stuck. About two months ago, perusing the book by Sokolov, investigator of extremely important affairs under Kolchak, I saw a photograph of those sleepers, and it said, here is a place covered with sleepers to let a truck through. So they dug up the whole area and did not figure out to look under the sleepers. I must say that everyone was so damned tired that they did not want to dig a new grave, but as usual in these cases, two or three started and the rest joined in. We lit a fire and while the grave was being prepared, we burned two corpses: Alexei and by mistake, instead of Alexandra Fyodorovna, we burned, apparently, Demidova. At the place of the burning we dug a pit, put in the bones, smoothed it out then lit a big fire and covered our tracks with ashes. Before putting the rest of the bodies into the pit, we poured sulfuric acid over them, filled the pit with dirt, put the sleepers over them, the empty truck drove over it, settled the sleepers better and put an end to it. At five or six in the morning, we collected everyone and told them the importance of what we had done and warned them that they had to forget what they had seen and never talk to anyone about it, we went into town. They had lost us and showed up when it was all over, the fellows from the regional Cheka: Comrades Isai Rodzinsky, Gorin, and someone else.

On the evening of the nineteenth I went back to Moscow with my report. I turned over the valuables to Trifonov, member of the Revolutionary Council III of the Army, and Beloborodov, Novoselov, and someone else I believe hid them in a cellar, on the land of some little house belonging to a worker in Lys'va and in 1919, when the Central Committee commission went to the Urals to organize Soviet rule in the liberated Urals, I was also going there to work, and Novoselov and someone else got the valuables out, and N. N. Krestinsky, who was returning to Moscow, took them there. When in 1921–23 I worked in the republic's State Security, putting the valuables in order, I remember that one of the strings of pearls of Alexandra Fyodorovna was valued at six-hundred thousand gold rubles [at the time approximately $120,000 U.S. dollars].

In Perm, where I worked on the former tsarist objects, another bunch of jewels was found, hidden in their things down to their underwear inclusively, and the goods of all kinds filled more than one railroad car.

From the reminiscences of Mikhail Medvedev (Kudrin), a participant in the execution of the royal family [written in December 1963]

The evening of July 16, 1918, in the building of the Extraordinary Commission on Fighting Counterrevolution [Cheka] of the Urals Province (located in the American Hotel of the city of Ekaterinburg, today the city of Sverdlovsk) the regional Urals Soviet was in session. When I—an Ekaterinburg Chekist—was called in, I saw familiar comrades in the room: Chairman of the Soviet of Deputies, Alexander Georgievich Beloborodov, Chairman of the Provincial Committee of the Bolshevik Party Georgy Safarov, military commissar of Ekaterinburg Filipp Goloshchekin, member of the Soviet Peter Lazarevich Voikov, chairman of the Provincial Cheka Fyodor Lukoyanov, and my friends, members of the collegium of the Urals Provincial Cheka Vladimir Gorin, Isai Idelevich (Ilich) Rodzinsky (now a personal pensioner living in Moscow) and superintendent of the House for Special Designation (the Ipatiev house), Yakov Mikhailovich Yurovsky.

When I came in, they were deciding what to do with the former tsar Nicholas II Romanov and his family. Filipp Goloshchekin was reporting on his trip to Moscow to see Ya[kov] M. Sverdlov. He could not get sanctions from the All-Russian Central Executive Committee to execute the Romanov family. Sverdlov had consulted with V. I . Lenin, who was for bringing the tsar's family to Moscow for an open trial of Nicholas II and his wife, Alexandra Fyodorovna, whose treachery during World War I had cost Russia dearly.

"An all-Russian trial!" Lenin had insisted to Sverdlov. "With publications in the press. Tote up the human and material costs the sovereign had created for the country during his reign. How many revolutionaries hanged, how many died at hard labor, and in the war no one needed! Have him answer before the people! Do you think that only some illiterate peasant believes in the 'good' tsar the father? Not only him, my dear Yakov Mikhailovich! Was it so long ago that our progressive Petersburg worker went to the Winter Palace with gonfalons? That was just some 13 years ago! It's that inexplicable Russian trust that I have to turn to dust in an open trial of Nicholas the Bloody."

Ya. M. Sverdlov tried to give him Goloshchekin's reasons: the danger of traveling by train with the tsar's family across Russia, where there were counterrevolutionary uprisings in cities, and the difficulties at the fronts near Ekaterinburg, but Lenin insisted.

"So what if the front is retreating? Moscow is now far in the rear, so evacuate them to the rear! And we'll have a trial the whole world will see."

In parting, Sverdlov told Goloshchekin, "You tell the comrades this, Filipp, that the Executive Committee is not giving official sanctions for the execution."

After his report, Safarov asked the military commander how many days he thought Ekaterinburg would last. Goloshchekin replied that the situation was dangerous—the poorly armed volunteer units of the Red Army were retreating and in three days, maximum five, Ekaterinburg would fall. A heavy silence filled the room. Everyone knew that evacuating the tsar's family from the city not even to Moscow but simply to the North meant giving the monarchists their long-awaited opportunity to kidnap the tsar. The Ipatiev house was a fortress to some degree: two tall wooden fences around it, a system of posts for external and indoor guards of workers, and machine guns. Of course, we could not guarantee such dependable security to a moving car or coach, especially outside the city limits.

Leaving the tsar for the White Armies of Admiral Kolchak was out of the question—this "favor" would threaten the existence of the young Republic of Soviets, surrounded by hostile armies. Hostile toward Bolsheviks, whom he considered after the Brest Peace [Treaty of Brest] as traitors to the interests of Russia, Nicholas II would have become the banner of counterrevolutionary forces inside and outside the Soviet republic. Admiral Kolchak, using the ancient faith in the good intentions of tsars, could have attracted the Siberian peasantry to his side, for they had never seen landowners and did not know what serfdom was, and therefore did not support Kolchak who was imposing landowner laws on the territories he captured (thanks to the uprising of the Czechoslovak corps). Word of "saving" the tsar would have increased tenfold the forces of embittered kulaks in the provinces of Soviet Russia.

We Chekists still had fresh in our memory the attempts of the Tobolsk clergy, led by Bishop Hermogen, to free the tsar's family from arrest. It was only the quick thinking of my friend, the sailor Pavel Khokhryakov, who arrested Hermogen in time and moved the Romanovs to Ekaterinburg under guard of the Bolshevik Soviet, that saved the day. With the deep piety of the people in the provinces, we could not give the enemy even relics of the tsarist dynasty, from which the clergy would immediately fabricate "holy miracle-working relics"—not a bad flag for Admiral Kolchak's armies.

But there was yet another reason that decided the fate of the Romanovs not in the way that Ilich [Lenin] wanted.

The relatively luxurious life of the Romanovs (the mansion of the merchant Ipatiev was a far cry from prison) in such troubled times, when the enemy was literally at the gate, created understandable outrage among the workers of Ekaterinburg and surrounding areas. At meetings and rallies in the plants and factories of Upper Isetsk, the workers said straight out:

"Why are you coddling Nicholas, you Bolsheviks? Time to put an end to him! Or we'll smash your Soviet to wood chips!"

These feelings were making it very hard to form units of the Red Army, and the threat of retribution was no joke—the workers were armed and for them word and deed were not divisible. There were other parties demanding immediate execution of the Romanovs. Back in late June 1918, members of the Ekaterinburg Soviet, S[ocial] R[evolutionary] Sakovich and Left SR Khorimsky (later a Bolshevik, Chekist, who died during the cult of personality of Stalin and was posthumously rehabilitated) insisted at meetings on the swiftest liquidation of the Romanovs and accused the Bolsheviks of inconsistency. The leader of the anarchists, Zhebenev, shouted at us in the Soviet:

"If you don't destroy Nicholas the Bloody, then we'll do it ourselves!"

Without sanctions from the Executive Committee for the execution, there was nothing we could say in response, and dragging it out without explaining the reason made the workers even angrier. Putting off the decision about the fate of the Romanovs in a war situation meant further undermining the trust of the people in our party. Therefore, in order to decide the fate of the royal family in Ekaterinburg, Perm, and Alapaevsk (where the tsar's brothers lived), the Bolshevist part of the Provincial Soviet of the Urals met. Our decision would determine whether we would lead the workers to defend the city of Ekaterinburg or the anarchists and Left SRs would lead them. There was no third way.

In the last month or two "curiosity seekers" kept approaching the fence of the House for Special Designation [Ipatiev house], usually suspicious characters who had come mostly from St. Petersburg or Moscow. They tried to pass notes and food, they sent letters by mail which we intercepted: all were assurances of loyalty and offerings of service. We Chekists had the impression that there was a White Guard organization in town stubbornly trying to get into contact with the tsar and tsaritsa. We stopped access to the house even for priests and nuns who brought food from the neighboring convent.

But it was not only the monarchists who had come secretly to Ekaterinburg who were hoping to free the imprisoned tsar; the family itself was prepared to be taken at any moment and did not miss any opportunities to make contact. The Ekaterinburg Chekists discovered this readiness in a simple way. Beloborodov, Voikov, and Chekist Rodzinsky composed a letter allegedly from a Russian officers' organization, which informed them of the coming fall of Ekaterinburg and suggested they be ready to flee on a specific night. The note was translated into French by Voikov and then copied in red ink in Isai Rodzinsky's good penmanship, and passed to the tsaritsa by one of the guards. The answer did not take long. They composed and sent a second letter. Observation of their rooms showed that for two or three nights the Romanov family stayed dressed—their readiness to escape was total. Yurovsky reported on this to the Provincial Soviet of the Urals.

Having discussed all the circumstances, we took a decision: that very night we would strike two blows: liquidate the two monarchist underground officers organizations, which could deal a blow to the back of the units defending the city (Chekist Isai Rodzinsky was given that assignment), and to destroy the Romanov family.

Yakov Yurovsky proposed making an exception for the boy.

"Who? The heir? I'm against that!" I countered.

"No, Mikhail, the kitchen boy, Lyonya [Leonid] Sednev, has to be taken away. Why kill the little cook. . . . He plays with Alexei."

"What about the other servants?"

"We gave them a chance to abandon the Romanovs from the very beginning. Some left, and the ones remaining said that they want to share the fate of the monarch. Let them share."

We resolved: to save the life only of Lyonya Sednev. Then we started thinking who should be sent to the liquidation of the Romanovs from the Urals Provincial Cheka. Beloborodov asked me, "Will you take part?"

"I was sent to prison on Nicholas II's order. Of course I will!"

"We need a representative from the Red Army," Filipp Goloshchekin said. "I recommend Peter Zakharovich Ermakov, military commissar of Upper Isetsk."

"Approved. And whom are you sending, Yakov?"

"Myself and my aide, Grigory Petrovich Nikulin," Yurovsky replied. "So that makes four: Medvedev, Ermakov, Nikulin, and I."

The meeting ended. Yurovsky, Ermakov, and I went together to the House for Special Designation, went up to the second floor to the superintendent's office, where Chekist Grigory Petrovich Nikulin (now a personal pensioner, living in Moscow) was waiting for us. We shut the door and sat for a long time, not knowing where to begin. We had to hide from the Romanovs that they were being taken out to be shot. And where could we execute them? Besides, there were only four of us, and the Romanovs with their doctor, chef, valet, and maid were eleven people!

It was hot. We couldn't think of anything. Maybe, while they slept, we could throw grenades into their rooms? That was no good—the noise would be heard all over the city, people would think that the Czechs had burst into Ekaterinburg. Yurovsky suggested a different idea: stab them to death in their beds. We even divided up who got to kill whom. We waited for them to fall asleep. Yurovsky went down to the rooms of the tsar and tsaritsa, the grand duchesses, the servants, but they were all awake—they must have been upset by the removal of the chef boy.

It was past midnight. It got cooler. At last, the lights went out in all the rooms of the family, they must have fallen asleep. Yurovsky came back into the office and suggested a third idea: wake the Romanovs in the middle of the night, ask them to come down to a room on the first floor on the excuse that anarchists were planning an attack on the house and the bullets could fly into the second floor windows where the Romanovs lived (the tsar and tsaritsa and Alexei in the corner, the daughters in the next room with a window onto Voznesensky Alley). There was no real threat of an anarchist attack that night, since not long before Isai Rodzinsky and I broke up anarchist headquarters in the mansion of engineer Zheleznov (the former Commercial Assembly) and had disarmed the anarchist troops of Peter Ivanovich Zhebenev.

We picked a room on the bottom floor next to the storeroom: there was only one barred window on the side of Voznesensky Alley (second house from the corner), the usual striped wallpaper, vaulted ceiling, and a dull electric bulb on the ceiling. We decided to put a truck in the yard outside the house (the yard was formed by an additional fence from the side of the prospect and the alley) and before the shooting start the motor, so that the engine noises would muffle the sound of the shots in the room. Yurovsky had already warned the outdoor guards not to worry if they heard shots inside the house; then he gave out Nagan pistols to the Latvians [who were serving in] the indoor guards—we thought it better to include them in the operation, so that we would not be killing some members of the Romanov family in front of the other members. Three Latvians refused to take part. Pavel Spiridonovich Medvedev, chief of the guards, returned their Nagans to the superintendents' room. Seven Latvians remained in the unit.

Long after midnight Yakov Mikhailovich [Yurovsky] went into the rooms of Dr. Botkin and the tsar, asked them to dress, wash, and [get] ready to go down into the semi-cellar shelter. It took the Romanovs about an hour to get ready, and finally, around three in the morning, they were ready. Yurovsky suggested that we take the remaining five Nagans. Peter Ermakov took two Nagans and stuck them in his belt, Grigory Nikulin and Pavel Medvedev took one apiece. I refused, since I already had two pistols: an American Colt in a holster on my belt and a Belgian Browning under my belt (I saved both historical pistols—the

Browning N 389965 and the Colt 45, government model "C" N 78517). Yurovsky first took the remaining revolver (he had a ten-shot Mauser in his holster) but then gave it to Ermakov, who stuck the third Nagan in his belt. We all smiled involuntarily at his martial appearance.

We went out on the second floor landing. Yurovsky went off to the royal apartments and then returned—following him in single file: Nicholas II (carrying Alexei, the boy has hemophilia, he hurt his leg somewhere and can't walk right now), after the tsar, skirts rustling, the corseted tsaritsa, then the four daughters (of them I can recognize only the youngest, chubby Anastasia, and the—older—Tatiana, who was mine in Yurovsky's dagger version, until I had asked Ermakov to give me the tsar), and after the young ladies came the men: Dr. Botkin, the chef, the valet, and the tsaritsa's tall maid, carrying white pillows. On the landing there was a stuffed she-bear with two bear cubs. They all blessed themselves as they passed the bears, before going downstairs. After the procession went Pavel Medvedev, Grisha Nikulin, the seven Latvians (two with rifles and bayonets over their shoulders), and Ermakov and I finished up the parade.

When we entered the lower room (the house had a very strange layout, so we first had to go into the inner courtyard of the mansion, then go back in on the first floor), it turned out that the room was very small. Yurovsky and Nikulin brought in three chairs—the final thrones of the condemned dynasty. On one of them, closest to the right arch, the tsaritsa sat on a pillow, and the three older daughters stood behind her. The youngest, Anastasia, for some reason went to the maid, who was leaning on the doorjamb of the locked door leading to the storeroom. In the middle of the room they placed a chair for the heir, and to the right of it Nicholas II sat down on a chair, and Dr. Botkin stood behind Alexei's chair. The chef and valet respectfully went to the column of the arch in the left corner of the room and stood against the wall. The lightbulb was so weak that the two women's figures standing at the locked door opposite sometimes looked like silhouettes and only the two white pillows in the maid's hands were clearly visible.

The Romanovs were completely calm—no suspicions. Nicholas II, the tsaritsa, and Botkin regarded Ermakov and me closely, since we were new people in the house. Yurovsky called Pavel Medvedev, and they went into the next room. Now to my left, opposite Tsarevich Alexei, stood Grisha Nikulin, opposite me, the tsar, to my right, Peter Ermakov, and beyond him an empty space, where the Latvians were supposed to stand.

Suddenly Yurovsky walks into the room and stands next to me. The tsar looks at him interrogatively. I heard Yakov Mikhailovich's carrying voice: "Would everyone please stand!"

Easily, in a military manner, Nicholas II stood; with an angry flash in her eyes, Alexandra Fyodorovna rose reluctantly from her chair. The Latvians entered and lined up opposite her and the daughters: five men in the first row, two—with the rifles—in the second. The tsaritsa made the sign of the cross. It grew so quiet that we could hear the truck engine through the window. Yurovsky took a half step forward and addressed the tsar:

"Nikolai Alexandrovich! Attempts by your followers to save you have not been successful! And so, in this difficult time for the Soviet Republic—" Yakov Mikhailovich raises his voice and waves his AMR, "we have been given the mission to end the House of Romanovs!"

Women's screams: "Oh my God! Ah! Oh!" Nicholas II quickly mutters, "Lord. Oh, my God! Oh, my God! What is this?"

"This!" says Yurovsky and takes his Mauser from the holster.

"Then we're not going to be taken anywhere?" Botkin asks in a hollow voice.

Yurovsky wants to reply, but I cock my Browning and fire the first bullet into the tsar. At the same time as my first shot come the bullets of the Latvians and my comrades to the right and left. Yurovsky and Ermakov also shoot into Nicholas's chest at close range. At my fifth shot, Nicholas II falls to the ground on his back.

Women's squeals and moans: I see Botkin fall, at the wall the valet sinks to the ground and the chef falls to his knees. A white pillow moved from the door to the right corner of the room. In the gun smoke a woman's figure dashes from the screaming women's group to the closed door and immediately falls, put down by Ermakov's shots, who is using his second Nagan. I can hear the ricocheting bullets coming from the stone columns, there is limestone dust flying. You can't see anything in the room because of all the smoke—now we are firing at barely visible silhouettes in the right corner who are falling. The shouts died down, but the shooting continues—Ermakov is firing his third Nagan. We hear Yurovsky's voice:

"Stop! Stop firing!"

Silence. Ringing in my ears. One of the soldiers is wounded in the finger and the neck—either by ricochet or he was creased by bullets from the rifles of the Latvians in the second row, who could not see in the gun smoke. The film of smoke and dust settles, Yakov Mikhailovich invites Ermakov and me, as representatives of the Cheka and the Red Army, to be witnesses and attest to the death of each member of the tsar's family. Suddenly from the right corner, where a pillow moved, a woman's joyous cry: "Thank God! God saved me!"

Swaying, the unharmed maid got up—she had been covered by pillows and the bullets got stuck in the down. The Latvians had used up all their bullets, and then the two with bayonets went to her, stepping over the bodies, and finish her off with the bayonets. Her death scream made the lightly wounded Alexei start moaning quickly—he was lying on the chair. Yurovsky came over to him and loosed his last three bullets in the Mauser. The boy grew still and slowly slid to the floor at his father's feet. Ermakov and I felt Nicholas's pulse—he was riddled with bullets, dead. We examine the others and finish off with the Colt and Ermakov's Nagan the still-living Tatiana and Anastasia. Now no one was breathing.

Chief of the guards Pavel Spiridonovich Medvedev approached Yurovsky and reported that the shots were heard in the yard. He brought in soldiers from the indoor guard to move the bodies and blankets in which to carry them to the cars. Yakov Mikhailovich assigns me to watch over the transfer of bodies and the loading into the car. The first one we place on the blanket is Nicholas II, who was lying in a pool of blood. The soldiers brought out the emperor's remains into the yard. I followed them. In the passage I saw Pavel Medvedev—he was deathly pale and vomiting. I asked if he was wounded, but Pavel said nothing and waved me away.

I meet Filipp Goloshchekin near the truck.

"Where were you?" I ask.

"Walking in the square. Listening to the shots. You could hear them." He bent over the tsar.

"The end, you say, of the Romanov dynasty? Yes. . . ."

A soldier brought Anastasia's lapdog on a bayonet—when we went past the door (to the stairs to the second floor) we heard a pathetic wail—the final salute to the Emperor of All of Russia. The dog's body was tossed in next to the tsar's.

"A dog's death to dogs!" Goloshchekin said scornfully.

I asked Filipp and the driver to stay by the truck while the bodies were brought out. Someone got a roll of soldier's cloth, and we spread it out on the sawdust in the truck's rear—and we laid the bodies on the cloth.

I accompanied each body: by now they had figured out to use two stout sticks and blankets to make makeshift stretchers. I noticed that the soldiers were removing rings and brooches from the bodies and hiding them in their pockets while they were putting the bodies on the stretcher. After everyone was put down, I suggested that Yurovsky search the bearers.

"Let's do it more simply," he said and ordered all of them to the superintendent's office on the second floor. He lined them up and said, "I want you to put on the table all the valuables you removed from the Romanovs. You have thirty seconds to think it over. Then I will search everyone. Whoever has it will be shot on the spot! I will not allow marauding. Do you understand?"

"We just wanted something, a souvenir of the event," the soldiers explained in embarrassment. "So it wouldn't be lost."

In a minute's time a hill of gold appeared on the table: diamond brooches, pearl necklaces, wedding rings, diamond pins, gold pocket watches belonging to Nicholas II and Dr. Botkin, and other objects.

The soldier went to wash the floor in the lower room and the connecting one. I went down to the truck and counted the bodies again—all eleven in place—and covered them with the free end of the cloth. Ermakov sat in the cab with the driver, and several guards with rifles got in the back. The truck started off, through the wooden gates of the outer fence, turned right, and drove along Voznesensky Alley through the sleeping city with the remains of the Romanovs.

Beyond Upper Isetsk within a few versts of the village of Koptyaki, the truck stopped in a large meadow with black, overgrown pits. We lit a campfire to warm up, the men in the back were chilled. Then we started bringing each body to the abandoned mine, tearing off their clothes. Ermakov sent the soldiers onto the road to keep people from the nearby village away. Using ropes, we lowered the bodies into the shaft—first the Romanovs, then the servants. The sun was out by the time they flung the bloodied clothes into the fire. . . . Suddenly, from one of the ladies' brassieres, a diamond stream splashed out. We trampled the fire and started pulling stones from the ashes and dirt. We found more diamonds, pearls, and some colored jewels sewn into the lining of two other brassieres.

A car rattled up the road. Yurovsky drove up with Goloshchekin in a car. They looked into the mine. At first they wanted to cover the bodies with sand, but then Yurovsky said to let them drown in the water on the bottom—no one would be looking for them here, since it was a region of abandoned mines and there are lots of shafts here. Just in case, we decided to collapse the upper part (Yurovsky brought a case of grenades) but then we thought: they'll hear the explosions in the village and fresh collapses are noticeable. We just threw old branches and stumps and rotten boards we found nearby into the mine. Ermakov's truck and Yurovsky's car started to go back. It was a hot day, everyone was exhausted, struggling with sleep, and no one had eaten in almost twenty-four hours.

The next day—July 18, 1918—information reached the Urals Provincial Cheka that everyone in Upper-Isetsk was talking about the execution of Nicholas II and the fact that the corpse had been thrown into abandoned mines near the village of Koptyaki. Some conspiracy! None other than one of the participants in the burial told his wife the secret, she told a friend, and it spread all over the district.

Yurovsky was called in to a Cheka collegium. They resolved: that same night send a car with Yurovsky and Ermakov to the mine to take out all the bodies and burn them. The Urals Provincial Cheka appointed my friend and member of the collegium, Isai Idelevich Rodzinsky, as their representative.

So, the night of July 18, 1918, began. At midnight the truck carrying the Chekists Rodzinsky, Yurovsky, and Ermakov, the sailor Vaganov, sailors, and soldiers (around six or seven) left for the region of abandoned mines. The truck was also carrying barrels of gasoline and crates with concentrated sulfuric acid in bottles to disfigure the corpses.

Everything that I will describe about the operation of the second burial comes from the account of my friends: the late Yakov Yurovsky and the still-healthy Isai Rodzinsky, whose detailed reminiscences must definitely be written down for history, since Isai is the only man left alive of the participants in this operation who could today identify the place where the Romanovs are buried. It is also important to write down the reminiscences of my friend Grigory Petrovich Nikulin, who knows the details of the liquidation of the grand dukes in Alapaevsk and of Grand Duke Mikhail Alexandrovich Romanov in Perm.

They reached the mine, lowered two sailors by ropes—Vaganov and another—to the bottom of the shaft, where there was a small ledge. When all the bodies were hauled up by the feet with ropes from the water to the surface and placed next to one another on the grass and the Chekists sat down to rest, it became clear how frivolous the first burial had been. Before them lay ready-made "miracle-working relics": the icy water in the mine had not only washed away the blood but had frozen the bodies so that they looked as if they were alive—the faces of the tsar, the girls, and the women even had rosy cheeks. Undoubtedly, the Romanovs could have been preserved in this excellent condition in the mine refrigerator for several months, and there were only days left before the fall of Ekaterinburg.

It was getting light. Along the road from the village of Koptyaki the first wagons were traveling to the Upper Isetsk market. Men sent to block the road from both sides explained to the peasants that travel was temporarily halted, because criminals had escaped from prison and the region was surrounded by troops, who were combing the woods. The wagons turned back.

The fellows didn't have a ready plan for reburial, where they were taking the bodies, no one knew, or where to hide them, either. So they decided to try to burn at least some of the victims, so that there would be fewer than eleven. They selected the bodies of Nicholas II, Alexei, the tsaritsa, and Dr. Botkin; they poured gasoline on them and set fire to them. The frozen bodies smoked, stank, and hissed, but they did not burn. Then they decided to bury the remains of the Romanovs elsewhere. They put all eleven bodies (four of them charred) in the back of the truck, got on the Koptyaki road and headed toward Upper Isetsk. Not far from the crossing (apparently, across the Gorno-Uralsk Railroad—have I. I. Rodzinsky show the spot on the map) in a swampy hollow the truck got stuck in the mud—wouldn't budge forward or back. No matter how hard they tried, it wouldn't move. They brought boards from the house of the railroad guard at the crossing and finally managed to push the truck out of the swampy hole that had formed. And someone (Yurovsky told me in 1933 that it was Rodzinsky) had the idea: the hole right in the road is the ideal secret fraternal grave for the last Romanovs.

They deepened the hole with shovels until they reached black peat water. They lowered the corpses into the swampy sludge, poured sulfuric acid over it, and covered it with dirt. The truck brought a dozen old railroad sleepers from the crossing and they laid them over the hole and drove over it a few times with the truck. The sleepers got pushed into the earth, looked dirty, as if they had always been there.

And thus in a random swampy hole the last members of the royal dynasty of Romanovs found a worthy resting place, a dynasty that had tyrannized Russia for three hundred and five years! The new revolutionary regime did not make an exception of the crowned robbers of the Russian land: they were buried the way highway robbers had always been buried—without a cross or tombstone, so that they would not catch the eye of people walking down the road to a new life.

That same day, via Perm, Ya. M. Yurovsky and G. P. Nikulin left for Moscow to report to V. I. Lenin and Ya. M. Sverdlov on the liquidation of the Romanovs. Besides the sack of diamonds and other valuables, they were bringing from the Ipatiev house all the diaries and correspondence of the royal family, the photo albums of their stay in Tobolsk (the tsar was a passionate photographer), and also the two letters in red ink that were composed by Beloborodov and Voikov to test the intentions of the royal family. Beloborodov thought that these two documents would show the Executive Committee that there was an officers' organization that had set itself the goal of kidnapping the royal family. Alexander was worried that V. I. Lenin would charge him with insubordination in executing the Romanovs without the Executive Committee's sanction. Besides which, Yurovsky and Nikulin were supposed to personally describe to Ya. M. Sverdlov the situation in Ekaterinburg and the circumstances that forced the Urals Provincial Soviet to take the decision to liquidate the Romanovs.

At the same time, Beloborodov, Safarov, and Goloshchekin decided to announce the execution only of Nicholas II, adding that the family had been taken away to a safe hiding place.

The evening of July 20, 1918, I saw Beloborodov, and he told me that he had gotten a telegram from Ya. M. Sverdlov: the All-Russian Central Executive Committee in a session on July 18 resolved: to consider the decision of the Urals Provincial Soviet on the liquidation of the Romanovs to be correct. Alexander and I embraced and congratulated each other—that meant that in Moscow they understood the complexity of the situation, and, consequently, Lenin approved our actions. That same evening Filipp Goloshchekin for the first time publicly announced at a meeting of the Provincial Soviet of the Urals that Nicholas II that been executed. The rejoicing of the audience was without end and the workers' mood improved.

A day or two later the Ekaterinburg newspapers carried the information that Nicholas II had been executed in accordance with the people's sentence, and the royal family had been taken from the city and hidden in a safe place. I do not know the real intention of this maneuver of Beloborodov's but I assume that the Provincial Soviet of the Urals did not want to inform the city's populace about the execution of women and children. Perhaps there were other considerations, but they were not known to me or Yurovsky (whom I frequently saw in Moscow in the early 1930s, and we talked a lot about the Romanov story). One way or another, this absolutely false statement in the press gave rise to rumors, still active to this day, that the children were saved, that Anastasia, the tsar's daughter, had fled abroad, and other legends.

Thus ended the secret operation to rid Russia of the Romanov dynasty. It was done so successfully that to this day no one has discovered either the secret of the Ipatiev house or the place where the tsar's family is buried.

chapter 4.

The search

Here is a cedar,
axed over and over,
Notches straight through the bark
By the root of the cedar
a highway
and in it an emperor—
buried.

—Vladimir Mayakovsky

■ The Inquiries ■

The evacuation of Ekaterinburg began on July 19; on July 21 there were a few clashes between the advancing White Army and a few Red Army units, which were retreating to Perm. On the night of July 24–25, 1918, troops from the Siberian White Army under the command of Colonel Voitsekhovsky occupied Ekaterinburg, meeting no resistance. The Ipatiev house, where the imperial family had been held, was empty and bore the traces of havoc and hasty flight. Announcements of Nicholas II's execution were pasted up all over town. On July 25, the head of the Ekaterinburg garrison, Major General Golitsyn, assigned a military sentry to the Ipatiev house, putting a stop to the looting that had begun there. He also appointed a special commission to be chaired by Colonel Sherekhovsky that consisted of officers, primarily graduates of the Academy of the General Staff, to investigate the execution.

The new civil authorities also took action. Kutuzov, the acting prosecutor of the revived Ekaterinburg circuit court, put notices in the newspaper inviting anyone with any information on the execution of Nicholas II or his family to come see him—since the night of the execution, rumors of all types had been circulating throughout town. At his instruction, Nametkin, special investigator of the Ekaterinburg circuit court, launched an investigation.

On July 27, Colonel Sheremetievsky appeared before the military commandant of the Eighth Municipal District to present burned pieces of clothing and objects that had been found by peasants at the Four Brothers. On July 29, Gorshkov, a resident of the town, appeared before Kutuzov and reported what his acquaintance, the former investigator Tomashevsky, had told him: that Chekists had executed not only Nicholas II in the Ipatiev house, but his entire family as well as their servants and Dr. Botkin. Before long, the same story was asserted by subsequent witnesses, including Pavel Medvedev, Letyomin, and Lyukhanov.

The commission compared this information with what was found in the Ipatiev house and then searched the Four Brothers area, where they found burnt clothing belonging to the tsar's family. They also found the mine shaft. On July 30, a party of officers led by Nametkin set out to search the mine. But the affair was bungled. Rather than following the route that Yurovsky and his men had taken, they went the easier way, along the railroad tracks. Thus, they approached the mine from the other side, but when they neared it they inadvertently destroyed most of the tracks from the vehicles and the sleds. They found trampled diamonds, emeralds, scraps of fabric, bits of a rifled hand grenade, and a few tiny bone fragments.

The officers acted energetically but amateurishly, without a plan. Nametkin himself, the investigator, would later be characterized as "an exceptionally dry and formal man, lazy by nature, careless in his inspections, inattentive to evidence, lacking in initiative or any notion of his work." It was said that "he took a nonchalant attitude toward his duties."[1]

The officers were angered by Nametkin's poor qualifications as an investigator and by his lack of zeal. On August 2, they launched their own independent inquiry, without the professional investigator. However, in two weeks of work, the officers had no luck either. Pumping the water out of the mine shafts brought a few new finds, such as a detached finger, shreds of skin, the empress's earring, false teeth, a tie fastener, braces, buttons, hooks—but they did not find any bodies.

Back in Ekaterinburg, once the court realized that Nametkin had not achieved the desired results, it used its authority to assign the investigator's duties to a member of the circuit court. On August 7, it turned the investigation over to Ivan Sergeyev, who examined the Ipatiev house much more painstakingly. He photographed the rooms, took samples from the walls and floor where there were bullet marks, and also established that the bodies had been reburied. In his report on the case, Sergeyev stated quite definitely:

> 1) according to the facts gathered by the investigation, the event of the crime has been proved;
> 2) the former Emperor Nicholas II, the former Empress Alexandra Fyodorovna, the Heir Tsarevich, and the Grand Duchesses Olga Nikolaevna, Tatiana Nikolaevna, Marie Nikolaevna, and Anastasia Nikolaevna were killed at the same time, in the same room, by multiple shots from revolvers;
> 3) at the same time, and under the same circumstances, the tsar's family retainers were also killed, physician Evgeny Sergeyevich Botkin, lady-in-waiting Anna Demidova, and the servants Kharitonov and Trupp;
> 4) the murder was planned in advance and executed according to that plan . . . and the murderers took their victims' property.[2]

He established who had planned and carried out the execution—but he also made the provocative assertion that the murder of the tsar's family was strictly an Ekaterinburg affair and that Moscow had had nothing to do with it. This belief conflicted with the view of White Army General Diterikhs, and cost him his job. He was removed from his post.

While Colonel Sherekhovsky's officers commission was being formed in July, General Golitsyn had also issued an order to the Ekaterinburg Military Criminal Investigation Department (commonly referred to as military oversight) to look into the disappearance of the tsar's family from the Ipatiev house using intelligence and counterintelligence methods. Kirsta, the assistant to the chief of military oversight for First Central Siberian Troop Headquarters, was appointed to run the commission. Kirsta's team questioned many people and obtained a great deal of information, varying in quality from the extremely valuable to the utterly fantastic. He compiled a complete list of the people who had taken part in guarding the "house of special designation," determined how the guard had been set up and how it operated, and drew up a list of the Ekaterinburg authorities who were involved in the "case of the tsar." He detained and questioned many of the friends and relatives of the guards, as well as some of the original guards who had remained in Ekaterinburg, such as Pavel Medvedev and Letyomin. In the process, he found Alexei's dog, a spaniel named Joy, who had been adopted by one of the guards, and several other objects originally belonging to the tsar's family that had somehow made their way into local homes.

The Military Criminal Investigation Department was quite successful in reconstructing the execution and the removal of the victims' bodies. Now all that was missing was the actual burial site with the actual bodies. However, in their haste to find leads, the department investigators rushed madly about, often believing whatever story came their way. Diterikhs complained angrily: "In this manner, of course, one only stumbles upon the truth by accident. . . . Usually those who work this way fall into traps set out to camouflage the other direction. This was the fate of the military criminal investigation. It took the path suggested by Soviet power itself: only the former tsar was killed and his entire family survived."[3]

Among the wild tales considered by the investigators was one claiming that the tsaritsa and her daughters dressed up in German pilot suits and were flown across the front to Germany,[4] despite the fact that neither the Czechs nor the Whites had a single airplane. They also grasped at confused rumors about the tsar's family being taken away by train to Perm and on to Moscow,[5] even though at least three-quarters of the railroad workers had not left with the Red Army, but had remained in Ekaterinburg where they were available for questioning. If Kirsta's investigators had interviewed them rather than chance passersby, they could have learned that the tsar's family had not left from the Ekaterinburg train station or any of the surrounding stations—it would have been quite impossible to send the tsar's family away without the rail workers knowing.[6]

Instead, though, Kirsta and his team went to Perm in late December 1918, where they continued to turn up new testimony and material "proofs." They established that the tsar's family had stayed in Perm for a short time—they even determined at which house they had been staying, based on the discovery of a used tsarist napkin. They decided that the family had then been transferred to Vyatka, eventually settling eight miles from Glazov. Grand Duchess Anastasia and Tsarevich Alexei had supposedly been separated from the rest of the family and had hidden separately. According to the testimony of one Dr. Utkin, Anastasia was then captured, soundly beaten, and returned to the Perm Cheka.

These fantastic versions drummed up by Kirsta diverged so stupendously from the results of Nametkin's and Sergeyev's investigations that on January 17, 1919, Diterikhs issued an order to the supervisors of the investigation stating that, in compliance with the order of Russia's supreme ruler, Admiral Kolchak, the work of the Military Criminal Investigation Department had been halted and Kirsta forbidden to conduct further investigations into the "case of the tsar." On February 7, 1919, Nikolai Alexeyevich Sokolov, special investigator for the Omsk circuit court, was put in charge of the preliminary investigation. He was given the complete investigative file and the material proofs that had been gathered by Sergeyev and Kirsta. His freedom of action was protected by a special resolution issued by Admiral Kolchak:

> Russia's Supreme Ruler
> March 3, 1919, No. 588/B–32
> Omsk
> TO ALL:
>
> I hereby order all places and persons to comply precisely and without deviation with all legal demands of Special Judicial Investigator Sokolov and to render him assistance in the implementation of the duties laid upon him at my behest in the preliminary investigation into the murder of the former Emperor, his family, and the Grand Dukes.
>
> [Signature:] Admiral A. Kolchak
> [Signature:] Acting Director of the Chancellery
> of the Supreme Ruler, Major General V. Martyanov[7]

Sokolov conducted his own investigation, interviewing many of the witnesses interviewed by the previous teams and uncovering many discrepancies. For example, when he reinterrogated Dr. Utkin on Anastasia being hidden separately from her family, Dr. Utkin was unable to distinguish Anastasia from her sisters in photographs.[8]

Sokolov continued his work on the investigation when he immigrated to France in 1920. He questioned many Russian émigrés, such as Kerensky, Milyukov, Guchkov, Shulgin, Maklakov, Lvov, and Sukhomlinov. He died in France on November 23, 1924, and the next year his book, *The Murder of the Tsar's Family,* containing unique historical and criminological material, was published. Over the decades, his archives containing the documents he used to research the book were moved several times and eventually disappeared. Some of these documents were returned to Russia in October 1997.[9]

A great deal of material has already been written on Sokolov's book. Here we will analyze only his concrete work: his tasks, methods, assessments, and the conclusions he reached based on data from the events of July 16–19, 1918. We will then compare this material with the material used by his predecessors and what is now known today.

According to official procedure, the court investigator and prosecutor determined the specific tasks for the individuals assigned to the investigation. Diterikhs, who supervised the investigation into the "case of the tsar," described Sokolov's task as follows:

> The Sergeyev investigation left the question of who was responsible for the crime—Medvedev, Yurovsky, the local or regional authority, the central authority, or some other group of people altogether—wide open. . . . Might the murder of the tsar's family and other members of the House of Romanov in fact have been inspired primarily by Jewish figures in the Soviet government? . . . Hence the tasks of the inquiry and investigation became to search for and gather not only materials that serve to uncover the crime, its executors, supervisors, and inspirers, but also materials that delineate the nationality of the murderers of the former Sovereign Emperor, Sovereign Empress, and Most August children. . . . The work of the inquiry and investigation was supposed to follow the plan, which stipulated simultaneous study of three aspects of the circumstances attending the crime: legal, historical, and national. Thus, in questioning a witness, questions were not limited to the legal aspect of the case but endeavored to exhaust the given witness in such a way as to shed light on the historical and national aspects of the matter.[10]

Diterikhs laid out the "national" aspect of the assignment even more specifically:

> In Russia one must never rule out the "Jewish question," an ever sensitive issue. . . . Whenever anyone confirms the exceptional attitude of the Jews in the Soviet government toward the murder of the tsar's family, the significance of nationality in this tragic event for Russia is underscored quite particularly. From this point of view, it was impossible not to take into account the fact that this case . . . would be a matter, primarily, for the Russia of the future, a reborn Russia, Christian and nationalistic, and would take on special historic significance with a decidedly national orientation.[11]

This is the perspective that Sokolov worked so hard to implement fully, even though he did not write a word in his book about the a priori historical and especially "national" orientation of his investigation. In spite of the prejudice inherent in the book, virtually every researcher who is familiar with it has remarked how scrupulous and systematic his work was, bordering at times on self-sacrifice. We agree with these assessments. But we will add to them and show, on the basis of the following examples, that Sokolov analyzed the material he collected only superficially.

The first question. The fact that a crime took place in the Ipatiev house was established. The perpetrators of the crime were specified. Eleven people were executed. But who exactly established the fact of this crime, and by what means did they establish it?

In Chapter 3 we analyzed the circumstances surrounding the execution and demonstrated that no one had ever established as fact the deaths of those who were shot. Sokolov had a complete list of the members of the firing squad, but he had no testimony that a doctor was present at the execution. When no one has legally confirmed a death, it is altogether possible that no death occurred. Sokolov, however, did not raise that issue.

The next question. Twelve men fired, but only twenty-six to thirty bullet marks were found on the walls and the floor.[12] Another fourteen bullets were found in the burial site excavations in 1991, meaning these had been lodged in the bodies of the victims.[13] Of course, some of the bullets remained lodged in the bodies. However, although the executioners fired at almost point-blank range, most of the bullets missed their marks because of the poor visibility caused by the gun smoke; it is therefore unlikely that more bullets remained in the bodies than in the walls and on the floor. The executioners should have fired at least three times as many shots. Why was the shooting halted? Sokolov scrupulously describes the pieces of floor and wall that Sergeyev removed from the half-cellar room. He cites the expert analysis of the types of bullets found and the angles from which they were fired, but he does not count them, nor does he compare the ones found with the number of bullets that should have been fired from so many guns in the hands of so many executioners. Was he afraid of an error? It is understandable to err by five or ten shots, but not by sixty.

Another question. From the testimony of the executioners,[14] the procedure during the execution consisted of firing a series of rounds and then "finishing off" with single shots those victims who, lying on the floor, still showed signs of life. But only six bullet marks were found on the floor.[15] Sokolov's witness Buivid testified to hearing individual shots fired after the series of rounds.[16] But how many individual shots did he hear? Were surviving members of the tsar's family really "finished off" or not?

And one more thing. Yakimov claimed that those lying on the floor "were finished off with bayonets."[17] Yet no bayonet marks were found on the floor. Also, we know that victims of bayonet stabs scream hideously. Yet, although the witness Buivid heard shots and was able to distinguish individual shots from rounds, he didn't hear any screams. So were surviving members of the tsar's family really "finished off with bayonets" or not?

Yet another question. A truck left the Ipatiev house without any guard vehicles and with only three or four men riding in the cab. This is what all the witnesses who saw it or heard it said.[18] Sokolov was quite familiar with the poor condition of the road. He had walked its length and taken photographs. It was obvious that a truck could not drive fast down a road like that. Not only would it have been forced to stop at every pothole, it would have tipped every time it navigated the deep ruts, which would have given anybody in the back who might still have been alive a very good opportunity to slip off. This question did not even occur to the investigator—or to Admiral Kolchak.

And finally, the most pressing question. Where were the victims' bodies? And how many of them were there? Sokolov is brief:

> Their main goal was to destroy the bodies. To do this first of all they had to cut the bodies up into pieces. This they did on the ground. . . . Some of the bodies were burned in fires with gasoline and destroyed with sulfuric acid. . . . The torn and shredded pieces of

> clothing were burned in the same fires. In some of them hooks and eyes and buttons were found. They had been preserved in burnt form. Some of the hooks and eyes had burned and could no longer be separated or unfastened.[19]

Sokolov has apparently come to the conclusion that the bodies had all burned in the fires, while somehow the hooks, eyes, and buttons had not burned. But we know very well that every metal melts at a strictly defined temperature. A metal alloy goes through an interval of fusibility, in which it softens and loses its original form before it is transformed into a liquid. The stages that organic material goes through while burning are broader: first it undergoes metric changes in its structure, called dry distillation; then it undergoes a partial incineration of its combustible components, its carbon fractions, and then its mineral parts; and only after this—at very high temperatures—does it burn to ashes. The fact that metal hooks, eyes, and buttons—all of which melt at relatively low temperatures—retained their original form is the best evidence that a high temperature was not achieved and that therefore human bodies, even if they were dismembered, would have burned only superficially. In the limited time the executioners had, eleven bodies simply could not have been burned without leaving some trace.

Also, let us recall that according to Yurovsky, the purpose of starting the fires was to burn the clothing and belongings. And even if the temperature of these supposed fires had been high enough to burn the bodies, there would still have been some bone remnants and, above all, teeth. So they found buttons but not teeth?

The story about using gasoline and sulfuric acid is also suspicious. Although at that time both items were still available and for sale, we have a requisition for acid signed by Voikov, but no requisition for gasoline.[20] Sokolov writes: "In the days when the mine was [in use], gasoline was brought here in large quantities. It was brought in on trucks,"[21] that is, by the metric ton. And in what was the gasoline carried? It must have been brought in in steel barrels. What happened to these barrels? Were they also burned without a trace? And what kind of combination is gasoline and sulfuric acid? Yes, gasoline will burn, yes, sulfuric acid will dissolve, but together they do not burn. Also, concentrated sulfuric acid must be diluted before it can be used. When untrained people attempt to work with it, they end up with terrible acid burns. However, not one of the witnesses reported any acid burns on their own bodies.

The story doesn't work any better with firewood. The area around the Koptyaki road and the Four Brothers tract is swampy, the woods are mixed, the trees are diseased, it had been raining, and no one had made any effort to prepare dry wood. Even with gasoline, a human body will not burn on a fire made from damp logs. Mikhail Medvedev notes in his memoirs that "the frozen bodies smoked, stank, and hissed, but they did not burn."

Finally, fires that were large enough to incinerate not one but several corpses would have been large enough for their glow to be seen at least from the village of Koptyaki, if not from Ekaterinburg. But none of the witnesses mentions a glow. And neither Sergeyev nor Sokolov mentions that the fires were of such dimensions.

Sokolov quotes a witness as recalling, "We had to cut the bodies up . . . striking blows with sharp-edged instruments."[22] But what kind of sharp-edged instruments? Knives? Axes? The executioners would have had to ready them beforehand—surely there were not a dozen axes lying around. Then, at night, in the confusion, not one ax was lost? And not one witness mentioned anything about what kind of sharp-edged instruments were used—whether they had knives or axes? And who exactly were these men, who, according to Sokolov, were hacking or cutting the bodies of women and children to pieces? Without answers to these questions, these so-called facts are merely ritual motifs in the legend of the murder of the tsar and his family.

The claim that the bodies of the executed Romanovs were burned has been refuted by experts for a long time. It has often been asserted that from a forensic medical standpoint, this version of the story is implausible. It was refuted most convincingly by the two American researchers Summers and Mangold in their book *The File of the Tsar.*[23] Yet some experts, even respected scientists, such as Dr. William R. Maples of the University of Florida and Vladimir Soloviev, the senior prosecutor and criminologist of the Russian General Prosecutor's Office, still pursue discussions on the subject.

On July 30, 1918, while inspecting the mine shaft, the original burial site of the victims, Nametkin collected small bone fragments of unknown origin. They were subsequently handed over to Sokolov, who considered them to be the remains of the burned bodies. It was then that he advanced the theory that the bodies had been chopped up and burned. But if unburned bone fragments with hacking marks remained, why didn't any teeth remain? In 1919, despite a great deal of digging, Sokolov did not find a single tooth. But he ignored this obvious contradiction in his book. The bone fragments are currently in the Russian Orthodox Church of St. Job in Brussels, Belgium, and have been declared by the Russian Orthodox Church Abroad to be the relics of the Romanov martyrs. Unfortunately, the head of that church, Metropolitan Vitaly, has opposed submitting the fragments to scientific analysis.[24]

Another question regarding the burning of the bodies is the time factor. It would have been impossible to burn even one human body in the time Yurovsky's team had. Most calculations agree that it takes approximately twenty-four hours for a human body to burn to ash; at the very least, it takes no less than ten hours. Let us trace the movements of the execution team hour by hour. This is a difficult task, however, because the Ekaterinburg Chekists made every effort to cover their tracks, and the Moscow leadership then "covered" their activities with disinformation. We will pause to look at the variety and extent of the disinformation before returning to the burial of the bodies.

On July 19, 1918, *Pravda* and *Izvestia* published the following text: "The Presidium of the Ural Provincial Soviet passed a resolution to execute Nicholas Romanov and carried it out on July 16. Romanov's wife and son have been sent to a safe place." On July 22, the same text was published in the *Ural Worker.*

The Soviet press published no specific reports that the entire family had been executed until 1926. On the contrary, in July 1918, the Bolshevik leader Karl Radek and the Soviet ambassador in Berlin, Adolf Ioffee, held talks with Germany about exchanging the tsaritsa and her daughters for Karl Liebknecht, Rosa Luxemburg, and other leaders of left-wing social democracy in Germany. The people's commissar of foreign affairs, Georgy Vasilievich Chicherin, asserted on September 20, 1918, that the tsar's daughters were alive, Bolshevik leaders Maxim Maximovich Litvinov and Grigory Evseyevich Zinoviev asserted the same on December 17, 1918, and July 11, 1920, respectively, and Chicherin reasserted it in an interview with the *Chicago Tribune* at the Genoa Conference on April 25, 1922.

Of course, even today people make this assertion. For example, a similar point of view is developed in *The File of the Tsar* by Summers and Mangold[25] and in *Nicholas II* by Marc Ferro,[26] as well as in numerous publications of an equally serious level.

The other side has not been quiet either. If on July 20 and 22, 1918, the Gavas agency in Paris and the *Times* of London, respectively, transmitted the official Soviet reports without commentary, soon afterward the tone of the European press concerning the fate of the tsar's family began to change. In 1920, a book was published in Istanbul titled *The Murder of the Tsar's Family and Their Suite,*[27] and in the same year in Harbin, China, *The Murder of Nicholas Romanov and His Family*[28] came out. In 1922, Diterikhs's two-volume *The Murder of the Tsar's Family and of the Members of the House of Romanov in the Urals*[29] was published in Vladivostok and later translated and reprinted on both sides of the ocean. The Soviet information service flew into a rage and demanded an opportunity to reply in a Western publication. It was in this context that the books of Pavel Mikhailovich Bykov appeared—in the Urals, not Moscow.

Chairman of the Executive Committee of the Ekaterinburg Municipal Soviet and member of the Ural provincial Soviet in 1917 and 1918, Bykov was very knowledgeable about the situation in the Urals and about the participants in the events that culminated in the tragedy of July 17. His essay "The Last Days of the Last Tsar" was published in 1921 in *The Worker Revolution in the Urals,*[30] a collection of essays. His book *The Last Days of the Romanovs* was published in 1926,[31] reissued in 1930, and published for a second time in 1990. Summers and Mangold believe that the book uses materials from Sokolov's dossier, which was stolen from him in Berlin and redirected to Moscow.[32] Indeed, part of Sokolov's investigation file was discovered in the archive of the Institute of Marxism-Leninism of the Communist Party's Central Committee in October, 1997.[33] Even the structure of Bykov's book follows Sokolov's, which had come out a year earlier.

For us, however, this is not important. What is important is that Bykov's articles and books are the first Soviet publications to describe in detail the Romanovs' execution and the Soviet's preparation for it, although they were suppressed for many decades. *The Last Days of the Romanovs* was relegated to a secret archive, where it lay hidden from the public eye for more than sixty years. Immediately after publication, *The Worker Revolution in the Urals,* with one of Bykov's articles in it, was confiscated and destroyed,[34] so none of the essays in this book was ever available to researchers. However, Bykov's book, together with the materials we have today—Soviet documents, memoirs of men who participated in the execution, and materials of the Russian state commission on the Ekaterinburg burial site—allows us to reconstruct the chronology of the events leading up to the execution.

In the opening chapters, Bykov pairs factual material with political quotations. The later chapters abound with factual distortions, omissions, and switched dates for individual events. Let us examine these errors and compare them against the documents and memoirs.

We know that in early July, the Ural provincial Soviet came out unanimously in favor of executing Nicholas Romanov, but since the majority of the Soviet did not want to take on this responsibility without the consent of Moscow, they decided to send the secretary of the Ural Provincial Party Committee of the RSDRP, Goloshchekin, to Moscow. There, Goloshchekin met with the Presidium of the VTsIK and its chairman Sverdlov and reported on military actions in the Urals. In light of the recent rebellions of the White Czechs, the Presidium suggested that Goloshchekin return to Ekaterinburg and prepare a trial against the Romanovs toward the end of July.[35]

In his book, Bykov writes that upon Goloshchekin's return from Moscow, "on the twelfth day of July" Goloshchekin delivered a report to the provincial Soviet on the Presidium's position toward the tsar's family. The provincial Soviet then made its own decision—to execute the Romanovs and destroy their bodies before the evacuation of the town began, that is, without waiting for a trial.[36]

In reality, the meeting Bykov described took place on the night of July 14–15; this date is documented in several places. The minutes of this meeting do not say a word about destroying the bodies after the execution. The man assigned to carry out the Soviet's sentence, Cheka member Yurovsky, wrote in his reminiscences that he received the order from Goloshchekin on the morning of July 15, carried out the order on the night of July 16–17, and received the order to destroy the bodies only on the evening of July 17.[37] These are the dates we will work from.

After the execution in the Ipatiev house, the bodies of the victims were loaded onto the truck in the middle of the night of July 16–17 and transported over the Koptyaki road to the Four Brothers tract. At dawn, around four or five in the morning, the truck reached the turnoff from the road into the tract. Here the truck could go no farther, so the bodies were reloaded onto sleds by Ermakov's brigade. At this point, the burial team discovered that two bodies were missing, and Yurovsky sent out a search party to backtrack on foot.[38] The remaining members of the team took the other bodies to the flooded mine shaft that Ermakov had selected. There they undressed the corpses, threw them down the mine shaft, and burned the clothing. The search party meanwhile was moving slowly—at no more than two and a half miles an hour—carefully examining the tracks on the road, and therefore did not reach the end of the road at the Iset River (the Upper Isetsk plant) before nine o'clock in the morning. They did not find the missing bodies on the road. The party then started back, checking again along the sides of the road, moving no faster than before, and returned to Four Brothers at around one o'clock in the afternoon.

At two o'clock Yurovsky set up roadblocks on the road to the north and south of the tract, and he and Ermakov left for Ekaterinburg by car to report "that things were not good." The decision was made to rebury the corpses. Toward evening on July 17, Ermakov returned to the burial site and began to organize the removal of the corpses from under the rubble and water in the mine shaft. No earlier than two o'clock in the morning on July 18, Yurovsky returned to the mine shaft with a slightly altered decision: to burn the bodies. However, "no one knew how to go about it."

On the morning of July 18, another group arrived to assist.[39] According to Medvedev: "They decided to try to burn at least some of the victims, so that there would be fewer than eleven. They selected the bodies of Nicholas II, Alexei, the tsaritsa, and Dr. Botkin; they poured gasoline on them and set fire to them. The frozen bodies smoked, stank, and hissed, but they did not burn. Then they decided to bury the remains of the Romanovs elsewhere. They put all eleven bodies (four of them charred) in the back of the truck, got on the Koptyaki road, and headed toward Upper Isetsk [where the road met the river]."

The same crew had a second opportunity to burn the bodies on the night of July 18–19, when the truck got stuck in the mud after leaving Four Brothers with the partially burned bodies. Yurovsky recalls: "Crossing the railroad tracks, we loaded the corpses back in the truck and soon got bogged down again. We struggled for two hours, and it was close to midnight. . . . At five or six in the morning, . . . we went into town."

Various sources indicate the dates and times of the events of July 17–19. According to Diterikhs, Yurovsky was seen in Ekaterinburg on the afternoon of July 17.[40] "On July 18, during the first half of the day, two trucks arrived in the Koptyaki forest," Diterikhs continues. "One had brought a supply of gasoline for the truck that had gotten stuck near Ganya's Pit, and a barrel, about 10–12 poods [350–450 pounds], of kerosene. The other truck brought barrels of something else. . . . Late that night [July 18] . . . one of the trucks left for town. . . . before dawn [July 19], so did the second."[41] Yurovsky ("at five or six in the morning") and Mikhail Medvedev give approximately the same time for leaving the Four Brothers area on July 19. Diterikhs and Sokolov also both indicate this time—and the roadblock was removed at six o'clock on the morning of July 19.[42] So according to all the sources, the burial crew had only a few hours, four or five (between midnight and 5 A.M.), no more, to burn the bodies.

Let us now turn to the research done by Paganucci, who asked U.S. forensic medical experts whether it was possible to turn adult bodies into ashes on a fire that was kept going for forty-eight hours, with kerosene and sulfuric acid periodically added. Opinions were diametrically opposed. Some expressed skepticism; others thought it was possible.[43] Thus, even at forty-eight hours experts are still divided over whether it is possible to burn bodies all the way down to ash. It is perfectly obvious, though, that with only four or five hours the burial crew did not have a chance in the world of burning even a single human body. They had neither the time nor the physical means.

Finding the Bodies

The year 1978 marked the first in an important chain of events for the "case of the tsar." A group of amateur researchers led by geologist Alexander Avdonin and writer Gely Ryabov found wood planking on the old Koptyaki road.

Avdonin writes:

> The investigation file [of Sokolov] had in it a photograph of the place where the truck carrying the Bolsheviks returning from the Four Brothers got stuck. Our first concern was to find that spot and verify that it was the only one connected with the transport of the remains. A search of all the low-lying spots on the Koptyaki road turned up no planking, though. Evidently it was concealed below the surface of earth. After extensive searching, geologist Mikhail Kuchurov and I, while probing the soil of the road with a large, corkscrew-type instrument that we screwed into the ground, did find it in the area of Piglet Gully. The wood area measured about 2 x 3 meters [6 feet 7 inches x 9 feet 10 inches]. We thought the underground wooden planking might be where the remains were concealed. This was in 1978. . . .
>
> In a letter addressed to G. Ryabov that accompanied the set of maps we

IPATIEV HOUSE
X
ASCENSION AVE.
UKTUSSKAYA
ПРУД
Масштаб в 1 дюйме 230 саж.
0
115
230
460
690 саж.
TRUCK ROUTE FROM THE IPATIEV HOUSE TO THE BURIAL SITE
TO THE UPPER ISET PLANT
Вторая
Луговая
Обсерваторская
Кузнечная
Васнецовская
Сибирская
Красноармейская
Ул. Ленина
Пл. Париж. Ком.
Пл. Энгельса
Пушкинская
Л. Свердлова
Мельковская пл.
Товарная станция
Троцкого
Л. Вайнера
Матроса
Хохрякова
Л. Шейкмана
Московская
Городская больница
Лесопильн
Глазная лечебница
Ипподром
Московский тракт
Кладбище
Горный институт
Добролюбова
Чернышевского
Володарского
Пл. Труда

ПЛАН
ГОРОДА
ЕКАТЕРИНБУРГА
map of
Ekaterinburg
1922
в Тюмень
в Челябинск
Екатеринбург I
Екатеринбург II
Староверческое кл.
Сибирский тракт
Ткацкая. фаб.
б. Макарова
Обсерваторская
№2
Исправдом
Пл.
Максима
Горького
Большакова
Декабристов
Сенная пл.
Казармы
Красноармейская
Сухаревская
Детский
городок
Цыганская
пл.
Стеньки Разина
Троцкого
Щепная пл.
Монастырь
Вуктус
Сибирский просп.
Рабочего
Большакова

> compiled for the area of the Four Brothers tract and the Koptyaki road, I wrote (September 1978): "We can state that we have found the site we were looking for. One thing astonishes me, though: in sixty years, nothing has happened to it. No one even started digging there, let alone dig it up. It's amazing! . . ."
>
> Numbers 1–6 are the burial site on the road. I went there with a colleague of mine who is an avid tracker and we immediately figured out the lay of the old road and two places where the burial site, as well as the board planking, might be.
>
> In 1979, A. N. and G. P. Avdonin, G. P. Vasiliev, V. Pesotsky, and G. T. and M. V. Ryabov excavated the place with the wooden planking, which was 30–40 centimeters [12–16 inches] from the surface. Immediately under the planking we found human remains. Taken from the dig were three skulls, which we examined briefly and then put back. We were not able to complete an expert analysis of the skulls. Nonetheless, after familiarizing ourselves with Yurovsky's note we became firmly convinced that these were the remains of the Romanovs.[44]

All the participants in the excavation then "swore to keep the secret of their discovery until better times."[45] Unfortunately, they committed lamentable errors in their excavation, which requires special expertise in order not to destroy evidence. To this day, researchers bemoan what happened then.

They kept their silence for ten years. Then, in April 1989, Ryabov reported the find in an interview with *Moscow Komsomolets* and, subsequently, in a large article in *Homeland*. A criminal case was opened on the murder of the as yet unidentified persons and on the cover-up of that crime. The investigation was assigned to Councilor of Justice Volkov, the senior assistant to the prosecutor of the Sverdlov province.

As usual, the first investigative action was an inspection of the crime scene, which lasted three days, July 11–13, 1991. Avdonin recalls:

> With the support of E. E. Rossel, chairman of the Sverdlov Provincial Executive Committee, a group of scholars was organized that included archaeologists, forensic medical experts, . . . criminologists, . . . workers from the investigative organs, representatives from the Recovery Fund, and other specialists.
>
> This group conducted [again, not without committing serious blunders] the scientific opening up of the burial site. In it they found nine human skeletons (four men, five women) almost completely lacking muscle tissue, hair, articles of clothing, and adornments. In the excavation

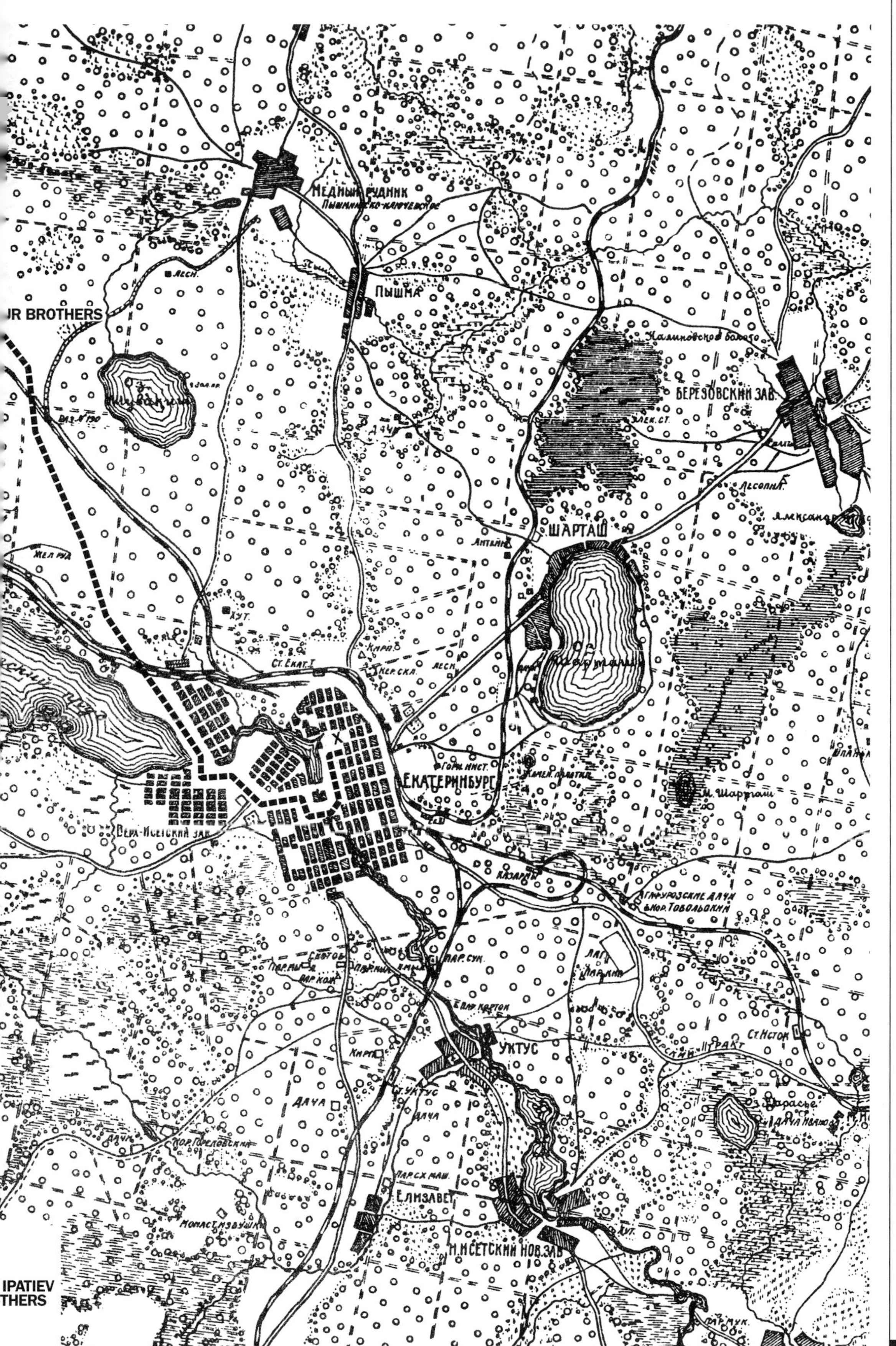
МЕДНЫЙ РУДНИК
ПЫШМА
БЕРЕЗОВСКИЙ ЗАВ.
ШАРТАШ
М. Шарташ
ЕКАТЕРИНБУРГ
ВЕРХ-ИСЕТСКИЙ ЗАВ.
Ст. Екат. I
ЛАЗАРЕТ
Ст. Исток
УКТУС
Ст. Уктус
ДАЧА
ЕЛИЗАВЕТ
Н.ИСЕТСКИЙ НОВ.ЗАВ.

they found more than ten bullets, rope remnants, and shards from ceramic vessels (presumably from the containers holding the acid). The facial parts of all the skulls were destroyed, and on some there were bullet openings.

Ever since the site was opened up, Russia's forensic medical experts and criminologists have been studying the remains. Lately, scientists from the United States led by Dr. Maples of the University of Florida have joined them. The research done has confirmed that the remains belong to the group of individuals murdered in the Ipatiev house. Scientists have established that the remains of the members of the family of Nicholas II have been found, except for the Tsarevich Alexei and one of his sisters, in the excavation on the Koptyaki road.[46]

Nikolai Nevolin, chief forensic medical expert in the Health Administration of the Sverdlov Provincial Government, relates the story:

The burial site was discovered 15 kilometers [9 miles] from the center of Ekaterinburg at the site of the old abandoned Koptyaki road. The graves were in a low-lying, swampy forest glade measuring 30 x 40 meters [98 x 130 feet], in a pit that had been closed over on the top (lying 30–40 centimeters [12–16 inches] from the surface) with brush, sticks, and half-rotten remains of boards (planks). The area of the burial site was rectangular and 1.6 x 2.2 meters [5 x 7 feet] in size. The depth of the grave was from 0.8 to 1.2 meters [2½ to 4 feet] deep. Its bottom had a gentle slope to the north and was formed from superficially deposited bedrock, which created a significant obstacle to making the grave any deeper. Clearing the burial site of soil revealed single skeletons and groups of skeletons laid helter-skelter without coffins. Found in addition were thirty-five ceramic fragments, eleven bullets, a firing mechanism from a hand grenade . . . and hair fragments. Formoplast [a type of plastic used to make dentures] was found in the cavities of two skulls. . . . There were no clothing remnants in the burial site. At a depth of about 80 centimeters [2½ feet] along the western portion of the pit, a 15 mm [½-inch] electric cable laid in 1972 was found. In that area, a disorderly scrambling of the skeleton bones that resulted from the violation of their integrity was observed.

During the excavation, no remains of charcoal or carbonized fragments of wood were found. . . . Signs of the effect of an open flame (high temperature) on the bones were not found. . . . The local nature of the destruction of the bones of individual skeletons . . . does not preclude the possibility . . . of the direct effect of acid used to destroy the bodies. . . .

The age of the burial is significant for each of the nine skeletons. It is measured in decades and probably amounts to at least fifty or sixty years, i.e., it could correspond to the time of the execution of the last Russian emperor, Nicholas II, and his family in the Urals in the summer of 1918.[47]

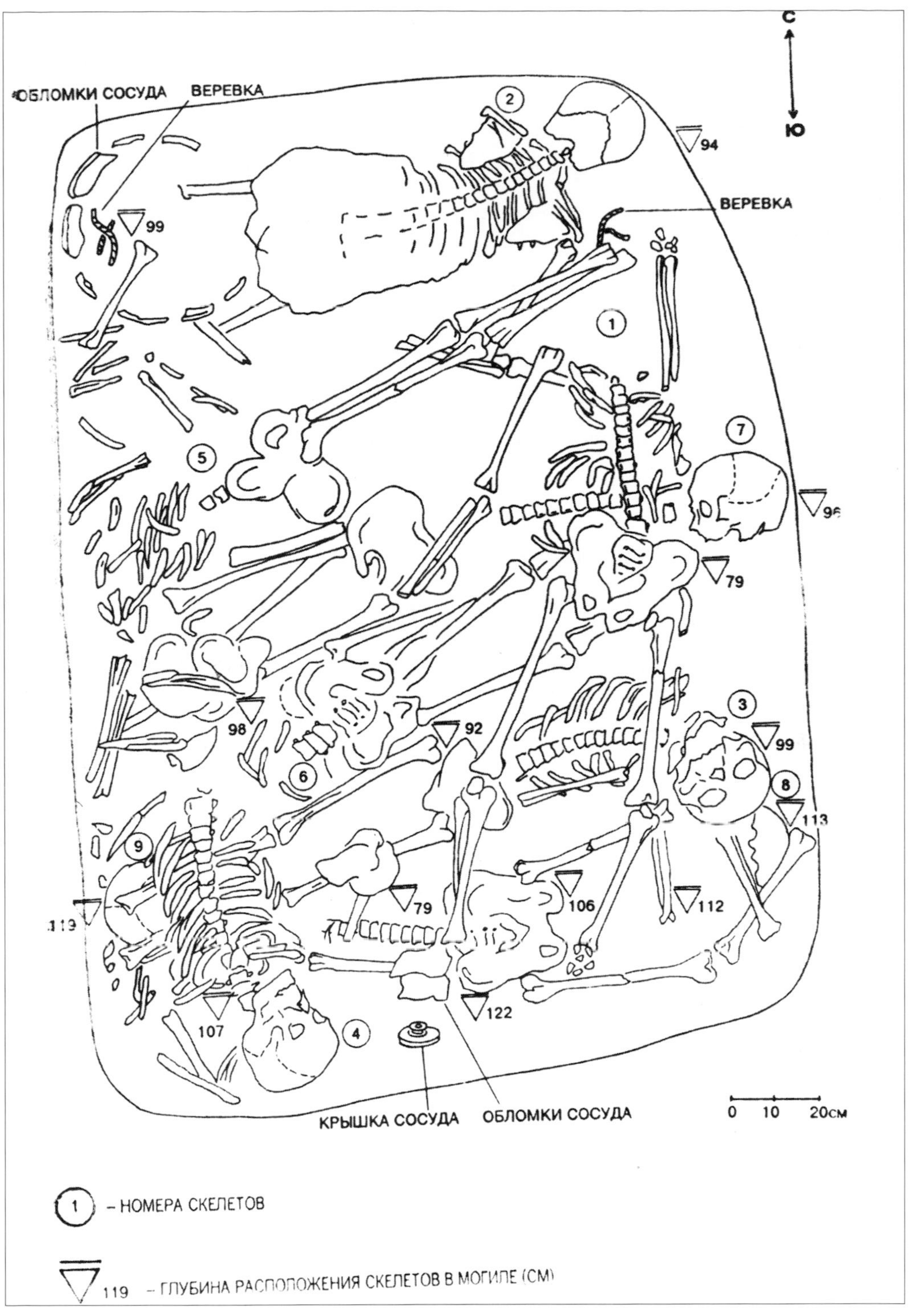

Burial layout of the bone remains found on the Koptyaki Road. The numbers in the circles indicate the number of the skeleton; the numbers in the triangles indicate the depth (in centimeters) of the skeleton in the grave. Skeleton No. 1: Demidova; Skeleton No. 2: Dr. Botkin; Skeleton No. 3: Olga; Skeleton No. 4: Nicholas; Skeleton No. 5: Marie; Skeleton No. 6: Tatiana; Skeleton No. 7: Alexandra; Skeleton No. 8: Kharitonov; Skeleton No. 9: Trupp.

On July 23–25, 1991, the remains were taken out and moved to the shooting range of the Upper Iset Police Department of Sverdlovsk (the name of Ekaterinburg during part of the Soviet period, named after Yakov Sverdlov, who had been head of the Ural Bolsheviks before assuming various posts in the Central Committee of the Soviets). There they were examined by a team of medical and forensic experts under the direction of investigator Volkov. In addition, a special commission was created under the provincial administration and chaired by the deputy administrator of Sverdlovsk province, Viktor Blokhin, a physician by training, whose assignment included facilitating the expert investigation.

The commission consisted of Russian experts in various fields who studied the original presentation of the site; sorted out which bones belonged to which person; analyzed features such as sex, age, and height for each person; analyzed the skeletal remains with the use of photo overlays made from photographs of the victims taken during their lifetimes; studied the bullet marks and other injuries on the bodies; and analyzed the bullets found at the site. In addition to the Russian experts, Blokhin's commission sought the research assistance of a group of American specialists led by the chief of the laboratory at the Florida Museum of Natural History of the University of Florida, forensic anthropologist Dr. William R. Maples.

The concrete results of the scientific analysis and the preliminary conclusions of the commissions are set forth in great detail in a special collection of materials from the conference "The Last Page in the History of the Tsar's Family: Results of Studies of the Ekaterinburg Tragedy"[48] and in the book *Where Are You, Your Excellency?*[49] by Professor Popov. Here we will limit ourselves to exploring the final conclusions and the various contradictions in the arguments. But first we must address the uproar in the press, which has drawn in even Russian President Boris Yeltsin,[50] over whether the remains discovered in Ekaterinburg are the real bones of the Romanovs.

It all started when the commission chaired by Blokhin set forth one condition that was not negotiable: all the research had to be done in Ekaterinburg. The skeletal remains were not to be taken out of the city. This condition was backed up by a decree from investigator Volkov, also a member of the commission. It resulted in an obvious incongruity. Although Ekaterinburg had relatively modern scientific institutions, it did not have the necessary facilities to address the complex analyses that experts from all over Russia had been invited to perform.

Moreover, both the analyses and the investigation itself were conducted in an absolutely unjustified cloak of secrecy. The medical research was done in a police building, and the researchers worked separately according to their own individual plans, and the result was they occasionally hampered the work of their colleagues and sometimes even destroyed material that was needed by other researchers. The commission had no single, unified work plan, and investigator Volkov, instead of giving the researchers the materials they so urgently needed for comparative research, passed resolution after resolution assigning the investigation first to one group of scientists and then another. For all intents and purposes, the experts worked independently, and any exchange of data was strictly private and voluntary. The two scientific conferences that were held in Ekaterinburg in April and July 1992 were, for the most part, merely a recap for the participants.

By the time the conferences took place, research was practically finished, but the official conclusion about whom the Ekaterinburg remains belonged to was still not announced.

The leading American expert, Dr. Maples, spoke directly and to the point at the second Ekaterinburg conference:

> The facts are so obvious that we can assume that this is the burial site of the imperial family and members of their servants. If this is so, then skeleton No. 1 conforms to Demidova, No. 2 to Dr. Botkin, No. 3 to Olga (by age), No. 4 to Tsar Nicholas II, No. 5 to Marie (by age and height), No. 6 to Tatiana (by age and height), No. 7 to Alexandra Fyodorovna, and No. 8 and No. 9 may have been servants, men. The remains of Tsarevich Alexei and Anastasia were not found.
>
> For the continuation of this work, we would like to make the following recommendations. The search must continue for data from their lifetimes for comparison, as well as for the dental plate of Dr. Botkin, as well as for the family's stomatological records. DNA testing must be done on all the skeletal remains in a highly specialized laboratory. The remains must be carefully preserved and they must also be photographed for documentary purposes. . . . Anastasia is not here because all the extant skeletons are too tall for her. There is also nothing among the bones that could belong to Alexei.[51]

Unfortunately, none of the Russian scientists, who had been working more intensively on the case than their American colleagues, made an official presentation at the July 1992 conference.

On August 12, 1992, the Russian deputy general prosecutor, Slavgorodsky, proposed to the acting government chairman, Gaidar, that a government commission be formed to organize a complete and accurate investigation into all the circumstances surrounding the death of the tsar's family and also that the necessary conditions be created for Russian scientists to complete the investigation so that the fate of the remains could be decided.

The investigation continued. On August 19, 1993, the General Prosecutor's Office opened criminal case number 18/123666/93, on "the premeditated murder of the people whose remains were exhumed in 1991 outside Ekaterinburg." Leading the investigation was senior prosecutor and criminologist Soloviev. On October 22, 1993, by order number 1884-R of the Russian Prime Minister Chernomyrdin, a special government commission was created under the chairmanship of Vice Premier Yarov to study the investigation and reburial of the remains of Tsar Nicholas II and his family.

Over the next two years, the commission's tasks changed, its composition changed, and its chairmen changed.

On September 15, 1995, the Russian deputy general prosecutor, Gaidanov, issued a statement that the investigation had fulfilled its purpose, the remains had been identified, and criminal case number 18/123666/93, originally opened as a case of premeditated murder, was being closed. A decree closing the case would probably be issued by the investigator, Soloviev.[52] On September 20, 1995, the government commission, together with the Russian scientific commission from abroad led by Prince

Shcherbatov, made its decision: the remains found outside Ekaterinburg had been identified and truly did belong to Nicholas II and members of his family; the remains of the tsarevich and one of the tsar's daughters had not been found.[53] Now it was up to the Russian Orthodox Church, the Romanov relatives, and the government of St. Petersburg (since this is where the burial site for the Romanov dynasty is located) to decide where to bury the tsar and his family.

Only in 1996, when Popov's book was published, were the details of the analysis of the Russian expert commission made available to the public. According to Popov, the conclusions of the commission are as follows:

The condition of the remains proved that they had been in the earth for more than fifty or sixty years. A summary of the results of the identification of the remains—sex, age, height, race, antigen characteristics, individual traits, the condition of the teeth-jaw system, and the photo overlays—are cited in the following table:[54]

Number	Sex	Age	Height	Kinship (stomatogenetic indications)	Quality of Dental Care	
					High	Low
1	f	40–50	161–168			+
2	m	50–60	171–177		false upper teeth	
3	f	20–24	158–165	+	+	
4	m	45–55	165–170			
5	f	approx. 20	166–171	+	+	
6	f	approx. 20	162–171	+	+	
7	f	45–50	163–168	+	+	
8	m?	40–50?	?			
9	m	over 60	172–181			
10						
11						

After the chart, the text follows:

> We are giving the reader an opportunity to make his own comparisons. For this purpose, let us recall the age of the people who were imprisoned in the Ipatiev house:
>
> The imperial family:
>
> Nicholas II, born May 19, 1868
>
> Alexandra Fyodorovna, born June 7, 1872
>
> Olga Nikolaevna, born November 16, 1895
>
> Tatiana Nikolaevna, born June 11, 1897
>
> Marie Nikolaevna, born June 27, 1899
>
> Anastasia Nikolaevna, born June 18, 1901
>
> Alexei Nikolaevich, born August 12, 1904

Members of the court:
Evgeny Sergeyevich Botkin, physician, born May 27, 1865
Anna Stepanovna Demidova, chambermaid, born January 14, 1878
Ivan Mikhailovich Kharitonov, cook, born May 30, 1870
Aloizy Egorovich Trupp, servant, born April 8, 1856

At the time he cited this streamlined analysis, Popov, himself an experienced forensic medical scientist, did not yet have all the results of the genetic fingerprinting research that was conducted separately by Dr. Pavel Ivanov and Dr. Peter Gill. However, he did have access to the various issues and contradictions brought up by the conclusions of the researchers.

The first two contradictions concern the identification of Nicholas II on the basis of certain characteristics of his skull. In 1891, when he was still the heir to the throne, Nicholas Romanov received a saber blow to the head while on a visit to Japan. A facsimile copy describing this occurrence is shown below.

A facsimile copy of the document describing this occurrence begins like this:

> On April 29, 1891, at about two-forty-five in the afternoon, upon the return of His Imperial Highness the Sovereign Heir and Tsarevich from his visit to the city of Karasaki and a trip to Lake Bili, via the town of Otsu, on one of the streets of that town, a Japanese policeman standing at his post among the other policemen stationed along the street rushed at the moving jinrikisha of His Imperial Highness and with a bared saber inflicted two wounds to the hair portion of his head, on the right side.[55]

To quote Popov:

> It is difficult to overestimate the significance of this document. . . . It was drawn up directly after the injury was received, and the description of the wound is efficient and professional in nature. The objectivity and accuracy of the description are confirmed by the collegial nature of the medical certificate. . . . This implies that there should have been traces from the saber blow on Nicholas II's skull. Only here is the question: did a bone callus form on the spot of this blow? The likelihood of this happening is minor, extremely minor. A bone callus almost never forms with skull fractures. . . . With time, the fracture spot gradually smooths over. However, the depression at the spot of the fracture does not disappear completely and can be noted, for example, when feeling the head, for many years. Therefore, we can believe Dr. Derevenko when he talks about the "deep spots" on the emperor's skull. But, Derevenko [also] says that Nicholas II did have a "bone callus" (a thickening of the bone) on his left temple.[56]

A statement to the prosecutor of the Kazan Legal Chamber, dated November 26, 1918, reads: "According to the statement of Dr. Derevenko . . . the characteristic and ineradicable mark of the body of Sovereign Nicholas II would be the bone callus on his left temple, following the old blow to the head during his visit . . . to Japan."[57]

Dr. Derevenko, in his role in the Ekaterinburg events of July 1918, seemed a rather curious individual even to Diterikhs,[58] and between Derevenko's autobiography and the accounts by Bykov[59] there are several factual inconsistencies concerning this period. Therefore, we do not follow Popov in unreservedly trusting the testimonies of Derevenko, and we do not think his comment that the skull of Nicholas II showed a bone callus on the left temple is necessarily true.

The second contradiction concerns the "legend of the tsar's head," originally advanced by Diterikhs[60] and remaining in circulation to this day.[61] According to the legend, the heads of the victims were cut off and taken to Moscow as evidence of the execution. Popov thoroughly refutes this legend, citing the condition of the teeth (the color of the teeth surfaces in each skull would have been different, due to humidity and temperature, if the skulls had been separated—as it was, they were all the same) and maintaining that the skulls had not been forcibly removed from the bodies.[62]

The third contradiction concerns the discovery of two separate upper teeth that doctors believe came from an adolescent, someone thirteen to sixteen years old, according to Popov.[63] These are the only remains that have been found that could possibly be attributed to the fourteen-year-old Alexei. However, Dr. Kovalyov maintains that these teeth could equally be from one of the younger daughters, Marie or Anastasia.

The fourth contradiction refers to genetic research conducted by Dr. Ivanov, the head of the genetic fingerprinting laboratory at the Bureau of Forensic Medical Expert Analysis in the Russian Ministry of Health. He and Dr. Gill conducted research using genetic fingerprinting at the Aldermaston Laboratory of the Forensic Science Service, part of the Ministry of Defence in Great Britain. The methodology of genetic fingerprinting is based on the following theories regarding DNA testing.

A person's hereditary information is carried by the chromosomes, which are made up of DNA (deoxyribonucleic acid). The latter, in turn, consist of four blocs, A (adenine), G (guanine), C (cytosine), and T (thymine), which are linked in pairs—A-T and G-C, so-called base pairs. The molecular structure of DNA is like a long spiral staircase (a double spiral) with steps that are the base blocs A, G, C, and T. Approximately 99.9 percent of the pairs of a single cell in all people are encountered in the same order, 0.1 percent in a characteristic individual order. By use of tagged atoms (radioactive isotopes), "pictures" of individually characteristic portions—"DNA fingerprints"—can be made and checked against the DNA of another person.

People inherit half their base pairs of DNA from their mother and half from their father, at least as far as the "core" DNA goes. Mitochondrial (extranuclear) DNA is inherited independently of the core DNA and only through the maternal line. The same genetic code will be identical for the granddaughter, daughter, mother, grandmother, great-grandmother, and so on, but will break off at a son.

In sum, using genetic fingerprinting analysis, it is perfectly possible to make a direct comparison of the genetic characteristics of individuals and state unambiguously who are and are not relatives among a group of unknown people or remains. Within a group of relatives, it is possible to establish the degree of kinship in the first generation of the type "parents–children" or "brothers–sisters." Kinship along the maternal line can be traced for many generations, since the maternal inheritance is unmixed. Analysis allows for virtually no errors in the event of negative results on familial ties. The only possible source of error is incorrectly drawn samples. For proof of familial relations, genetic fingerprint analysis is commonly accepted as part of the data needed, along with other data, to determine identity.[64]

Ivanov and Gill conducted genetic fingerprinting in Aldermaston on the basis of bone fragments from each of the skeletons found in the Ekaterinburg burial site. The scientists used various materials—blood, hair, and fingernail and toenail samples—belonging to individuals related to the Romanov dynasty—Prince Michael of Greece, Prince Rostislav Romanov, Prince Philip (the grandnephew of Alexandra Fyodorovna)—and compared them with blood remnants obtained in the exhumation as well as with the miraculously preserved lock of hair cut from Nicholas II's head with his bloody bandage after his attack in Japan in 1891.

As a result of this research, there are now substantive grounds for asserting blood kinship between the females (skeleton numbers No. 3, 5, 6, and 7) and to assert that they along with the male (skeleton number 4) belonged to the Romanov family. Skeleton number 4 was identified as belonging to Nicholas II not only on the basis of the "Japanese material" but also from the blood samples of one of the living descendants of the Romanovs connected to Nicholas II along the maternal line (the donor has asked that his identity be kept anonymous).[65] Gill and Ivanov successfully proved almost complete identity between the DNA of the bone remains of skeleton number 4 and the DNA of the blood of the descendant of Nicholas II.[66] In the summer of 1994, the remains of Grand Duke Georgy Romanov, Nicholas II's brother, were exhumed. Ivanov, working in the U. S. Armed Forces Institute of Pathology, established full genetic coincidence between the two.[67] In doing so, any lingering doubts that the remains from skeleton number 4 belong to Nicholas II were eliminated .

The pretenders

There is one problem, however, that is inevitable in suspicious historical situations. As Avdonin put it at the 1992 conference in Ekaterinburg:

> The story about the miraculous rescue of members of the Romanov family has conjured them up. P. Gilliard [Alexei's tutor] noted that in 1919, in Omsk, he was shown a boy purported to be Alexei. This allegation did not hold up to verification [in Admiral Kolchak's counterintelligence service], and the boy admitted he was a pretender. V. V. Shchetinin from Baghdad and M. Goleniewsky from the United States have tried to pass themselves off as Alexei saved from death. In 1991, a citizen of Spain, A. Brimeyer declared he was the grandson of Nicholas II, and a Romanov from Brazil declared himself to be the son of Nicholas II. An Alexei is known in the countries of the Commonwealth of Independent States.[68]

Another Alexei turned up in Bulgaria. On July 16 1997 Russian Public Television in Moscow (ORT) broadcast a report about the death of a resident of Bulgaria who called herself Anastasia Romanov and who had looked after the grave of her brother, allegedly Alexei Romanov, who had died much earlier. Of course, there have been several Anastasias, one of whom, Anna Andersen, was particularly well known because of her publicized trials in Germany and the United States in which she fought to be recognized as a Romanova.

The story of Anna Andersen was indeed a sensation all over the world. In February 1920, a Berlin policeman saved a young woman who had thrown herself into a canal. In the hospital, when she revived, she told a gripping story that boiled down to the fact that she was Anastasia Romanova. Rescued from the execution by a young Red Army soldier, she had run away with him to Romania, where he died. She had then made her way back to Berlin to meet Princess Irina, the sister of Russian Empress Alexandra Fyodorovna. The meeting never took place, though, because the woman threw herself off a bridge into a canal, was rescued, and was admitted to a psychiatric clinic under the name Fraulein Unbekannt ("unknown"). She was mentally unbalanced, had little do with the people around her, spoke German and English, and when she was asleep or in an unconscious state spoke Russian.

The story was publicized and the case was heard in various courts, but it ended unresolved because of a lack of proof, since the opinions of relatives diverged. Nicholas II's sisters, Olga and Xenia, recognized her as the genuine article, as did their cousin Andrei, the German Crown Princess Cecilia Hohenzollern, and a great many other relatives, even Mathilde Kschessinska (who had once been the tsar's mistress) and the children of the tsar's physician, Tatiana and Gleb Botkin. Many were uncertain, among them the man who taught the tsar's children, Pierre Gilliard. And many sharply objected, although most of them never laid eyes on her.

There was one weighty reason for the objections. The pretender stated that she had seen her uncle Ernest of Hesse in Petrograd in 1916. This put the grand duke in an extremely awkward position. As a general in the German army, Ernest of Hesse should not have been traveling to Russia at the height of the war without the knowledge of his government or, at the very least, the general staff. Because of this, he rejected the statement of his "niece" by fair means and foul. However, according to a statement made in court by the former kaiser's stepson, as well as by the Crown Princess Cecilia, Grand Duke Ernest did indeed travel to Petrograd in 1916 with the blessings of Kaiser Wilhelm II himself—less to visit his sister and brother-in-law than to propose the matter of concluding a separate peace.[69] Documentary evidence of this secret mission has not been preserved.

There were quite a few such stories connected with Anna Andersen's childhood memories. Several expert analyses were performed as well. Dr. Otto Reche, founder of the Society of German Anatomical Pathologists, conducted an expert portrait analysis and came to the conclusion that "a coincidence like this is possible only if this is the face of one and the same person or of identical twins." Dr. Minna Becker, who helped determine the authorship of Anne Frank's diaries, performed handwriting analysis and said: "After thirty-four years' experience testifying in German courts, I am prepared to make a sworn statement—both on my oath and on my honor—that Mrs. Andersen and Grand Duchess Anastasia are one and the same person."[70]

Other expert opinions were presented in court as well. Nonetheless, by the late 1970s, the courts still had not come to any final conclusions. A statement rather than a decision was issued that Anna

Andersen was not Grand Duchess Anastasia because she had been unable to prove that she was. Eight thousand pages of witness testimony were bound into forty-nine volumes, put on a shelf, and forgotten. But not forever, as later became clear.

On February 12, 1984, Anna Andersen died of pneumonia in Charlottesville, Virginia. Four and a half years before her death she had undergone intestinal surgery at a local hospital. The removed tissue was sent to a pathology laboratory, as usual, and samples were preserved and put in long-term storage. When it became known that the remains of Anastasia and Alexei had not been found at the Ekaterinburg burial site, interest in the biological samples from Anna Andersen increased sharply.

In May 1994, Dr. Gill obtained tissue samples from Charlottesville, conducted genetic fingerprinting analysis, compared the results with the data bank he had at his disposal, and established that Anna Andersen could not have been a relative of the Romanovs who were executed in Ekaterinburg or of any of the other Romanovs. Moreover, opponents of the Anastasia story presented biological samples of Polish peasants by the name Shantskovsky who had admitted, way back in 1927, that Anna Andersen was their relative. The analysis performed by Gill proved a 100 percent compatibility showing complete identity between the biological samples of Anna Andersen and her Polish relatives. The legend that had lasted seventy-four years was dispelled.

In 1963, a book came out entitled *Anastasia: The Autobiography of the Grand Duchess of Russia,* written by a Eugenia Smith in Chicago. Photograph and handwriting comparisons did not support her claims. In 1995, it was suggested that she give blood for genetic fingerprinting research. She refused.

On July 12, 1993, Mikhail (Michael George) Goleniewsky died in New York. In the past he had been a colonel in the Polish intelligence service and had actively collaborated with the CIA. According to the author and historian Robert Massie, from 1958 to 1960 Goleniewsky was responsible for bringing down several Soviet agents.[71] Upon his arrival in the United States in 1963, Goleniewsky began publicly asserting that his true title was Grand Duke Alexei Nikolaevich Romanov. True, Alexei was born in 1904 and the pretender in 1922, a difference of eighteen years that was hard to conceal. None of the Romanovs recognized him. The CIA declined his services and pensioned him off. In 1964, the archpresbyter of the Synod of Bishops of the Russian Orthodox Church Abroad, Count Georgy Grabbe, had the imprudence to register Goleniewsky on his marriage to Irmgard Kampf as "Alexei Nikolaevich Romanov, son of Nikolai Alexandrovich Romanov and Alexandra Fyodorovna Romanova, née von Hesse." A scandal broke out in Russian émigré circles, and the church leadership barred Father Georgy from christening the Goleniewsky's daughter, Tatiana. The pretender was acquainted with Eugenia Smith; the "brother" and "sister" recognized one another.

In 1986, in Scottsdale, Arizona, "Prince Alexei Romanov" passed away. He had been an entrepreneur, the picture of health, a dashing horseman and a ladies' man who sold "Alexei" vodka. According to him, he had broken bones eleven times horseback riding, but that didn't bother him. On August 26, 1992, Ivanov received the following letter:

> VINK Corporation. Letter sent at the recommendation of Professor Maples. To Dr. Pavel Ivanov.

Esteemed Dr. Ivanov!

I represent the family of a recently departed gentleman by the name of Alexei Romanov. His entire family solemnly believes that the dead man was the tsarevich, i.e., the son. After Alexei's death, his wife gave me his autobiography, which he had worked on for the past forty years. In connection with the events in Russia, including the publication of official documents, I look on this autobiography as quite realistic. Given the new situation, verification has become even more important for the family. Therefore, all the members of the family have asked me to find out how this can be done and how much it will cost, since we now know that the method of genetic fingerprinting would be used to identify the remains. We are certain that this method will allow us to establish whether our Alexei was the real one or not.

For this we will consider presenting the remains of our Alexei for research. His son and grandsons are also prepared to submit samples.

Thus, I have been authorized to contact you at the instruction of the wife and son of Alexei Romanov, who died in Arizona in 1986, and am prepared to facilitate the necessary research to compare the DNA samples in order that my clients might know the truth about their relatives once and for all.

I want to assure you that my clients have no other motives than the natural desire to learn the truth about the recently deceased and respected head of the family. And naturally, this could bring us closer to a solution to one of the most enigmatic secrets of the century.[72]

It was an open letter printed in one of the Russian-language newspapers published in the United States.

In 1949, Semyonov, a patient in a psychiatric clinic in Petrozavodsk, had declared his tsarist origins, although he did not demand the restoration of his true name. He had persistent hematuria (blood in the urine, as a possible symptom of hemophilia, from which Alexei suffered) and cryptorchidism (Alexei had an analogous disease). Semyonov knew society life before 1917 in minute detail. He had been sent to the northern camps diagnosed with paranoia, and there he languished.

In 1993, the Latvian legal scholar Gryannik published a book, *The Testament of Nicholas II.*[73] In it he states that neither Nicholas II nor his family were executed in Ekaterinburg but rather they made their way safely to Sukhumi, where the head of the family died on February 6, 1957, and where other members of the family died at other times. Apparently some are alive to this day. Gryannik relies on the results of scientific analysis number 129 conducted in the first half of 1992 by Dr. Kislis at the Latvian Scientific Research Laboratory for Forensic Analysis. Unfortunately for Gryannik, the identification of the Ekaterinburg remains places his book in the category of fiction. Popov cites a detailed critical dissection of the portrait analysis done by Dr. Kislis.[74] We agree with his conclusions.

In 1992, in a letter to the United Nations, "Grand Duke Nicholas Alexeyevich Romanov-Dalsky, elect and heir to the throne," declared his existence. According to some sources he was a junior sergeant in the Soviet army who had spent his military service in a song-and-dance ensemble in the Moscow Military District; according to others, he was either a rear admiral or a colonel general, the only Soviet general to be a member of neither the Communist Party nor the Komsomol.[75]

On December 19, 1996, in the Cathedral of the Epiphany in Bogorodsk (near Moscow), a coronation was held for "their Imperial Highnesses the grandson of the Emperor of All the Russias Nicholas II, Nicholas II Alexeyevich Romanov-Dalsky, and his Most August spouse Natalya Evgenievna, née Musina-Pushkina." (Musina-Pushkina is also an old, aristocratic Russian name.) The ritual was performed by priests Andrian, Rafail, and Sergy, who belong to a sectarian Ukrainian church led by Metropolitan Filaret.[76] The biography of the newly crowned "emperor" paints him as the son of Alexei Romanov, who was rescued by Yurovsky himself and then passed off as the little cook Sednev. This emperor graduated from the Military Medical Academy and the conservatory in Saratov, simultaneously, and has a doctorate in economics. This incredible tale would not merit such detailed consideration if it were not for the following tidbit: "On June 16, 1997, Citizen Nikolai Nikolaevich Dalsky received a new passport in Moscow in which he is now called Nikolai Alexeyevich Dalsky-Romanov."[77]

Even more grandiose claims to the Russian throne have been made by a man named Edvard Borisovich Shabadin,[78] an engineer, inventor, and entrepreneur, on the following quite romantic grounds. According to court rumors in the second half of the eighteenth century, the willful heir Pavel Petrovich secretly married Princess Prozorovskaya before his official marriage to the Princess of Hesse-Darmstadt. Varvara Prozorovskaya bore Pavel Petrovich a son, Simeon, in 1772, before being married off to Suvorov. As we know, this marriage brought Suvorov no happiness. According to the same rumors, Simeon served as a naval officer and under the command of Admiral Travenev participated in battles against the Swedes in 1788–90. In the army seminary created by an edict of his father in 1800, Simeon received a theological education and became a professor of divinity by the name of Koltunov.

It is through him that Shabadin traces his lineage. The pretender believes that when Emperor Pavel I rescinded Peter the Great's law on the right of the reigning monarch to appoint his heir and introduced an edict of inheritance exclusively through the elder male line, he actually had his older son Simeon in mind to succeed him on the throne. On the basis of this, Shabadin considers all Romanovs, starting with Alexander I, usurpers and believes that after the abdication of Nicholas II, the Russian crown should have returned to the dominant branch, that is, to the descendants of Pavel I through Simeon, the Koltunov family.

And finally, one more story occurred literally as these lines were being written.

On January 30, 1998, the Independent Television Company of Moscow (NTV) broadcast an interview with Edvard Edvardovich Rossel, the former governor of the Ekaterinburg region, who stated that the Ekaterinburg scientist Avdonin had discovered the burial site of Alexei and Marie Romanov, which would be dug up and studied only after the remains of all the Romanovs (who have been found to date in Ekaterinburg) had been buried in Ekaterinburg. Those remains have now been buried. Far be it from us to consider this original interview merely anecdotal, especially since Rossel cited Avdonin, who said in an interview in spring 1998 that "two places where burial sites were possible." We do not yet know whether the second spot has been excavated, whether a burial site or anything else has been found there, or whether anyone has scientifically analyzed whatever may have been found there. We certainly do not exclude the possibility of adding a second set of Ekaterinburg remains, should such a thing present itself, to our research.

■ Report by Dr. William R. Maples ■
"On Studying the Skeletal Remains in July 1992 in Ekaterinburg"

Published: *Taina tsarskikh ostankov. Materialy nauchnoi konferentsii "Poslednyaya stranitsa istorii tsarskoi sem'i: itogi izucheniya ikaterinburgskoi tragedii."* [The Mystery of the Tsar's Remains. Materials of the Scientific Conference: "The Last Page in the History of the Tsar's Family: Results of Studies of the Ekaterinburg Tragedy."] Ekaterinburg, 1994, pp. 109–13. The international working conference took place in Ekaterinburg on 27–28 July 1992.

William R. Maples was head of the laboratory at the Florida Museum of Natural History at Florida State University, Gainesville, Florida, U.S., and a forensics anthropologist.

My thanks to Dr. Blokhin and Dr. Avdonin for inviting me to participate in this work and also to the colleagues who made reports about their findings and analyses. At the request of Dr. Blokhin and Dr. Avdonin, from July 24 to 25, 1992, we studied the skeletal remains, their X-rays, and other existing evidence. And in that period we came to the following conclusions.

Skeleton No. 1 belongs to a white female (Indo-European), height approximately 168.4 cm [5 feet 6 inches]. At time of death her age was around 40–50 years. The skeleton is incomplete—missing are central portions of the face part of the skull, including the upper jaw, and the ribs. Changes in the joint surfaces of the ankle bones show evidence of extension (stretching), connected to frequent crouching. The lower jaw has a gold bridge, consisting of six units, and a filling in one tooth. The technology of fillings and dental prostheses corresponds to the level of technology used at the start of this century. The lower jaw is damaged.

Skeleton No. 2 belongs to a white fifty-year-old male approximately 175.2 cm tall [5 feet 9 inches]. There are bullet holes in the skull, the entry opening on the left forehead 2.5 cm [1.13 inches] from the temple line and the exit in the right temple area. The central sections of the face are severely damaged and recently restored. The upper jaw has no teeth and probably had a removable prosthesis. We know that one bullet was found in the vertebra and another in the soft tissue of the pelvis.

Skeleton No. 3 belongs to a young white female in her early 20s, height around 159 cm [5 feet 3 inches]. There is a bullet wound. The bullet apparently entered the left side of the lower jaw, went through the palate, ethmoid bone, and exited through the forehead near the ridge. The central sections of the facial part of the skull were severely damaged, the left part of the upper jaw is missing. The cranium of the skull from the side of the exterior surface is significantly damaged—the compact plate and the underlying spongy bone matter are almost completely corroded. There are many fillings and caries in the teeth, which could be useful in identification.

Skeleton No. 4 belongs to a white male aged 45–55, height 168.3 cm [5 feet 6 inches]. The central sections of the facial part of the skull are damaged and incomplete. A significant resorbtion (loss, dissolving) of the bone tissue in the alveolar appendices and remaining teeth was the result of disease—periodontosis. Along the edges of the heads of the femurs there are extensions of the joint surface. These changes are usually observed in people who spent significant time on horseback.

Skeleton No. 5 belongs to a young white female age 17–20 or slightly over 20, height, 171 cm [5 feet 7 inches]. The central sections of the facial part of the skull are damaged, the right half of the upper jaw is missing. Many dental fillings were found which can be used for identification. A bullet was found next to the skeleton in preserved soft tissues.

Skeleton No. 6 are the remains of a young white female 20 years old or a bit more, height around 170.7 cm [5 feet 7 inches]. The central sections of the facial part of the skull are significantly damaged, but restored. There are bullet wounds through the skull, the entry opening found behind the ridge of the left temple bone and the exit near the right sygmoid notch. The minimal diameter of the exit wound is 8.8 mm, which corresponds to a .32 caliber bullet, with a diameter of approximately 7.7 mm. The bones of the forearms are not identical or symmetrical. The absence of similarity between them is seen also under ultraviolet light—the bones have different colors of luminescence (glowing under ultraviolet rays). There are many fillings in the teeth, which can be used for identification.

A comparison of the posthumous dental X-rays allows us to suppose that skeleton No. 5 is younger than skeleton No. 6, and No. 6 is younger than No. 3, which also corresponds with the anthropological findings.

Skeleton No. 7 belongs to a white female approximately 45–50 years old. The fact that the long bones were sawed does not permit us to establish her height. The central sections of the facial part of the skull have been reconstructed. There are complex and well-made dental prostheses and three crowns of a silver-colored metal. When compared to the others, they seem to be temporary, perhaps part of an unfinished treatment less than a year before the death.

Skeleton No. 8 is very severely damaged, incomplete, and belongs to a mature white male, probably aged 40–50 years. There is an old break in the lower third of the elbow bone, the head of the right femur is destroyed. The right femur shows the presence of thickening, the left does not. The upper jaw is missing and the part of the lower jaw has alveoli for 10–11 teeth.

Skeleton No. 9 are the remains of a white male, probably around 50 years old, with a height of approximately 181 cm [5 feet 11 inches]. There is a 2 cm stabbing-cutting wound on the breastbone. On the outside left hip bone there is a gunshot wound. The bullet channel goes through the synovial membrane and comes out the middle part of the bone. The teeth have not been restored; the overbite caused heavy wearing. There are indications of periodontosis.

Most of the skeletons, especially the second, have adipocere [a waxy substance produced when water combines with fatty tissue]. The lambdoid sutures on the bones of skeletons No. 3, 5, 6, and 7 presuppose a family connection. The teeth on some of the skeletons have lye regions formed by the acid. Probably, it also caused the erosion of the cranium No. 3. The skeletons are missing many ribs and vertebrae.

Thus, the facts are so obvious that we can assume that this is the burial site of the imperial family and their servants. If that is the case, then skeleton No. 1 conforms to Demidova; No. 2 to Dr. Botkin; No. 3 to Olga (by age); No. 4 to Tsar Nicholas II; No. 5 to Marie (by age and height); No. 6 to Tatiana (by age and height); No. 7 to Alexandra Fyodorovna; No. 8 and No. 9, may have been servants, men. The remains of Tsarevich Alexei and of Anastasia were not found.

For continuation of this work, we would like to make the following recommendations:

The search must continue for dental records of the family and of Dr. Botkin for comparison, as well as for the family's stomatological records. DNA analysis must be done on all the skeletal remains in a highly specialized laboratory. The remains must be carefully preserved and they must also be photographed for documentary purposes.

Questions for the speaker:

1. What you have just said, is that guesswork or are you certain?

   No one can make a final conclusion without comparing medical records and charts. According to the information we have now, we can make a rough estimate of who the skeletons belong to.

2. I would like to be sure, did you say that upper jaw of skeleton No. 2 had a full row of teeth?

   There are no teeth, only the prosthesis.

3. Which bones and what method are used to determine age and height?

   With the adults, age was established by the degree of obliteration of the seams of the cranium; with the young girls, the teeth are used as well.

4. Is the information accurate that Anastasia's skeleton is missing? How can you tell them apart? After all, Maria was only a bit older and not much taller.

   The younger daughters were the same height, both taller than Nicholas. Anastasia is not here because all the extant skeletons are too tall for her. There is also nothing among the bones that could belong to Alexei.

5. Does the theory that Anastasia survived still exist today?

   That is outside my sphere.

6. Tell us, please, is the research done by Russian scientists very different from yours?

   Upon our arrival in Ekaterinburg we were given a lot of additional information that we did not have, although there have been many books printed in the West on this question. I read my first book about the murder of the Romanovs when I was twelve. Since then, I have been following events. Russian scientists have done everything that we usually do in analogous situations.

7. Is there total certainty that all the bones forming skeleton No. 8 belong to a man?

   No.

chapter 5.

The Rescue of Tsarevich Alexei

A time to get, and a time to lose;
A time to keep, and a time to cast away;
A time to rend, and a time to sew;
A time to keep silence, and a time to speak.

—Ecclesiastes 3:67

■ Investigations into the Filatov-Romanov Kinship ■

In September 1996, the authors were approached by a Russian man named Oleg Vasilievich Filatov, who informed us that his father, Vasily Ksenofontovich Filatov, and Alexei Nikolaevich Romanov, the son of Tsar Nicholas II, were the same person.

Igor Vladimirovich Lysenko, one of the three authors, explains how he met Oleg Filatov:

> In August 1995, I learned from the official reports issued by the state commission researching the Ekaterinburg burial site that the remains of the heir to the throne, Alexei, and one of the younger daughters of Nicholas II, either Marie or Anastasia, had not been found. In October of that year I learned of someone who thought that his father's life may have been linked to the fate of the Romanovs executed in Ekaterinburg in the summer of 1918. This piqued my interest, and I went to meet with this man, Oleg Vasilievich Filatov, at the apartment of Archpriest Nikolai Golovkin, along with the journalist Konyaev and the priest Alexei Morozov.
>
> It was a Sunday evening. I sat in the corner of a large room and listened to a man of average height with large, gray, heavy-lidded eyes. He narrated his story evenly, without agitation, telling what he remembered. He was obviously restraining his emotions as he relived his father's story of the execution, his rescue, and his subsequent wanderings.
>
> I recalled the story of the trip Oleg Filatov, the priests Nikolai Golovkin and Vladimir Basmanov, and police major Sergei Simonenko made to Ekaterinburg and Shadrinsk in early October 1995. During this trip, Golovkin had made a videotape of the burial site.
>
> Ekaterinburg was the place of the execution and at that time was still the tem-

Oleg Filatov, 1998.

porary burial site of the Romanov family. Shadrinsk is a town 230 kilometers [143 miles] away where, according to official documents, Vasily Filatov was born. Vasily Filatov told Oleg that the wounded Alexei Romanov had been brought to this town and that there he had become Vasily Filatov. I noticed the bitterness with which Oleg recounted the pathetic state of the burial site.

At the end of our meeting, I told him about myself and expressed an interest in seeing his documents and photographs and in meeting the people who had helped him. Oleg showed me the documents and introduced me to the people who had volunteered their assistance. I offered my assistance as well and joined the collective of volunteers who were working to establish an identity between Vasily Ksenofontovich Filatov and Alexei Nikolaevich Romanov.

A year later, in September 1996, I learned from my teachers at the St. Petersburg Theological Seminary about the Bishops' Council of the Russian Orthodox Church, which was scheduled to be held in February 1997. On the schedule was the topic of the canonization of the executed tsar and his family, with an examination of materials. One of my teachers, Archpriest Georgy Mitrofanov, was a member of the Commission on the Canonization of Saints of the Russian Orthodox Church's Holy Synod. The commission had never considered the possibility that some of the family may have been rescued.

Emperor Nicholas II.

This was the context in which researchers working on the story of Tsarevich Alexei Romanov's possible rescue recognized the need to create an independent research organization to field inquiries and work with the archives, the press, and the official organs as well as to coordinate the efforts of individual researchers to improve efficiency. The Living History of the Fatherland National Humanitarian Foundation was established for this purpose in early October 1996. Professor Georgy Borisovich Egorov, who has a doctorate in engineering and specializes in the field of systems research and control technology, was invited to be the research director.

Archpriest Nikolai Golovkin, Oleg Filatov, Professor Popov, and Archpriest Vladimir Basmanov (far right) at the site of the Ipatiev house in Ekaterinburg.

The foundation summarized all the information that had been received about Vasily Filatov and sent it, along with the reports by the priests Basmanov, Golovkin, and Popov, to the Commission on the Canonization of Saints. (See documents on pages 200–202 in the Appendix.) A brief synopsis of this information follows.

According to his birth certificate, Vasily Ksenofontovich Filatov was born on December 22, 1907, in the town of Shadrinsk, in the Isetsk District,

Vasily Filatov, 1936.

Tyumen Province. His father's name was Ksenofont Afanasievich Filatov and his mother's name was Elena Pavlovna Filatova. On the 1995 trip, it was discovered that there is also an entry for his birth (also dated December 22, 1907) in the birth register of the Flor-Lavrskaya Church in Shadrinsk. Ksenofont Filatov was a shoemaker who worked independently until 1918 and, after that, in the shoemaker's shop at the trade cooperative until his death in 1921. Elena Filatova died before 1917.

The only testimony we have about Vasily Filatov's life before 1934 is from his autobiographies of 1937 and 1967 (see documents on pages 191–92 in the Appendix) and from the stories he told his family. In his 1967 autobiography, he indicates that from 1918 to 1922 he studied at the polytechnic school in Shadrinsk; in 1921 he was orphaned, and from 1922 to 1928, he lived on his own and in children's homes in various cities throughout western Russia (according to his children's stories, he lived in Nizhny Novgorod, Kostroma, Murom, Yaroslavl, Tula, and Kaluga; spent some time in Moscow, Yalta, Batumi, Tbilisi, Sukhumi, Baku, and Magnitogorsk; and from there went to Shadrinsk). In 1928 he enrolled in a course of study for elementary schoolteachers in Grozny, and then worked as a teacher in the village of Aisengur (now called Novogroznensk) until 1932, when he enrolled in the Workers' School of the Urals Pedagogical Institute in Tyumen, from which he graduated in 1934 (see page 181 in the Appendix).

However, in the 1937 autobiography he indicates that he completed elementary school in Shadrinsk in 1918 and then worked as an apprentice shoemaker in various towns throughout the Soviet Union from 1921 to 1930. He continues that in 1930 he matriculated at the Road Building Workers' School in Shadrinsk and graduated from the Workers' School of the Urals Pedagogical Institute in 1934.

We have been able to obtain Vasily Filatov's certification of graduation from the Workers' School of the Urals Pedagogical Institute dated June 1934 (he must have transferred from the Road Building Workers' School); a certificate stating that Vasily Filatov graduated from the Teachers' Institute in Tyumen in 1936 and was qualified to teach middle school (see page 182 in the Appendix); and a certificate from the Tyumen State Pedagogical Institute in 1939 stating that he was qualified to teach geography (see page 183 in the Appendix). He earned this last degree by attending school part-time while working as a teacher at the local high school in a village of Upper Beshkil, in the Isetsk District of the Omsk Province, where he had been living since 1936.

According to Vasily Filatov's work record from the Isetsk Regional Department of Public Education (see page 185 in the Appendix), in August 1938 he was transferred to Isetsk High School as a geography teacher, and he worked there as a teacher, a school inspector for the region, and acting director

Vasily Filatov, 1939.

of the Isetsk District Education Department until 1946. From 1946 to 1952, he was in charge of academics at Sloboda-Beshkil High School, and in 1952 he became a geography teacher in the village of Krasnovo. In 1953, he married Lydia Kuzminichna Klimenkova, a mathematics teacher in the same school, who was born in 1917. In 1953 their first child, a son, Oleg, was born, and in 1955 a daughter, Olga.

The family has kept the certificate of Vasily Filatov's immediate release from military duty, number 973, issued by the Isetsk District Military Commissariat to reservist Vasily Filatov. After a medical exam on December 5, 1942, he was deemed unfit for military service under paragraph 1, article 12, of the Schedule of Illnesses of Order No. 336 of the USSR People's Commissariat of Defense and was excluded from registering and removed from the military lists (see page 188 in the Appendix and the illustration on page 123). Note that on the Certificate of Exemption from Military Service, article 12 is cited as the reason for his exemption. However, upon closer examination of the certificate, it looks as if the number "2" was written over another number—the number 9. Therefore, it appears that Vasily Filatov was exempted from military service under article 19, not under article 12. Article 19 stands for hemophilia and blood-related diseases, while article 12 stands for chronic illness of the muscular system of a neuropathic character (see page 191 in the Appendix).

Vasily Filatov received decoration "For Valorous Labor during the Great Patriotic War," for his work during World War II helping children who had been evacuated from blockaded Leningrad to the Urals. He helped find them housing and arranged care, food, and clothing for them. In addition, he received decorations for "40 Years of Victory in the Great Patriotic War" and "For Labor Excellence." His family has kept all these decorations.

In 1955, Filatov and his family moved to the village of Pretoria, Novosergievsk District, Orenburg Province. Filatov worked as a geography teacher at Pretoria High School until his retirement in 1967. In 1957 a daughter, Irina, was born, and in 1961 another daughter, Nadezhda.

Oleg Vasilievich Filatov, the oldest of Vasily Filatov's children, graduated in 1976 from the Astrakhan Pedagogical Institute, worked as a teacher, served in the army, married, worked for nine years at Pulkova Airport customs, and is now a consultant at Vitabank. He has two daughters and lives in St. Petersburg. Olga Vasilievna Filatova graduated from the Astrakhan Art Institute and the Repin Institute in Leningrad. An art scholar, she has a daughter and lives in St. Petersburg. Irina Vasilievna Filatova graduated from the Moscow Textile Institute. She is a chemical engineer and lives in Germany with her son. Nadezhda Vasilievna Filatova graduated from the Leningrad Institute of Music Pedagogy and lives in Germany.

Upon retiring, Vasily Filatov moved his family to the village of White Brook, Vytegorsk District, Vologda Province, and three years later, in 1970, moved to the village of Ikryanoye in Astrakhan Province. There he died on October 24, 1988, from heart failure (death certificate IKV No. 432838).

Upon first meeting the Filatov family, one is struck by the resemblance between Vasily's daughters—Olga, Irina, and Nadezhda, and female members of the Romanov family—Empress Marie Feodorovna (Nicholas II's mother), Grand Duchess Xenia Alexandrovna (Nicholas II's sister), and Empress Alexandra Fyodorovna (Nicholas II's wife). (See pages 135–37.) There is a similar resemblance between Vasily's son, Oleg, and emperors of the House of Romanov—Alexander II, Alexander III, and Nicholas II. (See page 138.) Such an obvious degree of similarity along both the female and male lines between one entire generation of the Filatov family and so many members of the Romanov family merits serious attention.

The modern fields of forensic medicine and criminology have contributed numerous investigative methods and experience to the studies of personal identification (the field of establishing an identity between two people, either dead or alive). In September 1994, after studying materials presented by the Filatov family, scientists Andrei Valentinovich Kovalyov[1] and Vyacheslav Leonidovich Popov[2] presented Professor Bonte, director of the Institute of Forensic Medicine of Heinrich Heine University in Dusseldorf, with a proposal to conduct a joint investigation to prove or disprove the genetic kinship between the Filatovs and Romanovs. The scientists began working together, and three families of Filatovs (the families of Oleg, Olga, and Irina) underwent clinical examination of their teeth and the mucous membrane of the mouth. Plaster casts were taken to determine their stomatological status, X-rays were taken of their jaws, skulls, rib cages, and spines, and samples were obtained for genetic and fingerprint testing.

Unfortunately, the investigation was never completed because the scientists concluded that to

Oleg Filatov, circa 1955.

Three of Vasily Filatov's children: Oleg (born 1953), Olga (born 1955), and Irina (born 1957).

continue the genetic testing, it was necessary to exhume the remains of Vasily Filatov. However, based on the research that was completed, the scientists were able to reach the following conclusion:

> In studying the frontal and lateral X-rays of the cervical section of the spines of Oleg, Olga, and Irina, which was carried out within the framework of the expert forensic medical analysis into the death of members of the House of Romanov in 1918–1920, fourteen similar individual structural features were discovered that indicate, in our opinion, genetic kinship between the individuals studied. . . . Independent research conducted at the Institute of Forensic Medicine at Heinrich Heine University using DNA analysis also confirmed the results we obtained. Thus, the results of the research show that blood relatives display a similarity of anatomical structure in the cervical section of the spine. These results have major practical significance, since they allow us to establish, either independently or combined with the methods of genetic analysis, genetic kinship between the individuals investigated.[3]

Considering the size of the data bank that has been compiled on the Romanov remains found in Ekaterinburg, we might think that completing this research would not require much more work, especially since the absence of negative results at the initial stage of the research seems to promise a positive result at the final stage. (The correspondence between the scientists is cited on pages 193–95, and excerpts from Kovalyov's doctoral dissertation are cited on page 209 in the Appendix).

Popov relates the results of his research:

> On September 9, 1994, my colleague Kovalyov and I met with the children of Vasily Filatov: Oleg, Olga, and Irina, who believe their father may very well have been the Tsarevich Alexei. Their opinions are based on their father's erudition and level of education and cultivation, and the stories he told them while they were growing up that correspond to the content and chronology of prerevolutionary events and the facts that are now known about the fate of the last Romanovs. Vasily Filatov never told his children directly about his origins and always evaded direct questions on this subject. He spent his last years in Astrakhan, where he died in 1988. He asked that his ashes be left where they were laid to rest and told his children to move to St. Petersburg. After their father's death, they honored his request.
>
> The children have declared their desire to get closer to the truth and were prepared to have their father's body exhumed and to conduct and finance the identification research, but they had to have samples from known Romanovs for comparison. Who would agree to give them fragments of the remains from the burial site in Ekaterinburg? Who of the surviving Romanov relatives would donate blood for genetic analysis? [Given the extensive bank of genetic information existing on the Romanovs, the authors do not believe this is necessary.] Their appeals to the government commission have yet to receive a reply, hence their logical decision to seek independent experts. Russian, American, and British specialists were already taking part in the investigation, so they decided to seek additional assistance from forensic medical experts in Germany and Finland, who offered to conduct genetic research to prove or disprove the genetic kinship between the Filatovs and the Romanovs. Clearly, only comparative genetic research on the biological tissues of their father and the Romanov remains from Ekaterinburg, or the blood of surviving Romanov descendants, could provide scientific proof.
>
> The German scientists suggested that the Filatovs donate blood for genetic research. But what could a comparison of the blood of the children of the purported heir (a male heir, not a female!) with the results of the British analysis yield? Success was doubtful, since hereditary genetic information is transmitted along the female line. Therefore, it became necessary to conduct a genetic study of the remains of their father, Vasily Filatov.[4]

The authors are in full agreement with the methodology of Popov and Kovalyov. The sole point on which we disagree is with their pessimism regarding the existing identification of the Romanov remains. We did not plan to conduct our own analysis of the remains. We have confidence in the quality of the existing bank of genetic information on the Romanovs and we do not think the disputes over the authenticity of the remains affect the legitimacy of this information.

In addition, we would like to point out that genetic research is only a part, albeit a substantial one, of identification studies. A comprehensive proposal to establish the identity between Alexei Nikolaevich Romanov and Vasily Ksenofontovich Filatov was drawn up in 1996 by Professor Vadim Petrovich Petrov, who holds a doctorate in medicine.[5] He began work on the project, and his son—Vadim Vadimovich Petrov, who also holds an advanced degree in medicine and is continuing his studies at the Legal Scientific Research Center of the St. Petersburg University Law School[6]—continued it after his death. The scientific research was conducted by Leonard Nikolaevich Gavrilov,[7] a legal scholar, and Vadim Petrov. The results of our analyses are set forth here.

The scientific identification of an individual requires comparative materials from the same time for each of the people whose identity is being established. These materials can be photographs of the face (head), stomatological diagrams, X-rays of various parts of the body, molds of the jaws and teeth, handwriting samples, genetic-fingerprinting descriptions, and so on. The best comparative materials in criminology, according to accepted practice, are the prints from the palmar surfaces of the nail phalanges for fingerprint research. These were not taken from Alexei Romanov or Vasily Filatov since the investigation began after their deaths. However, we have analyzed the photographs of Vasily Filatov and Alexei Romanov as well as handwriting samples from each of them. In conducting the handwriting analysis, we used the following materials:

Six letters and five diary pages from Tsarevich Alexei

Seven documents and six personal letters from Vasily Filatov (provided by his son Oleg) and two more photocopies of manuscript documents (provided by the Tyumen Provincial State Archive)

The handwriting analysis was conducted using traditional criminological methods (the text is cited in full beginning on page 203 in the Appendix). We quote the conclusion here:

> EVALUATION OF RESULTS
>
> Evaluating the results of this comparative investigation allows us to arrive at the following opinion: The small number of differences discovered in the general and specific features of the records studied can be explained by the large interval of time that elapsed between the six letters and diary pages that were written in 1916–1918 and the letters and manuscripts written later [between the years 1939 and 1985] by Vasily Filatov. The differences that were discovered in a few general features, and in a small number of specific features, in the handwriting samples are not sufficient grounds for concluding that the writing samples studied were executed by different people. In the process of an individual's personal development, the level of one's writing changes, the general features of one's handwriting change, and improve, and the specific features of one's handwriting can

Handwriting samples of Alexei Romanov.

The top sample is taken from one of his letters; the bottom sample is taken from his diary.

Л.Н.Гаврилов В.В.Петров

Автобиография.
Я, Филатов Василий Ксенофонтович, родился 22 декабря 1907 г. (~~по старому стилю~~) в г. Шадринске, Курганской области. До революции мой отец работал сапожником по найму у частных лиц. После революции в сапожной мастерской [illegible] в г. Шадринске. При жизни отца я закончил городскую начальную школу и поступил учиться в Шадринский Политехникум, в котором обучали и учили детей различным ремеслам. Окончить его мне не удалось в связи со смертью отца в 1921 г., а также голодовки, которая началась в нашем

A handwriting sample taken from the autobiography of Vasily Filatov.

Photographs of Alexei Romanov, taken from the photographic analysis comparing depictions of Alexei Romanov and Vasily Filatov.

change as well. No inexplicable differences were discovered in the investigation between the executor of the diary and the six letters of 1916–1918 and Vasily Filatov's handwriting samples taken later. The differences in the general features and in a small number of specific features that were found during the course of the research can be fully attributed to the development of his writing (written speech) over the course of time.

The research has revealed similarities in the general and specific features of the handwriting. Each of the coinciding general and specific features taken alone is not unusual or rare. However, the discovery of such a large number of specific features coinciding in the handwriting samples studied as compared to the very small number of differences allows us to arrive at a very high degree of confidence in our conclusion that the writing samples studied (the six letters of 1916–1918, the five diary pages, and the handwriting samples from Vasily Filatov) were written by one and the same person.

CONCLUSION

Our research allows us to conclude that the writing samples we studied (the six letters of 1916–1918, the five diary pages, and the handwriting samples from Vasily Filatov) were written by one and the same person.

Specialists: L. N. Gavrilov (signature), V. V. Petrov (signature)

For the scientific portrait analysis, using photo registering, and sectoral coincidence, we studied seventeen black-and-white photographs of the Tsarevich Alexei (both alone and in groups), twelve black-and-white photographs of Vasily Filatov (both alone and in groups), and eleven photocopies and com-

Photographs of Vasily Filatov, taken from the photographic analysis comparing depictions of Alexei Romanov and Vasily Filatov.

puter printouts of photographs. As is usual in identification research, the work began with a separate study of each subject. In the photographs of both Alexei Romanov and Vasily Filatov, we studied the general structural features of the faces as a whole and their separate parts applicable to the elements of a "verbal portrait." Then, in these same photographs, we studied specific features in the structure of the same parts of the faces. We summarized the results in tables and compared. In the comparative research we juxtaposed the same features and drew conclusions about their correspondence or lack thereof. Utilizing television technology in pairs of depictions of Alexei Romanov and Vasily Filatov, we created various combined portraits that contained elements of the depictions of both of these individuals. After this, on each combined portrait, we studied the degree of correspondence between elements of Alexei Romanov's face and Vasily Filatov's face. The research is cited in full on page 211. Here we quote the entire conclusion:

> EVALUATION OF RESULTS
>
> Evaluating the results of the comparative investigation allows us to arrive at the following opinion: An investigation of the portraits presented in the photographs revealed a large number of coinciding general and specific features in the structure of the heads and faces of the adolescent and the man. Also, despite the long interval between the time the photographs of the adolescent and the man were taken, we discovered no significant differences. The discovery of such a large number of coinciding general and specific characteristics in the absence of significant differences allows us to conclude, with a high degree of certainty, that the photographs and printouts portray the same person at different times in his life.
>
> CONCLUSION
>
> Our research permits us to conclude, with a high degree of certainty, that the photographs and printouts portray the same person at different times in his life.
>
> Specialists: L. N. Gavrilov (signature), V. V. Petrov (signature)

Given the absence of negative results from the initial genetic testing and given the similarity of the anatomical structure of the cervical sections of the spine that is applicable to close relatives (as stated earlier, these two studies have not yet been completed), the positive results of the handwriting and

Фото 10. Та же фотография, что и на фото 1.

Фото 11. Та же фотография, что и на фото 9.

Л.Н.Гаврилов

В.В.Петров

Two photographs from the photographic analysis comparing depictions of Alexei Romanov (left) and Vasily Filatov (right).

Фото 12. Та же фотография, что и на фото 1 и 10, с нанесенной разметкой. Цифрой 1 со стрелкой указан перерыв контура левой брови.

Фото 13. Та же фотография, что и на фото 9 и 11, с нанесенной разметкой. Цифрой 1 со стрелкой указан перерыв контура левой брови.

Л.Н.Гаврилов

В.В.Петров

The same photographs of Alexei Romanov and Vasily Filatov as above, with a superimposed layout over each. The numeral 1 with the arrow indicates the break in the contour of the left eyebrow.

Two photographs from the photographic analysis comparing depictions of Alexei Romanov (left) and Vasily Filatov (right).

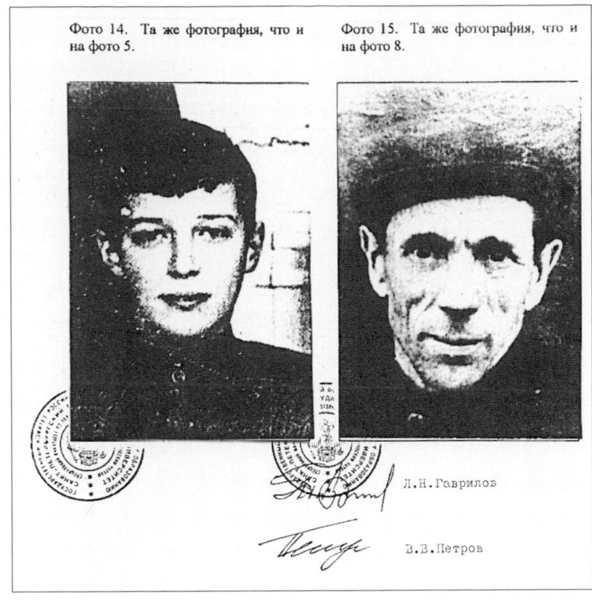

Фото 14. Та же фотография, что и на фото 5.

Фото 15. Та же фотография, что и на фото 8.

Л.Н.Гаврилов

В.В.Петров

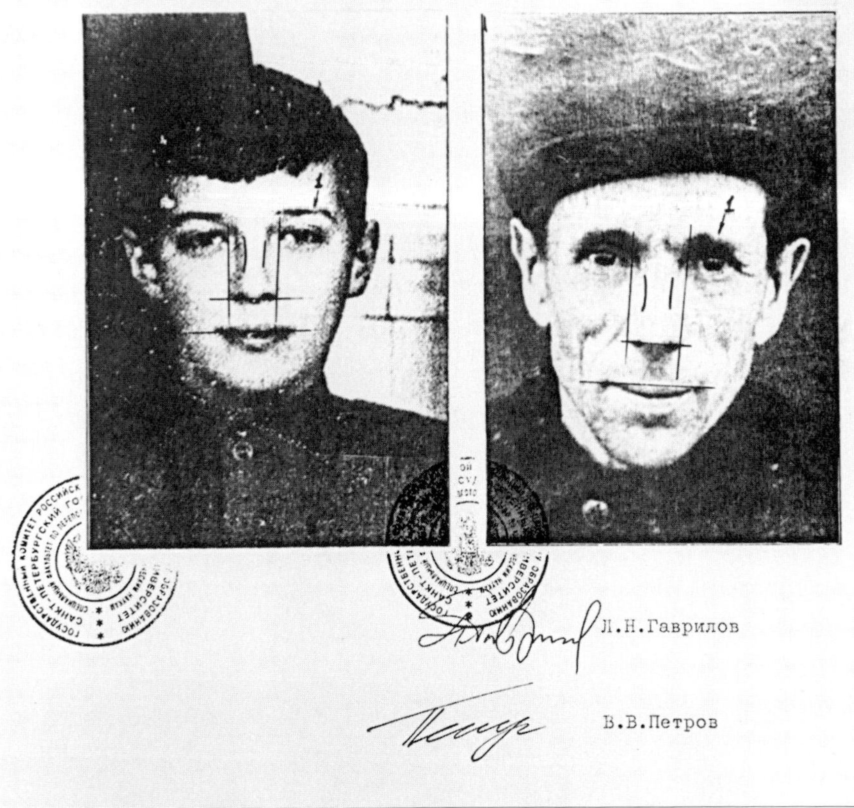

Фото 16. Та же фотография, что и на фото 5 и 14, с нанесенной разметкой. Цифрой 1 со стрелкой указан перерыв контура левой брови.

Фото 17. Та же фотография, что и на фото 8 и 15, с нанесенной разметкой. Цифрой 1 со стрелкой указан перерыв контура левой брови.

Л.Н.Гаврилов

В.В.Петров

The same photographs of Alexei Romanov and Vasily Filatov as above, with a superimposed layout over each. The numeral 1 with the arrow indicates the break in the contour of the left eyebrow.

portrait research allow us to draw the preliminary conclusion that Alexei Nikolaevich Romanov and Vasily Ksenofontovich Filatov were one and the same person.

Nor is this conclusion contradicted by our many other observations.

According to the testimony of his wife and children, Vasily Filatov suffered from hemiparesis of the muscles of his left leg: his right foot was size 42 [U. S. size 10], his left size 40 [U. S. size 9], and his left leg was shorter than his right. He experienced major discomfort but made no adaptations to his left boot (the son of a shoemaker who worked as an apprentice in a shoemaker's workshop for nearly nine years!). We know that Alexei Romanov's left leg suffered a trauma in 1912 and that after heavy internal bleeding he endured a temporary deadening of the nerves, a loss of sensation that was not restored even after lengthy treatment.

According to the family's testimony, when Vasily Filatov accidentally hit himself on the arms or legs, the place where he was struck swelled, there were signs of internal hemorrhaging, and his temperature rose. The process of reabsorption (the uptake into the bloodstream of substances previously filtered out of the blood) was accompanied by acute pain and lasted several days. As we stated earlier, article 19, the article number that was originally written on Vasily Filatov's military service release papers (see illustration page 123), stands for hemophilia according to the Schedule of Illnesses of the USSR, NKO (People's Commissariat of Defense) 1942.

We know that Alexei Romanov suffered from hemophilia. However, prior to the 1930s, no clear diagnostic methods existed for differentiating between "true" hemophilia and other blood diseases that involved the symptoms of hemorrhaging. It may be that the doctors' pessimistic prognoses at the beginning of the century that Alexei had a "life-threatening disease" were seriously exaggerated from our modern point of view. In the 1980s and 1990s, the average life expectancey of hemophiliacs was over sixty years, and we know instances of hemophiliacs fighting in World War II.

Recalling Vasily Filatov as a person, his children describe his love for his family, his erudition, and his love of music, art, and literature. In the evenings he liked to read out loud surrounded by his family, and he loved to play music. Oleg writes, "What astonishes me most of all is where a former homeless child learned to play keyboard instruments. . . . [He] not only played the harpsichord, piano, and organ, but also knew how to tune them. He loved the balalaika. . . . he played the concertina, bayan, and accordion and taught them to us. . . . He was very fond of classical music: the mazurkas and waltzes nos. 6 and 7 of Chopin, Beethoven, Tchaikovsky . . . and the polonaise. He played Russian waltzes on the piano . . . He knew the marches of all the tsarist regiments. . . . He taught us to sing without tensing the vocal cords, but achieving a smooth tone without strain. His manner of singing was quiet and calm, but very expressive. He sang ballads, operatic arias, and long Russian folk songs."

The entire Filatov family would prepare long and intensively for the New Year, their favorite holiday, sewing costumes and making masks for home theatrical productions. The family made toys, garlands, boats, and snowflakes from colored paper and drew pictures for each other with inscriptions in verse. Olga and Oleg write: "Just before New Year, we would decorate a tree, which was always large and tall—up to the ceiling—and give each other presents. In our family, everyone cared for everyone else, the older children helping the younger. . . . Father and Mother would deck themselves out as the Snow Maiden and Granfather Frost, take the presents out from under the tree, pass them

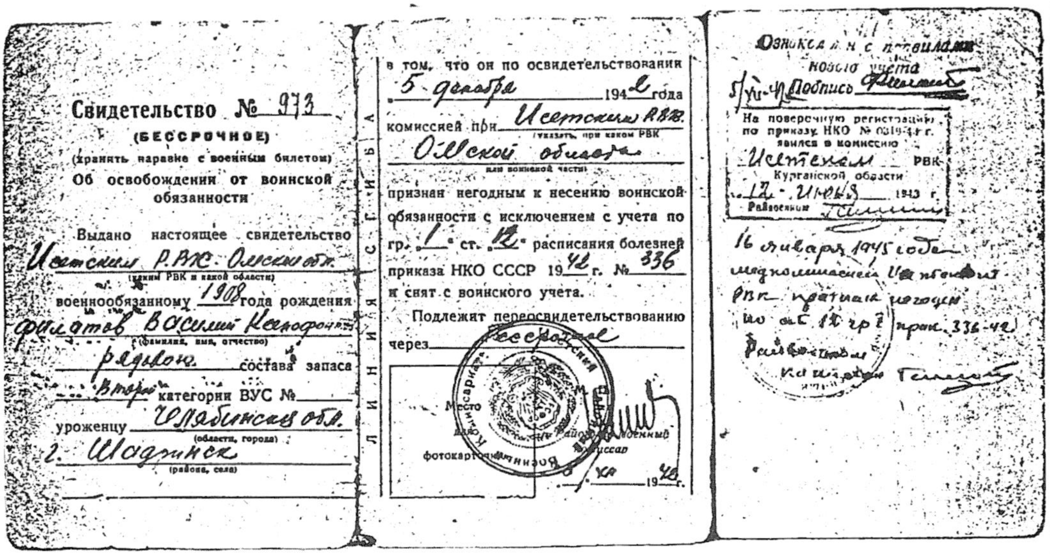

Свидетельство № 973
(БЕССРОЧНОЕ)
(хранить наравне с военным билетом)
Об освобождении от воинской обязанности

Выдано настоящее свидетельство Исетским Р.ВК. Омской обл.
(каким РВК и какой области)
военнообязанному 1908 года рождения
Филатов Василий Ксенофонтович
(фамилия, имя, отчество)
рядового состава запаса второй категории ВУС №
уроженцу Челябинской обл.
(области, города)
г. Шадринск
(района, села)

ЛИНИЯ СГИБА

в том, что он по освидетельствовании 5 декабря 1942 года комиссией при Исетском РВК (указать, при каком РВК) Омской области (или воинской части) признан негодным к несению воинской обязанности с исключением с учета по гр. 1 ст. 12 расписания болезней приказа НКО СССР 1942 г. № 336 и снят с воинского учета.

Подлежит переосвидетельствованию через бессрочно

Место для фотокарточки

Районный военный комиссар

.. XII 1942 г.

Ознакомлен с правилами нового учета
5/XII-42 Подпись

На поверочную регистрацию по приказу НКО № 0319-4 г. явился в комиссию Исетском РВК Курганской области 12 июня 1943 г.
Райвоенком

16 января 1945 года медкомиссией Исетского РВК признан негоден по ст. 12 гр. I прик. 336-42
Райвоенком

Vasily Filatov's certificate of release from military service.

around, and congratulate us, and we would give them our gifts, sing a song about the tree, and dance around it."

These details may be typical for an educated Russian family with traditions from the early part of the century, but they are far from typical for the family of an orphan shoemaker. Georgy Shavelsky, an archpriest in the Russian army who knew the Romanov family well, wrote about their rare love for one another and their patriarchal traditions. Pierre Gilliard, the teacher of the tsar's children, wrote about the Romanov family as well: "The Sovereign often read out loud while the little duchesses did handwork or played with us. The empress . . . would also pick up some work or recline on her couch. We would spend the long winter nights in this peaceful family atmosphere as if we were lost in the limitless tracts of distant Siberia."

Vasily Pankratov, commissar of the Provisional Government, recalled that Nicholas II loved Russian history and taught his son history himself. "The former tsar truly did know Russian military history, but his knowledge of his nation's history in general was very weak. He either forgot or had a very poor understanding of the Russian historical periods and their significance. All of his discussion along these lines came down to the history of wars."[8]

Oleg Filatov recalls that his father taught the children history, telling them the stories of major battles from different periods. "My father had a great enthusiasm for history, especially military history, and knew it thoroughly, including the troop dislocations and the alignments of forces in specific battles. In demonstrating his knowledgeability in these matters, my father seemed to include himself in the military caste. All his life he used to say: 'We Filatovs have always stood on guard for the state.' When he described battles on the ice, he recounted in detail the German and Russian tactics—the wedge and the ambush. He would compare Suvorov's alpine marches and the 'ravine' battles of Kutuzov and Barclay de Tolly. Describing naval battles from Ushakov to Makarov, he emphasized the precision of Russian artillery fire and the quality of the army." For Vasily Filatov, too, then, military history was of paramount interest.

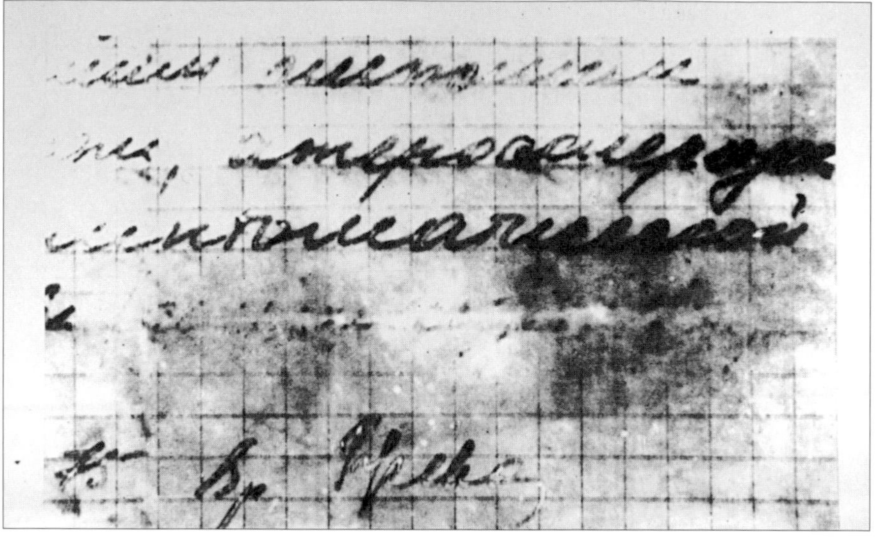

A fragment from a report on the health of Vasily Filatov, 1975. The last word has been erased.

Vasily Filatov was a family man. He spent a good deal of time with his children, and took great pleasure in teaching them. Oleg writes, "He knew the traditions of his own country and other states well. He had mastered foreign languages—German, Greek, Old Church Slavonic, Latin, English, and French—although he did not use them actively. . . . He could recite from memory [the poetry of] Fet, Pushkin, Lermontov, Tyutchev, Esenin, Chekhov, Kuprin, Heinrich Heine, and Goethe in German. . . . He made an embroidery stand himself and made me learn how to embroider on it—cross-stitch, satin stitch, and other ways. When I would ask him why I needed this, he would reply: 'What do you mean? This is simply something one must know how to do.' He taught us to draw. After that we moved on to watercolors, and later to oils."

Lydia Kuzminichna Filatova—Vasily Filatov's wife—remembers him as follows:

> In 1949, I was sent to work at the seven-year school in the village of the Sloboda-Beshkil . . . where the dean was my future husband, Vasily Ksenofontovich Filatov, a geography and history teacher. My first impression was of a crippled man who swayed when he walked. He would drag his left leg and then throw it forward. He wore a wrinkled cotton suit, a wrinkled pink shirt, and boots with turned-up toes. . . . He had a pale face with regular features animated by sorrowful, dark, deep-set eyes. He won me with his selflessness, his kindness, his vitality, his courage. . . . He was often sick, he had terrible headaches and pains in his legs, shoulders, and waist. . . . To distract himself from the pain, he would pray, and when it let up, he would play chess.

His children talk about how he would work through at least two chess matches a day, read chess literature, and play chess by correspondence: . . . "Chess was his passion. He played chess when he was laid low by pain. He said that he played instead of taking medicine."

In his profession as a teacher, Vasily Filatov enjoyed the respect and friendship of all, although he had no close friends and did not invite his students (even his favorites) to his house. He did not give bad grades. He almost never argued. He swam well, liked to fish, and went hunting with his colleagues from work. He said very little about his past and was very circumspect.

The Escape and Rescue of Alexei

The testimonies of Vasily Filatov's family members have allowed the authors to draw a possible picture of what happened to Alexei Romanov immediately after the execution:

On July 3, the White Czech General Gaida and Colonel Voitsekhovsky's units captured Zlatoust and Kyshtym. Less than 62 miles separated them from Ekaterinburg. On July 4, the Fifth Congress of Soviets opened in Moscow, and on the agenda, among other items, was the issue of a trial against the former emperor, Nicholas Romanov. In Ekaterinburg, the commandant of the Ipatiev house was replaced: Yurovsky, the deputy chairman of the provincial Cheka, and Nikulin replaced Avdeyev and his assistant, Moshkin. Yurovsky and Nikulin changed the entire inside guard of the house, but kept the outside guard, in which the brothers Alexander and Andrei Strekotin had been serving since April 1918. Vasily Filatov used to refer to them as his uncles and rescuers.

In 1928, Andrei Alexandrovich Strekotin wrote an account of those days guarding the tsar and his family. He describes the walks the tsar's family took:

> He [the tsar] would cautiously lift him [his son] up and hug him to his broad chest, and his son would hold his father . . . The tsar would carry him out of the house like that, put him in a special carriage, and then wheel him down the lanes, stop, gather pebbles, snap off flowers for him or branches from trees—and give them to him, and he, being a child, would throw them into the bushes. There were hammocks for them in the garden, but only the tsar's four daughters used them. Two of them were blondes with gray eyes. They were of average height and looked very much alike. Another, Tatiana, was plump and healthy, a beautiful brunette. The other, the eldest, Olga, was above average height, skinny, palefaced, and sickly looking. She took few walks in the garden and did not associate with any of her sisters. She spent more time with her brother.[9]

So far we know virtually nothing about the Strekotin brothers' personalities. That work lies ahead. We turn the reader's attention now to just one fact: their reminiscences were written calmly, without prejudice, with evident interest in their charges. This alone distinguishes them significantly from the other reminiscences we have from the guards and soldiers who came into contact with the Romanovs during this time.

From July 4 to 9, the White Czechs and Kolchak's army were developing their plan of attack on Ekaterinburg and the surrounding area. Direct communication between Ekaterinburg and Moscow was cut. On July 6, Left Socialist Revolutionary riots broke out in the capital, and people in Moscow had other things on their minds besides a trial against Nicholas II. Filipp Goloshchekin, secretary of the Urals Executive Committee of the Russian Social Democratic Workers Party (Bolshevik) (RSDRP[b]), a member of the Ural Provincial Soviet's Presidium, and military commissar of the Ural District, gave the Ural Soviet an instruction from the All Russian Central Executive Committee to conduct the legal trial there. But no time was left. General Gaida's shock troops were on the move from Kuzino Station to Ekaterinburg, and the city's days were numbered. On July 14, at a session of the Ural Soviet Executive Committee's Presidium, Goloshchekin suggested "liquidating the former tsar Nicholas Romanov and his family, as well as the servants now with him." A resolution was passed, and Yurovsky was assigned responsibility to implement an execution—by July 18 at the latest.

On July 16, at eleven-thirty at night, Goloshchekin arrived at the Ipatiev house and handed Yurovsky the text of the execution decree. After midnight, a truck pulled up at the entrance to the house on Ascension Lane, a one-and-a-half-ton Fiat. Behind the wheel sat the driver, Lyukhanov, and in the cab, assigned to assist Yurovsky, were the Chekists Ermakov and Mikhail Medvedev. Yurovsky, Ermakov, and Medvedev rang the electric buzzer at the Ascension Avenue entrance, summoned Dr. Botkin, who was sleeping in the anteroom, and asked him to awaken the prisoners and assemble them downstairs.

In the middle of the night, eleven people gathered in the small half-cellar room: Nicholas, Alexandra, Olga, Tatiana, Marie, Anastasia, and Alexei, Dr. Botkin, the cook Kharitonov, the servant Trupp, and the lady-in-waiting, Demidova. The twelve executioners lined up across from them: Latvian Chekists (former Austro-Hungarian prisoners of war) from the "special team" formed on Yurovsky's order: Khorvat, Fisher, Edelshtein, Fekete, Nagy, Grinfeld, and Vergazi, as well as Vaganov, Pavel Medvedev, and Nikulin, along with Yurovsky, Ermakov, and Medvedev. There was no physician or clergyman present. Yurovsky read out the execution decree and the rounds of firing began.

But the execution did not go at all as Goloshchekin, Yurovsky, and Ermakov had planned. After the first few rounds were fired from the revolvers and pistols, the cramped, unventilated room filled with gunpowder gases. The smoke prevented the executioners from seeing not only whom they were shooting but even the weapons in their own hands. They were firing bullets loaded with both smoke-free and black gunpowder, and the combination of those two gases is extremely acrid. The shooters were overcome by tearing, coughing, and vomiting and had to quit the building immediately, having fired less than half the ammunition allocated and not taking the time to ascertain which of the victims were dead and which were still alive. They shot repeatedly only at those who sat down or stood up. The victims were transferred quickly to the truck, whose engine had been kept running to drown out the noise of the shooting. Military Commissar Goloshchekin had stood by to make sure the noise couldn't be heard outside. Given this lack of organization, it is likely that there were some survivors interspersed among the dead in the back of the truck.

While transferring the victims' bodies from the house to the truck, there was a brief five- or ten-minute break. When Yurovsky discovered that some of the men had absconded with the victims' jewels, he assembled the marauders upstairs and forced them to give back their plunder. During these few minutes, Nikulin ordered Andrei Strekotin, a shooter from the outside guard, to continue searching the bodies of the executed. Strekotin must then have discovered signs of life in the unconscious Alexei.

Once he had dealt with the marauders, Yurovsky went outside, got in the cab with Ermakov, Vaganov, and the driver, Lyukhanov, and the truck, loaded with the victims' bodies, set off through the nighttime city.

But where did it go?

The route via the Upper Isetsk plant to the Koptyaki road has been described many times in different accounts—the miserable condition of the road that caused the truck to get stuck more than once, eventually bringing it to a complete halt. The weak engine—no more than 50 horsepower—of the one-and-a-halfton Fiat overheated and would not pull, so the executioners had to unload the vehicle. Edvard Radzinsky in his book *The Last Tsar: The Life and Death of Nicholas II* mentions just such a halt at railroad crossing number 184.[10] It was there that Alexei could have left the truck.

According to the reminiscences of Filatov's children, it was during this reloading that Alexei hid under the bridge near the railroad, and, after the truck left, moved along the right-of-way, reaching Shartash Station by dawn.

This coincidence in the story of Vasily Filatov and in the account related in Edvard Radzinsky's text stumped the authors for a long time.

The map (see pages 88–89) shows clearly that from railroad crossing number 184 to Shartash Station it is at least nine miles. A sick and possibly wounded adolescent simply could not have covered that kind of distance in a few nighttime hours.

The situation seemed hopeless until we were able to come up with a detailed diagram of Ekaterinburg during those years (see pages 88–89). We then saw that there was more than one bridge near crossing number 184 where the truck could have become stuck in the mud and required unloading.

From the Ipatiev house, two routes led through, or past, the Upper Isetsk works to the Koptyaki road. The first went over the dam at the town pond, a guarded site where a truck on a secret mission would not have wanted to go. But a block downstream on the Iset River, which turned into a brook right below the dam, was a small bridge and next to that, the machine shop rail branch, which led to the Rezhevsky plant. It was about two-and-a-half miles from here to the Shartash Station. Alexei could have covered this distance in two hours in the dark. The search party did not go in that direction and could not have found him.

The other route went from the Ipatiev house on Ascension Avenue to North Street, left over the bridge across another brook, past the new and old stations, past the Upper Isetsk plant, and out onto the Koptyaki road. The truck could have become stuck at this bridge, too. Once again, alongside it was the railroad right-of-way, which continued for about three miles to Shartash Station. Alexei could have covered this distance in two hours as well.

In 1918, there was not a third route.

According to the reminiscences of Vasily Filatov's children, on the morning of July 17, the Strekotin "uncles" found Alexei at Shartash Station, and drove him 140 miles to Shadrinsk. The road to Shadrinsk—the terminus of what was at the time a blind branch of the Ekaterinburg–Sinarskaya–Shadrinsk line—was still open. Voitsekhovsky and Gaida's shock troops were moving toward Ekaterinburg from Chelyabinsk in the south and from Kuzino Station in the west. Easterly

Shartash Station, in the 1990s.

directions—toward Tyumen and Shadrinsk—were still open during the week of July 17–24. Alexei could have reached Shadrinsk with an escort during that week.

How could the Strekotin brothers have found him at the station? Quite easily. In the morning, the search party that Yurovsky had sent out from Koptyaki arrived at headquarters in Ekaterinburg and reported the disappearance of the two bodies. It is unlikely that anyone in the search party thought they had actually escaped. More likely, they assumed that passing peasants had gathered up the victims' bodies in order to bury them according to Orthodox ritual. But the Strekotins could have known that they were still alive. And if so, they also would have known that since the search party had not found them, then the two lost victims had obviously moved in the opposite direction from the search party—that is, in the direction of Shartash Station.

We still do not know why the Strekotin brothers decided to search for Alexei. The circumstances surrounding his disappearance from the truck still need to be reconstructed. The researchers have not yet sufficiently examined this aspect of the story; and Vasily Filatov would talk about this part of his story only sparingly and reluctantly. However, his children Oleg and Olga, and Oleg's wife, Anzhelika Petrovna Tămaş, have pieced together what Vasily Filatov told them in September 1984.

En route to the burial site, Alexei woke up in the back of the truck from the pouring rain, tumbled out of the vehicle, crawled under the little bridge, and then made his way to Shartash Station following the rail line. The Strekotins found him there, and drove him to Shadrinsk to live with the Filatov family. Alexei Romanov was adopted into the family—Ksenofont Filatov had one son who had died from the Spanish flu—and assumed the name Vasily Filatov.

chapter 6.

The End of the Romanovs?

Neither take away nor augment
Thus on earth has it always been.

—Alexander Tvardovsky

We have followed an eighty-year trail in the wake of the death of Nicholas II. Now let us look back at the fall of the Russian imperial family and revisit the principal landmarks along the path.

The reign of the Romanov monarchical dynasty came to an end in Russia on March 2–3, 1917, when Nicholas II abdicated in favor of his brother, Grand Duke Michael Alexandrovich, who in turn abdicated in favor of the Constituent Assembly. After the Senate confirmed the two abdication documents, the abdication became irrevocable under the laws of the Russian Empire. On September 1, 1917, Russia was declared a republic by a decree of Kerensky, the head of the Provisional Government. The populace perceived this as a fait accompli, and Russia's monarchy passed into the realm of history.

Theoretically, of course, there was still some possibility that the monarchy could be restored. At the time of the abdication, the Constituent Assembly was supposed to decide what new form of government Russia would have. Even if Russia had continued with a monarchy, it would not necessarily have been an absolute monarchy, or even a Romanov monarchy. There were other legitimate contenders for the Russian throne—descendants of Rurik, the Scandinavian prince who founded the Russian monarchy in the ninth century, could always show up.

However, the Constituent Assembly—which consisted almost entirely of socialist parties—lasted only a day and never had the opportunity to consider the structure of Russia's future government. The newly powerful Bolsheviks viewed the Romanovs solely as vanquished tyrants guilty of bloodshed, unwarranted war, greed, and the cause of hunger and poverty among the masses.

Revolutionary leaders pushed for a trial against Nicholas II for his "crimes against the people." A trial against the ex-tsar was on the agenda at the Fifth Congress of Soviets, but uprisings by the Socialist Revolutionaries and the worsening civil war forced the Bolsheviks to hand the trial (and the retribution) over to the Ural Provincial Soviet, which was then holding the Romanovs.

Between Moscow and Ekaterinburg, both of which were trying to maintain Soviet power in July 1918, lay the immense territories of the Volga and Trans-Volga regions, which at this time were under the control of the Czech rebels. In the south were the Orenburg steppes, which had been seized by the White Cossacks, and in the east lay Siberia, under the control of White Army Commander

Kolchak. The only connection with Moscow was the northern railway through Petrograd, the sole line of communication under Soviet control.

It was under these conditions that, on the night of July 14–15, 1918, the Bolshevik leadership in the Urals—the Presidium of the Regional Soviet's Executive Committee, the leadership of the RSDRP(b) Regional Committee, and the Military–Revolutionary Committee —decided to liquidate former Tsar Nicholas II, his family, and their retinue before July 18, 1918 (the date the town was to be evacuated). The texts of the resolution and the protocol of execution were drawn up formally, despite these urgent conditions, in full compliance with the proper procedures.

The question of whether the execution of the Romanovs was legal under the RSFSR (Russian Soviet Federative Socialist Republic) constitution that had been adopted only a week before continues to be discussed even today.

From the standpoint of national sovereignty, the Bolsheviks rejected the principle of separation of powers. According to this first constitution, the RSFSR was the source of the legislative, judicial, and executive power that constituted the framework of the Soviets' sovereignty. Thus, when the Presidium of the Ural Soviet's Executive Committee made the decision to execute Nicholas II, it was a perfectly legal decision according to the constitution of the day. The "legality" of this decision reflects the monstrosity of this interpretation of the law and, of course, has no moral bearing on the events in question.

History shows that any revolution is cruel and bloody. Three hundred years ago, history saw the execution of an English king, two hundred years ago a French king, and almost a hundred years ago a Russian king. Each execution was a tragedy. The first two have long since become a part of history and no longer inspire objections or strong emotions. The tragedy of the executed Russian tsar should also be perceived as a historical event—but first the whole truth about it needs to be told so that Russia—and the world—can understand and accept the tragedy.

In our opinion, the main obstacle to societal acceptance is the following. When the VTsIK Presidium instructed the Ural Soviet to try former Tsar Nicholas II, everyone knew what the outcome of such a trial would be. However, the Ural Soviet condemned everyone to death—including the children and the servants—thereby evoking persistent distaste in society for this criminal deed.

According to our calculations, the Romanov family now numbers about thirty people. Eleven live in the United States, six in France, five in England, three in Italy, one in Denmark, and one in Uruguay. Five branches of the family have been maintained: the Mikhailoviches, Vladimiroviches, Pavloviches, Konstantinoviches, and Nikolaeviches. The Mikhailoviches trace their line from Michael Nikolaevich, the son of Nicholas I; their branch is the most numerous. The Pavloviches continue the line from Pavel Alexandrovich, the uncle of Nicholas II. The Konstantinoviches descend from Nicholas I's son Konstantin Nikolaevich, the Nikolaeviches from Nicholas I's son Nicholas Nikolaevich the elder. These four branches have joined together in the Association of the Family of the Romanovs.

None of their members holds the title of grand duke any longer. The last grand duke, Andrei Vladimirovich, died in 1956, and the last grand duchess, Olga Alexandrovna (the sister of Nicholas II), in 1960. The head of the association is Prince Nicholas Romanovich Romanov, son of Grand Duke Roman Petrovich and Countess Praskovya Dmitrievna Sheremeteva. The prince asserts that the mod-

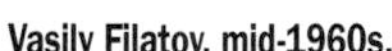

Vasily Filatov, mid-1960s.

Grand Duchess Olga Alexandrovna, 1959.

ern status of the House of Romanov remains in compliance with the "establishment" of Pavel I, and "the Romanov family, in exile, has shown itself in this particular respect to be much stricter and more captious than the royal dynasties that have managed to hold on to their thrones to this day."[1]

Neither he nor the other members of the association have made any claims to the title of heir to the throne of the Russian Empire; rather, they share the view once expressed by the widowed empress Marie Feodorovna and Grand Duke Nicholas Nikolaevich the younger, that the final arbiter of whether there is a monarchy in Russia, and who would reign, must be the Russian people.

The Association of the Family of the Romanovs remains in permanent conflict with the fifth branch of the Romanov family, the Vladimiroviches. The source of this conflict is back in the 1920s, when Grand Duke Kirill Vladimirovich, who left Russia in mid-1917, declared himself the "guardian of the imperial throne" on August 8, 1922 and "Emperor of All the Russias" on September 13, 1924, thereby causing not merely a scandal, but a schism in monarchist circles of the Russian emigration. Opposing him were the most active members of the emigration, who had retreated from Russia with weapons in hand and who united around their former supreme commander, Grand Duke Nicholas Nikolaevich. They accused Kirill Vladimirovich of abandoning his honor and dignity. The Dowager Empress Marie Feodorovna also opposed Grand Duke Kirill. However, Grand Duke Peter Nikolaevich supported his brother, as did others. Eventually, the Association of the Family of the Romanovs was formed, which opposes the claims of the Vladimiroviches to this day. No end to the schism is in sight.

The issue of the Vladimiroviches' claims is ambiguous and multilayered. According to Pavel's "establishment," when an emperor dies and his brother and his son also die in short order, the eldest of his male cousins becomes the heir to the throne. Indeed, the eldest male cousin of Nicholas II was Kirill Vladimirovich. Had this happened during ordinary times, and had the eldest cousin been someone other than Kirill Vladimirovich, he would have been recognized as heir to the throne without objections. However, in 1924 there was neither empire nor throne, and it was not appropriate to demand an "automatic" succession without taking into account the opinions of the empire's defenders.

Grand Duke Kirill Vladimirovich, in the 1930s.

In Chapter 1 we wrote that on March 1, 1917, before the emperor's abdication, Grand Duke Kirill Vladimirovich was one of the first Russian officers to commit an act of betrayal to his oath of loyalty and to his dynastic duty. While commanding the Marine of the Guard, which was responsible for guarding the imperial family at Tsarskoe Selo, Kirill Vladimirovich marched them into Petrograd to declare their allegiance to the Duma. If this does not qualify as desertion, then his emigration in July 1917 while he was a rear admiral in active military service in a country at war cannot be called anything but desertion. It is not difficult to understand why military men may have refused to recognize a man of such high "valor" as their monarch.

The problems of the self-proclaimed emperor did not end here. Pavel's establishment prohibited grand dukes from marrying outside their religion and without the consent of the church and the permission of the reigning emperor. By marrying a Lutheran, Grand Duke Vladimir Alexandrovich (the father of Kirill Vladimirovich) violated article 60 of the establishment on the imperial family in the Code of Laws of the Russian Empire, which states: "Marriage between a male person of the imperial house in line to succeed to the throne and a person of another faith cannot be accomplished otherwise than by her acceptance of the Orthodox confession." So Vladimir Alexandrovich lost the right to succeed to the throne, not only for himself personally but also for his elder son Kirill Vladimirovich.

The marriage of Kirill Vladimirovich himself to his own cousin Victoria Melita, who had been married previously to Ernst of Hesse, the brother of Empress Alexandra Feodorovna, took place in 1905 without the consent of the church or the permission of the emperor, who retired the transgressor from the service and barred his entry to Russia. Subsequently, Kirill Vladimirovich obtained forgiveness and returned to the tsar's service, but he concluded it, as we have seen, ingloriously and without the right to transmit his title to his heirs. He died on October 12, 1938, and his son, Prince Vladimir Kirillovich, died in 1992 without male children; therefore, the Vladimirovich branch ended with him. Vladimir Kirillovich's daughter, Maria Vladimirovna, married Prince Franz-Wilhelm of Prussia (Hohenzollern) in 1976 and became the princess of Hohenzollern.Their son, George, also Prince Hohenzollern, who was born in 1981, has found himself at the center of a new controversy. Prince Vladimir Kirillovich conferred on Prince Franz-Wilhelm the title Grand Duke Michael Pavlovich and on George, his grandson, the title Grand Duke George Mikhailovich, as if to resurrect the claims of a broken line to the throne. On behalf of the Association of the Family of the Romanovs, Vasily Alexandrovich, a nephew of Nicholas II, issued the following statement on the birth of George:

> The Association of the Family of the Romanovs hereby states that the joyous event in the Prussian royal house bears no relationship whatsoever to the Association of the Family of the Romanovs, inasmuch as the newborn prince is a member neither of the Russian imperial house nor of the Romanov family. All issues of dynastic importance can be decided only by the great Russian people on Russian soil.[2]

Nonetheless, the self-proclaimed "head of the Russian imperial house," Princess Maria Vladimirovna Hohenzollern, persists in pursuing the family's claim, often playing rather freely with Russian laws.

On October 11, 1997, St. Petersburg television reported that a certain Mr. Lukyanov, representing the "interests of the descendants of Mrs. Kirby (the mother of Maria Vladimirovna Hohenzollern) and Prince Vladimir K. Romanov, had obtained death certificates for Tsarevich Alexei and his sister."[3] Reluctant to state this without substantiation, we show on page 197 the reply of the Register Office of the Central District of St. Petersburg to the inquiry of the Legislative Assembly of St. Petersburg. Without appropriate grounds, the inappropriate organ issued an inappropriate document. Both the officials and the recipients of these documents need to be held accountable for this.

In principle, the death of Alexei Nikolaevich Romanov can—and ulitmately should—be determined only by the court.

On July 17, 1998, a funeral was held for the remains of Tsar Nicholas II's family in the Sts. Peter and Paul Fortress in St. Petersburg. However, the funeral did not close the case of the execution of the family of the last Russian tsar.

There is nothing incredible about the idea that some of the tsar's family who were supposedly executed eighty years ago in the cellar of the Ipatiev house in Ekaterinburg may have actually survived. Such things have happened often enough during mass executions. It is only the long concealment of the truth that still inspires doubt.

Even the most exacting scientific research is powerless in a country without the necessary judicial mechanisms in place to establish and restore lost familial ties. Therefore, as we bring this book to a close, we propose to exert our future efforts in precisely this direction, while not forgetting, of course, the issues that have not yet been clarified from our first stage of work.

Whether we have arrived at a convincing vision of what happened in July 1918 and after is for you, esteemed readers, to judge.

Emperor Alexander III, in the 1880s.

Grand Duke Alexander Alexandrovich.

Olga Filatova, 1973.

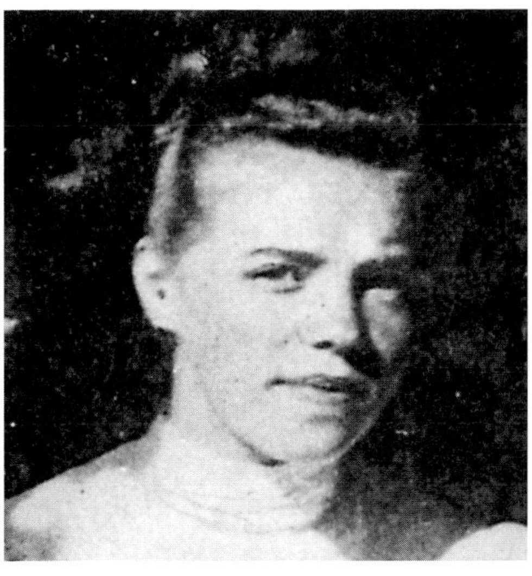

Grand Duchess Olga Alexandrovna.

Empress Marie Feodorovna with her son Nicholas, 1871.

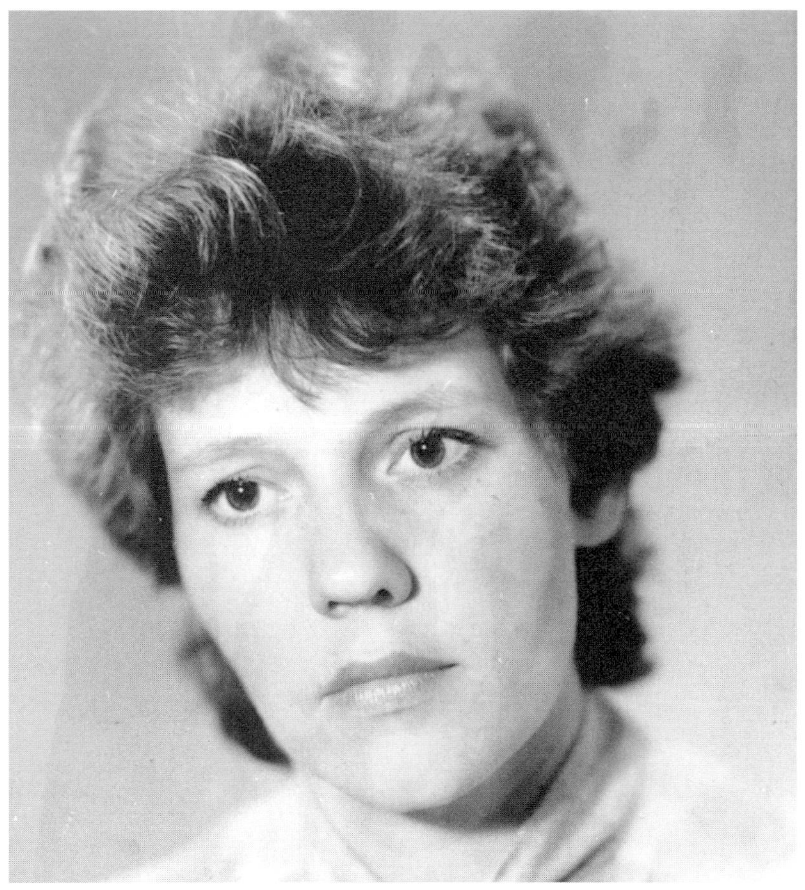

Irina Shünemann (Filatova), 1977.

LEFT: Nadezhda Härting (Filatova), 1993.

BELOW: Grand Duchess Xenia Alexandrovna.

RIGHT: Nadezhda Härting (Filatova), 1982.

BELOW: Empress Alexandra Fyodorovna.

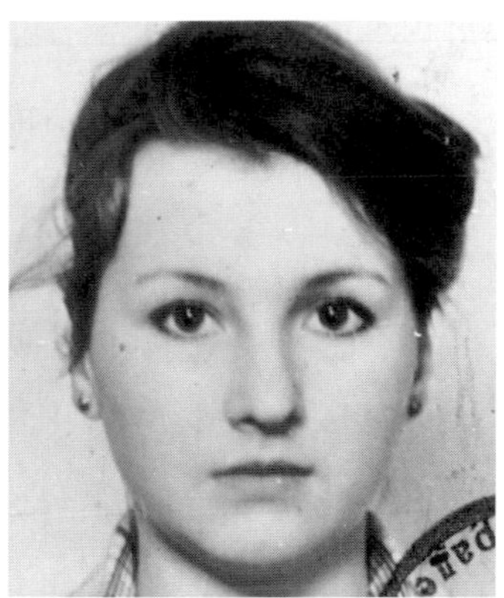

Oleg Filatov, 1961.

Tsarevich Alexei Nikolaevich.

Oleg Filatov, 1998.

Emperor Nicholas II.

chapter 7.

personal reminiscences by the family of vasily filatov

■ reminiscences of oleg vasilievich filatov ■

Forced to conceal his true origins, he had to recast his knowledge and upbringing and make himself as unremarkable as possible.

In 1988, as he was dying, my father said: "I have told you the truth, and you must know the pass to which the Bolsheviks have led Russia." We, his children, are certain that he was not deceiving us. Unfortunately, he told us very little, and we find we still have questions for him. His spirit, though, seems to be with us. And we ask him our questions, and it feels like we are going through time and communing with him. While your parents are still alive, you accept it as your due, not giving any real thought to the fact that they are not immortal. This is why now we have to gather the crumbs of what he said, filling in his story with our own thoughts and the new facts recently uncovered. That is why my father's story is interspersed with my own thoughts. The inquiries are not over. We have been helped to bear this heavy cross that was placed upon us by our friends, relatives, comrades-in-arms, and scholars who have taken an interest in this story. I hope that as a result we will all learn the truth.

Oleg Filatov, circa 1988.

When I began thinking in earnest about how to tell the truth about my father, I spoke with my friends, colleagues, and acquaintances and came to the conclusion that it had to be told the way he himself would talk about it, not as a historical figure out of a distant era but as our contemporary, a man born at the beginning of the century who suffered through all the hardships, trials, famine, and repressions with his people. It is difficult to imagine what it was like for him, realizing who he was, to remain silent for so many years. How much he had to see and endure for the sake of saving himself and his family, his children. We may never find out the whole truth, but obviously that is what we must strive for. *Non progredi estra gredi*—if you are not moving forward, then you are moving back.

My father lived a long life. He compensated for his physical disadvantages through his constant effort to achieve harmonious development and knowledge. This gave him the motivation to go on. We children were born when he was already far from young, and he was heartened by this development, sensing new meaning in his life. When grandchildren were born, he finally opened up and told their mother, my wife, Anzhelika Petrovna, about his tragic fate. This was in 1983, five years before his death. Before that he had told us about it allegorically, a certain segment to each of us. Now we are collecting all his stories and our recollections of him in order to arrive at a better understanding of what happened. Some of the memories of members of our family—his children and his wife, Lydia Kuzminichna Filatova (thanks to whom, actually, he survived for so many years)—have already been published in newspaper articles and have been the basis for the special research conducted by scientists that is continuing even now. Unfortunately, there are many gaps in these reminiscences. He was sparing with his stories, and because we were children, we did not ask unnecessary questions but simply believed him. How can you not believe your own father when you see him suffering and realize that his life might have turned out very differently?

I may have to repeat myself in this account, but there is nothing so terrible in that. What is most important is to be honest. This is the basic principle: to tell the truth no matter what it is. Of course, the archives might suggest a great deal, both the closed and the open archives, to which we do not have access due to several circumstances—partly a lack of money and partly the bureaucracy and the fear that lives on in people. But if we don't read this page, which obliges all of us to prevent a repetition of something similar, we will never find out how the history of our state might have taken shape had there not been a revolution. If we are talking about repentance, then we still have to sort out who committed the murder of the last Russian emperor, Nicholas II, and why to this day none of the country's leaders and none of the forensic medical experts or attorneys has proposed a standard version of those events of July 1918, or of how the lives of the people who participated in this Ekaterinburg tragedy turned out.

My father told us almost nothing about his parents. When we would ask where the photographs of our grandmothers and grandfathers were, he would reply: "There aren't any, everything was lost." There was nothing surprising in that. There had been a civil war and everything burned up and was lost. But when we began questioning him, he would fall silent. All he said about his own father was that he had been a soldier all his life, that he went on his final march of sixty kilometers [almost forty miles], drank some cold water from a well, came down with consumption, and died in 1921. About his mother he said that she was a schoolteacher and taught language and music and was shot as a Left Socialist Revolutionary when he was still a boy. He also used to say that he had relatives but he didn't know them because they abandoned him in Sukhumi when they went abroad during the civil war. When my mother occasionally asked him in a fit of temper, "Here you are saying that we are doing everything wrong, but where are your relatives?" he would shut down, move off, and stop talking. By the way, he could say nothing for long periods of time—go several days or a month without talking. On the other hand, he was sometimes like a child, especially on days when his health was bad. He would just look in silence. He was mulling over something privately, but there was no sadness in his eyes.

In discussing my father's destiny, I have to say that he possessed exceptional abilities and extensive connections. Recalling him, I come to the conclusion that this man was obviously not who he made himself out to be. Officially, he came from the family of a soldier who due to disability became a shoemaker, a man who went to church school as a child, became homeless as a child, and later became a teacher. Today I reconstruct my reminiscences of him from my own childhood and come to the conclusion that this story is not true and that many of his actions were conditioned by his education, sufferings, and illness.

My father had an extremely broad outlook and a thoroughgoing knowledge of life, history, geography, politics, and economics. He knew the traditions of his own country and other states well. He had mastered foreign languages—German, Greek, Old Church Slavonic, Latin, English, and French—although he did not use them actively. He explained his knowledge of languages and his excellent motor and visual memory by saying that he had always striven to be a harmoniously developed person. He used to tell us: "You are as many times a man as the number of languages you know." He meant that if you know the language, culture, traditions, and customs of a people who live in some other world, you expand your own possibilities. He read with amazing speed and in great quantities, remembering what he had read very easily. You got the impression that he was extracting information like an automaton. He could recite from memory [the poetry of] Fet, Pushkin, Lermontov, Tyutchev, Esenin, Chekhov, Kuprin, Heinrich Heine, and Goethe in German. He loved Goethe's *Faust*. He explained this by saying that in their family they used to gather in the evenings and read aloud to one another: plays, poems, novellas, and novels in Russian and foreign languages. In this way, the family bonded, relaxed, and conversed.

My father had a great enthusiasm for history, especially military history, and knew it thoroughly, including the troop dislocations and the alignments of forces in specific battles. In demonstrating his knowledgeability in these matters, my father seemed to include himself in the military caste. All his life he used to say: "We Filatovs have always stood on guard for the state." When I watched films about the Great Patriotic War [World War II], I often had questions—for example, why at the beginning of the war our troops retreated. My father would answer my question very thoroughly, both about the beginning of the war in 1939 and about the initial testing of the Russians' strength during the invasion of Poland by Soviet troops. He would explain to me what caused the difficulties with our armaments in the first days of the war. Despite the fact that he, as an invalid, was released from serving in the army, he cited amazingly detailed examples.

For example, he used to talk about how during the Second World War we had to take Rostov twice because the Germans left a barrel of alcohol there—not a barrel really, but a cistern. The Russian soldiers got thoroughly drunk, and the Germans retook Rostov back. So we had to take it a second time. But when the Germans attacked initially, the Russians used electric fences for the first time. They placed them on the banks of the Don and dug them into the sand. It was dreadfully hot, and the Germans were thirsty. When they crawled toward the river, the circuit was completed, and they stayed right there. I don't know where he got this kind of information.

He used to tell us a great deal about the Russian tsars who built the state and as an example often cited Ivan III, the assembler and organizer of the Russian land, who gave the Russian people the chance to free themselves from the Mongol horde and get on their feet. He recommended that we read *Primordial Rus'*, by Ivanov, to get to know Russia's history better.

When he used to talk about the civil war, he would also mention the move the tsar's family made from Tobolsk to Tyumen. He used to say that a brigade arrived under the command of the Cossack captain Gamin, or Gatin (unfortunately, I don't remember precisely), for their rescue. He told us how well White intelligence functioned, especially on the railroads. The family had already been warned, men were ready, and it was just a matter of exploiting the situation at the proper time, but in Tyumen the guard was replaced, and the plan failed. Unfortunately, events followed a different scenario, although everything had been made ready to free them.

His artistic qualities were also outstanding. After they already had us, he and mama would perform in amateur shows, and he was invited to transfer to join a professional theater. What astonishes me most of all is where a former homeless child learned to play keyboard instruments. To this question of mine he would reply in the orphanage in Kaluga. . . . Moreover he not only played the harpsichord, piano, and organ, but also knew how to tune them. He loved the balalaika, and although he did not play the guitar he told me that the piano and guitar have identical pitch. He played the concertina, bayan, and accordion and taught them to us. His favorite artists were Shchepkin, Okhlopkov, Chaliapin, Sobinov, and Caruso. He used to say that his mother played the piano, usually Chopin or Beethoven. He himself liked to listen to Tchaikovsky, Mussorgsky, and Rimsky-Korsakov. He taught us to sing without tensing the vocal cords, but achieving a smooth tone without strain. His manner of singing was quiet and calm, but very expressive. He sang ballads, operatic arias, and long Russian folk songs and knew an enormous number of *chastushki* [humorous folk ditties].

He called chess the game of tsars. Chess was his passion. He began teaching us various chess openings at the age of three. He spoke about such chess players as Capablanca, Alekhin, and Eive. He spoke especially warmly of Alekhin, who was an excellent chess player and played 265 games blindfolded and won. My father used to demonstrate this method of play for us, but he said it was harmful because it sapped so much energy. He himself played chess when he was laid low by pain. He said that he played instead of taking medicine. It distracted you and made you forget about the pain. He had many books on chess and subscribed to chess magazines, analyzing and taking notes. He liked to take clippings from specialized magazines and newspapers and he collected crossword puzzles and interesting comments. He collected hooks and gear for fishing, all kinds of screws and nuts. He had fitted out several boxes for this, in each of which he kept something. We used to laugh at this weakness of his, but whenever we needed something, we would immediately go to him and he would locate what we needed.

My father loved photography and started teaching it to us when we were children. He bought us Smena-8 cameras and books for amateur photographers. When there was time, we did photography from morning till night. Lessons with my father were very interesting for us. My parents provided everything we needed for all this. And he would talk about his own childhood a little. He said that he had liked to play cops and robbers. That was a fashionable game at the time. He used to tell us that he was very mischievous and never gave the adults a moment's peace. For instance, once at a lesson in divine law he played a joke on the priest, nailing his boots down. He was punished for that.

Two of us, his children, are absolute blonds, and two are dark. He was quite dark, too, but he said that as a child he had fair, curly hair. "Everyone loved me. They called me fluff and cut my hair very simply, bowl fashion. It was later that life changed me." His hair was jet black and only beginning to show gray just before his death.

Oleg Filatov, 1963.

He often used to say that one needed to know how to speak well and cogently and how to declaim. It is interesting that as an example of eloquence he cited not only Horace and Socrates but Trotsky as well. He used to tell us that during the civil war, when the Red Army units were retreating, Trotsky could talk for hours. The soldiers who heard his speech would attack the enemy and fight to the death. He used to tell us that a person must know how to do that, inasmuch as God has given him the ability to speak. You must construct sentences and set forth your ideas correctly. Each word must be substantive and in no way ostentatious.

He dreamed that I would become a lawyer. When I would ask him why he wanted that so much, he would reply: "Well, why, then you could sort matters out. You would know what to do." He also made me study foreign languages. I would ask him why he did not speak to me in German, which he knew well, or teach it. He replied that this language had grown hateful to him ever since the war with the Germans.

In childhood, I had no trouble remembering all this. There is no barrier, nothing to fear, especially when it is your parents teaching you. I never felt fear when I was with my father. I felt as though I was living in clover with him. He was an exemplary family man, spending a lot of time with his children and teaching us nearly everything. For example, to write with our left hand in order to develop both hemispheres of the brain. He said that the nobleman could fence with both hands and switch his sword from his injured arm to his healthy one. He made an embroidery stand himself and made me learn how to embroider on it—cross-stitch, satin stitch, and other ways. When I would ask him why I needed this, he would reply: "What do you mean? This is simply something one must know how to do." Then he would check my work when I embroidered handkerchiefs for Mama and my sisters for their birthdays. He taught us how to draw. First how to hold the pencil, then how to draw with it, and then he gave us colored pencils. He showed us how to draw on a grid in order to observe symmetry and, later, from memory. Only after that did we move on to watercolors, and later to oils. My father wanted me to show my work in art contests, so I did. He did sculpture with us—using plasticine and clay. He taught us to write compositions, selecting the material we needed from books, examining pages along the diagonal, and selecting what we needed to develop our theme. So that we would know how to express our thoughts figuratively, he would have us write, for example, how the birds fly in spring. He himself made starling houses and taught us to love and study nature. Generally speaking, he loved the spring and always became despondent when autumn arrived. We did not have a church in our settlement, so his soul refreshed itself in nature. By the way, he was very knowledgeable about medicinal herbs.

Oleg Filatov with his brigade counselor at Camp Eaglet, August 1965.

He did not try to impose his knowledge and abilities on us. A flock of birds or geese would fly overhead and he would suddenly ask, "How many?" If you saw it once, you had to remember it instantly—that was his system of childrearing. I was supposed to remember after one time the names of streets, buildings, people, transportation, and even which way the wind was blowing when they took me to Orenburg. Leaving an unfamiliar building, I was supposed to describe to him what objects were there and how they were laid out. He himself was very observant. When you walked with him in a crowd, he would say, "Did you see that man who passed? He has a peculiar gait. Do you see this one? He keeps looking around, searching for something." He noticed all kinds of insignificant details and made me remember everything.

Now it seems unusual to me that from my very childhood, somewhere around nine years old, he taught me to remember everything he said the first time. He used to say, "Remember what I say the first time because I'm not going to repeat it for you. You have to know this in order not to repeat mistakes and not to tell anyone, or there will be trouble." Even then I realized that he was concerned not only for us but for other people as well. He used to tell us about them and show us their photographs, saying: "I'm showing you one time. I'm not going to show you again. Remember these people." But whether or not they were alive at the time, we didn't know.

Sometimes certain people from some unspecified place would pay him very brief visits. He would go out with them and discuss something with them. We never saw them before or after. We could not get him to tell us who they were or why they had come. He smiled and said nothing. Probably he didn't want us to know his former life and didn't want us to expose ourselves or those people to danger. In the 1960s, my father would write postcards to someone and give them to my younger sisters, who could not read yet, to drop in the mailbox. If we asked him whom the postcards were for and what was written there, he only smiled and said nothing.

He had amazing friends. For example, there was the old man Yavorsky, who lived in our village. Once my father took me along to see him, when I was about nine. There was an old man wearing a belted white peasant shirt lying on the stove. My father suddenly said to him: "Tell me, grandpa, how did Nikolai Ivanovich Kuznetsov die?" The old man raised up onto one elbow and looked at me: "And who's this with you?" "This is my son, you can talk in front of him." And then the old man told us about waiting for Kuznetsov with Strutinsky. That was their assignment. He was in the Signal Corps in Poland. They were waiting for him outside Lvov, but he never did come. Then they received the news that Nikolai Ivanovich Kuznetsov had died—he had blown himself up when he fell wounded into the hands of the nationalists. For me what was most interesting is where my father met him. He himself said it was at Uralmash [Urals Machine-Building Factory], where he had been trying to get a job.

Often in our childhood years we would see how lonely he was, despite the fact that he had a wife, our mama, who slaved away indefatigably to raise us. All those years, especially in the 1960s, he spent a lot of time at his radio, listening to "The Latest News" from morning till night. This is when he began telling me about the revolution, politics, and Chamberlain. He was constantly thinking about Kerensky. He knew not only who Kerensky was but for some reason how he had fled and where he lived. He said that Kerensky made himself out to be a leader but in fact was an adventurist. My father would keep returning to the idea that tsars worried constantly about the state, the treasury, and the army, without which there was no state, and watched over their Orthodox Church. He told us how they killed Trotsky in Latin America.

My father was an invalid. (He used to say: "I was born a cripple like this.") His left foot was withered, size 40, and his right a size 42. Once he said that his foot did not wither until about 1940. He had a curvature of the spine, many scars on his back and arms, and the traces of shrapnel wounds at his waist, under his left shoulder blade, and on his left heel. This evoked puzzled questions from us. The man had never been in a war, but he was so crippled. Where? When? But it was not done to talk about this in our family. Once as a child I saw his wounded back and asked him what had happened. "Well," he said, "there was a certain business. They were shooting in a basement, killing people." When I asked him what happened to his foot, he waved his hand and said that if they had cut off his other foot he would have been totally incapable of work. "But this way I can work and earn my living." His foot always hurt, he had cut himself with a razor somehow on the heel, and he had a terrible scar there. He went especially to Leningrad to buy "general's boots," which had a high instep and were sometimes sold in the 1960s. He said that previously he had had an orthopedic insert, they had given him massages, stretched and massaged his foot. He had wanted to have an operation, but he was afraid his heart couldn't take it, even though he was relatively young.

It must be said that he never went to doctors and no certificates of his illness remain. Only once, in 1975, we made him go for a physical. This is the only information we have about the state of his health. By the way, we have never had photographs of my father in his younger years. There are a few from before the war, and those there were had been taken much later. Generally speaking, we have very few documents for him, although he taught us to store every document and every paper carefully and never lose anything. He would tell us that his birth certificate had been lost and so he had had to reconstruct it from the church's registers. "So it was a dentist who established my age. But he was wrong." My mother remembers that he confessed to her in 1952 that he was forty-eight.

Despite his disability, he possessed stunning endurance. He could go great distances without a stick, favoring first one leg and then the other. He made these treks daily, especially in the summer on his days off, when he walked a couple of miles to the river to fish. He was very strong spiritually and carried himself with the greatest dignity. I don't remember an instance when he was humiliated by anyone or called an invalid. He himself simply came undone whenever his illness kept him from doing something. This would get discussed and then he would calm down. All his life he did certain special calisthenics and said that without them he would be as skinny as a rail.

Often he would suddenly fall ill. We couldn't figure out what was wrong, but he never went to doctors. He would put himself to bed and lie there for hours on end. He swallowed certain tablets and was always taking ascorbic acid. When I would ask him what was wrong with him, he would answer: "I got this from my parents. And I was left a cripple my whole life. People said my parents should not have married, but they did and gave birth to me the way I am." When he was in pain from being hit by something in the foot, he would bandage up the bruise and put himself to bed or sit hunched over, muttering something nonstop. Once I heard him repeating the Our Father. This was his defense. He used to say: "There couldn't be anything more terrible in life. The most terrible thing of all is the Ipatiev cellar." Of course, these phrases sank into our minds.

Usually he got up early, did his calisthenics, splashed himself with cold water, and always shaved very carefully. This amazed me and I would ask, "Papa, what are you, a soldier?" He would answer: "No, but my ancestors were all soldiers." He was painstaking and neat about his apparel, and if he was going anywhere, then the packing was an entire process. He went off to work with dignity, and we saw that this was his principal business. After I was 16, he began having me lift weights and dumbbells. In the summer I loved to swim and did this very well. He told us it was easiest of all to swim on your back or do the butterfly, if you didn't make noise.

It was pure pleasure to see him wield an ax when he was chopping wood. We thought it took half a lifetime to learn how to do that so well. He taught us how to chop wood, too, so we wouldn't injure ourselves. He told us how Russian warriors knew how to defend themselves with an ax, switching it from hand to hand. He even tried to teach us how to throw an ax. At school there was a military office where they kept small-gauge rifles. He taught us how to shoot with them: how to hold the butt and press it to your cheek, how to lower the trigger while you hold your breath, and how to aim.

He had a reasonable attitude toward food. He loved fish, cocoa, wine, and champagne. I remember, when we were children, sitting down at the table and each of us being given a starched napkin. There was a soup tureen on the table and everything was very formal. We were not allowed to pick up our spoon first. For that you could get a smack on the forehead. When he taught us to sit at the table and use a fork and knife, and what the table setting should be, my mother would say: "There you are again with your silly White Guard ways. I just hope to God no one finds out." When we got older, all this came to an end. The china disappeared, and we started eating like everyone else. Any information was passed on to us before a specific age. Evidently, he felt that this ability [to be well mannered] no longer had any application.

I think that he knew and experienced enough to fill several books and films. He used to say that all you had to do was read *My Universities* and *Journey among the People* by Maxim Gorky to know what his youth had been like. When I read *How the Steel Was Tempered,* I asked, "Papa, was it you who was Nikolai Ostrovsky?" He smiled and answered, "No, I wasn't Nikolai Ostrovsky. Anyway I had a worse fate than he did." My father often told us how he traveled around in his childhood. As an example he cited Mark Twain's book about Tom Sawyer, and he liked Jack London, too. He watched films about the war and intelligence agents very attentively. He noticed what demeanor one needed to have and how one needed to educate oneself to say nothing extra. He liked certain sayings: "My tongue is my enemy" and "We were given a tongue to hide our thoughts." I don't know where he got this kind of information, but he would tell us that the Germans had a spy school where they studied Orthodoxy and divine law. Then they were dropped into Russia. According to him, these people were caught once at the railroad station in Tyumen when they tried to poison the food and sprinkle poison in the milk cans.

We lived in a German–Dutch settlement founded during the days of Catherine II in the Novosergievsky District of Orenburg Province. The settlement had an unusual name: Pretoria. It was either Holland or Germany in miniature—with its windmills, cheese factory, and particular way of life. The houses were made out of huge boulders, the large roofs and doors out of thick wood. If you pulled on a rope, half of the door would open—the carved, wooden half. And everything was always left unlocked. No one ever stole anything. It was tidy. My father worked there as a geography teacher at the high school and was always highly regarded. His pupils loved and respected him. Many people knew him in the town and the province as well. He was a sociable man and was also involved in civic activities—he was a deputy.

He was always comfortable with people of other nationalities. He never taught us to treat them in any special way. He said that one had to study another person's experience in order to learn how to live better. He called upon us to be tolerant. He did not recognize Baptists or sectarians. In his understanding, they created a superfluous background, not being a major spiritual movement in religion like Orthodoxy. He remembered prayers and created them for himself. He said that by age fourteen he knew them all by heart.

Our family's life was spent in villages removed from large cities and communications, so our only connection with the world was the radio, and later, in the 1960s, the television.

Holidays had a special significance for the family, because they bonded the family, creating warmth, coziness, and a special mood. We children always looked forward to them, especially New Year's, birthdays, and so on. The New Year always had special meaning for our family. Mama and Papa tried to make us part of the general preparations not only at school, where they were always the leaders, taking part in the amateur theatrics. Mama organized carnivals, sewed costumes, embroidering them with beads by herself and with our help.

Father read by heart: poetry, Koltsov, Lermontov, Pushkin; Krylov's fables. And he liked reciting the works of Anton Chekhov, like "Boots," "The Boor," "The Horsy Name, "Lady with the Lapdog," "Nasty Boy," and "Surveyor," and Kuprin's "The Duel."

Mama sang love songs, accompanying herself on the guitar. At home, we put on plays, learning the roles for the fairy tale "Kolobok," "The Tale of the Golden Fish," "Filipka, "Tom Thumb," "Speckled Hen," "Nasty Boy," and so on.

The school in the village of Pretoria was a wooden structure dating to 1905, with a large assembly hall, where we would put a 30-foot tree and the teachers would gather around it with their children. Children of various ages waltzed with their parents. I always wore a large bow tie and I liked to dance. Father liked to dance, but only the slow tango. We had a teachers' choir, in which my parents sang. The director was Turnov Alexander Alexandrovich, the music teacher.

At home, my parents also set up a tree, which we kept up for two weeks starting December 30. My parents and sisters and I made toys from paper, ships, crackers, we glued and drew pictures, we liked to illustrate scenes about the boy from "Snow Queen," how he suffered and searched for his sister. We also had glass ornaments for the tree. We set the tree on a crisscross stand or in a box with sand. Papa helped us embroider kerchiefs with themes from nature or from stories like "Kolobok" and "Inchman," the little man who lived in a music box.

Mama and Papa put presents under the pillows on birthdays, but for New Year's they would dress up as the Snow Maiden and Grandfather Frost, take our presents out from under the tree and congratulate us, and we would give them our gifts, sing a song about the tree, and dance around it.

Papa often recalled how he celebrated New Year's as a child. "But back then," he said, "It was different. We also had Christmas, and that was a big family holiday." We would ask, "What was that holiday and why don't we have it now?" He would reply evasively and say that it was hard to talk about it now. We did not have a church in the village, but he would mark the occasion by recalling his life and talking about the "old" New Year's, because after the Revolution all the dates were changed and people went to church then, but we lived in a German–Dutch village and the locals had their own holiday, which father did not recognize and said that it was a holiday based on a different calendar.

At New Year's some residents went to Baptist prayer houses; some dressed up and visited friends.

My father's birthday was around that period, and he always said that the certificate he was given in the 1930s indicated that he was born December 22, 1908, but he counted and figured that in the new style [the Gregorian Calendar] it was January 4; but he told Mother that it was January 28, and she asked him, "So which is your birthday?" and he would say that it was all mixed up.

We never had guests for his birthday. We celebrated it in the family. He recalled his parents, who died early in life. We wrote him cards, made drawings, gave him books on chess, fishing, hunting, and history, and embroidered hankies for him. Unfortunately, because we moved often, it was all lost, even though Mama often exhibited her work at school, where she ran the sewing club, and in regional shows, as were our drawings, especially the ones I did with Father, for the holidays. I don't know what could be found of that now. In connection with Christmas Father often talked about "Christ's egg" and the suffering of Christ at the hands of bad people. He told us about how the first holiday trees appeared in Russia, about how the holidays were celebrated by the Slavs in ancient pagan times and later, starting with the Russian tsars until Peter the Great, and how he traveled around Russia, a "wandering beggar," and said that he had to keep in his memory everything that happened to him. And he told us that the Russian tsars loved to hunt in those days. He told us that there was a fast before Christmas, that people prepared themselves for the feast day, and that he used to be like that, he observed Advent, but now few people remember it.

On holidays Kagor wine was served, which my father always called "church wine." Mama made pies filled with cabbage and with berries, jellied fish, and roast goose or suckling pig. (Father often told us that as a child he and his father "at night" cooked goose "African style," cooking it without removing the feathers, in clay in a bonfire, and that the feathers came off when you removed the clay. They also cooked pheasant and quail that way.) Our family loved desserts, we children had cakes, and our parents drank champagne.

We children spent the holidays outside, making snowmen, playing with snowballs, building fortresses out of snow. I spent my whole childhood far from cities, and came to know large cities only later.

In school we studied the history of Russia and the history of the Party. Everyone knows what kind of sciences these were. For him, history was a favorite subject, the basis of his children's upbringing. He believed that all the misfortunes in Russia were due to a lack of upbringing and education, that this was the greatest of shortcomings and led to misunderstandings, incomprehension, a reluctance to penetrate to the essence of events, and, in the final analysis, to wars. He used to say that to know history we must read not only textbooks but other books as well. For example, we needed to read about Emelian Pugachev, Suvorov, Catherine II, and Peter I and know much more about them than we got in school.

We would ask him whether he knew the history of his own family. And he would tell us how his people grew up on the river Uvod in Kostroma, where his ancestors lived in wooden huts and hunted and fished. "They always hunted with dogs. You must never beat dogs. If, God forbid, anything happened and you offended it, it could betray you during a hunt." He told us about some distant ancestor of his who went hunting for bear in the winter, but his dogs abandoned him in the forest because he had beaten one of them. The bear was full, of course, and only laid the hunter low with a fallen branch. When the hunter came to, he shot the dogs. "But," he said, "my people also went after bears without guns. They made an iron ball with spikes and threw it at the bear. He caught it with his paws and the spikes cut into them. Then they had to ride up to him and slit open his belly. That was their idea of entertainment." (My father was a marvelous marksman and loved to hunt. He used to say that in the old days he had had a dog, a rust-colored Russian hound.) He used to say that all his ancestors were very blond and very fair-haired. "And our name," he said, "came from Filaret. Once there was a man named Filaret, and we are descended from him." Today I understand why he said this. "Filaret" comes from the Greek, *filat*. Later, when we were attempting to sort out his allegories, we asked, "So does that mean that you are the boy who was rescued during the execution of the Romanov family?" And he answered: "Of course not, I descend from Filaret."

I learned from my father about the execution of the tsar's family for the first time in about the seventh grade, when we began going through the history of the Revolution. That was when I first heard the name of Yurovsky, who, as my father said, organized the entire affair. I could not understand how the boy could have lived (in his stories, he spoke about the tsarevich only in the third person and called him "the boy"). He used to say that this boy saw the entire crime and what happened afterward and that they hunted for him all the rest of his life. I asked him, "So where did he hide?" And he said: "Under a bridge. There was a bridge there at the crossing, and he crawled in there when the truck shook." "But how do you know this?" He fell silent. "My uncles told me." "But who are these uncles?" "Uncle Sasha Strekotin and Uncle Andrei Strekotin, who were in the house guard. After the front, they were stationed there. Oh, and also Uncle Misha."

He also used to tell me how the bodies of the executed were thrown into tiny mine shafts. "If you want to see how it all was, go watch the movie *The Young Guard*. There you'll see large mine shafts, like in Alapaevsk, but you'll have a notion of those events." To my question of why I would care about that, he replied: "Why do you need a reason? You'll know history." I went to those movies and all my life I remembered the mine shafts the people were thrown down in the film. About the grave he said that he remembered the place, where it was. And that there were no traces left.

It was not until later that I began asking myself how this could be, if this were a boy, a chance witness of a certain episode, he could easily have lost control and cried out or given himself away somehow. In order really to know everything from the beginning (Tobolsk and the Ipatiev house) to the end (the burial site), he had to have passed through the entire chain of events. Could there have been several boys? All of them would have had to have a diseased left foot. How many such boys with a sick foot (specifically a left foot) could end up in the same place at the same time so that one of them saw the execution, another the road along which the bodies were transported, and so on. Which means there was one boy. In addition, there was nowhere to read about the details he told us at that time. This was not publicized or popularized in the official press, and there was no such thing as reading something on the topic in the library, which is why this stuck in my memory especially. He used to talk about these events when the conversation turned to tsars and history, and this was embedded in our memory. My father did not often return to these stories (it would drive anyone crazy to talk about this all the time). He raised us very competently and sensibly, stage by stage, step by step. He spoke about what had happened to him cautiously, so that his story would stay in our memory like little specks. He did not tell us very much about the Revolution. He did say that they broke up and smashed everything, murdered people, and destroyed everything the Russian people had created, because they had lost their faith in God.

My father used to say that the Strekotins were very fond of this boy. They used to talk to him through the fence and exchanged handkerchiefs and other small objects with him. They came from working-class families—ordinary Red Army soldiers from the Orenburg front. One of the Strekotins, Andrei, perished on the Iset River during Bliukher and Kashirin's retreat to Perm on July 18, 1918. As my father said, Uncle Sasha Strekotin used to tell the story of how on that day Andrei had had a premonition and had said: "Melancholy is swallowing me up. They'll kill me today, Sasha." And no sooner had they said goodbye to one another than that is what happened. He raised his head too high out of the trench and a stray bullet struck him right in the forehead. I would ask my father how the Strekotins managed to save themselves after helping the tsarevich. According to him, they fled with Bliukher into the forest, where everyone forgot about them. Under the command of the famous civil war hero Kashirin, the brigade left Ekaterinburg on July 18, 1918, and got as far as Perm. On August 12, 1918, Bliukher had joined up with Kashirin and was his second in command. I often wonder about another coincidence: in our village there were some Kashirins who looked after us in our childhood. For the most part their family lived in the next village, but they would come to see my father and help him out.

Mikhail Gladkikh.

In talking about the Strekotins' participation in rescuing the tsarevich, my father made it very clear that they were aided by tsarist intelligence. And indeed, as of April 1918, the Academy of the General Staff had been transferred to Ekaterinburg. Many of the officers who studied there had already been through the war and, naturally, regardless of whether the boy was called Alexei Romanov or Vasily Filatov, there was no need to prove anything to them because they simply knew him by face. According to my father, in Ekaterinburg information was exchanged with the help of semaphores, which were done from the attic using a candle, which they turned "on" and "off" with their hand. By the way, my father taught us Morse code. He said that the most important thing in this alphabet, as in music and semaphore, was the concept of the pause, and that Morse code had been widely introduced in Russia and the tsar's ships had started using it. He did not tell us about the people he communicated with in this way, but he did show us several photographs. I remember he always loved films about secret agents, and when we watched them with him, he always drew our attention to their knowledge and restraint, which was essential to possess in order not to say an unnecessary word.

The further story of the rescue is this. With the help of several workers, Mikhail Pavlovich Gladkikh (Uncle Misha) took the "boy" to Shartash Station and from there to Shadrinsk. They brought him to the Filatov family, who laid him down next to their ailing son Vasily, who was approximately the same age as the "boy." After a while Vasily died of fever or, as they said at the time, the Spanish flu. Thus my father became Vasily Filatov. They established his age by looking at his teeth, and later they found a birth certificate, and everything fell into place and matched up quite logically. Thus, in 1933, at the Road Building Workers' School where he was studying, he was asked whether he had been deprived of his voting rights. In the reply it says he hadn't and was the son of a shoemaker. [If one was considered a White, or a member of the bourgeois classes, the Soviets would revoke his or her right to vote.] For a man with this kind of legend, everything had to match up. Of course, the people who helped save him and who worked out the legend by which he lived his life had to have been relatively well educated.

At the time [of the rescue], Shadrinsk was an important center in Perm Province. They treated many wounded in these places, taking advantage of the local medicinal springs. My father used to say that he was rendered his first medical assistance at Shartash Station. After he was given his new name, they took him to Surgut, where they treated him for loss of blood. Naturally, this could be done only by people who knew in detail both his illness and the methods for treating it, considering the local natural conditions. After all, the boy was very sick. These people had to have known beforehand where to take him, where they would be able to help him using traditional and folk medicine and to provide him with a devoted and experienced physician. In those regions there were many folk healers, and my father put great faith in them. I remember when we were living in the Urals he would travel to the next settlement of Kichkas to a healer and study with her. She taught him to gather broken human bones. She would smash a clay pot, sprinkle the broken pieces into a sack, and make the person gather them by touch. At the river, my father searched for clay for mud baths and treated himself. The healer helped him do this. All his life, my father was good at identifying herbs and used them for his treatment. He used to tell us that he had learned this from northern peoples, when he was living in Surgut. The Khanty-Mansy and Nenets tribes had taught him this. It is a well-known fact that they have methods for stanching blood, as they are constantly battling scurvy.

With the assistance of Archpriest Golovkin, we are able to obtain from the Russian State Archives a copy of the autobiography of Vladimir Nikolaevich Derevenko, the tsar's family physician. We know from Derevenko's autobiography and works by contemporary researchers that shortly before the execution, a General Ivan Ivanovich Sidorov arrived from Odessa to contact the tsar's family (evidently an emissary from Nicholas II's mother, Marie Feodorovna Romanova). He made contact with Derevenko, who was also in Ekaterinburg at that time but living not in the Ipatiev house, together with everyone else, but separately, at liberty, and he was allowed to visit the tsar's family regularly to examine the tsarevich. In Nikolai Ros's book *The Death of the Tsar's Family,* which was published in Frankfurt in 1987, I read that in one instance Nicholas II asked Dr. Derevenko to take out of the Ipatiev house the most precious thing they had, Rasputin's letters, and that Derevenko managed to get them past the guard. I think that this can serve as confirmation that it was he, a man devoted to the tsar's family to the end, as well as a physician intimately familiar with the boy's ailments and the means for helping him, who was involved in his rescue.

The official fate of Vasily Ksenofontovich Filatov took shape as follows. In an autobiography written in 1967, he wrote that while his father was still alive he completed elementary school in Shadrinsk and went to study at the Shadrinsk Polytechnic School, where children were taught various trades. "I was unable to finish up there due to with my father's death in 1921. I went through the famine that began in our district after a failed harvest, and as a result these circumstances forced me to abandon my studies in 1922 and find work. I had to leave my native region, to save myself from starvation. By that time I had almost no relatives left. From 1922 to 1928 I lived and worked in various towns in the European part of our country, including orphanages. In 1928 I began taking courses for elementary school teachers in Grozny, and in 1929 I was sent to work in the village of Aisengur, now Novogroznensk, where I worked for about three years. In 1930 I returned to study by correspondence at the workers' faculty of the Urals Pedagogical Institute in Tyumen. In 1932, I transferred to daytime classes, and after graduating from the workers' faculty in 1934, I continued my studies at the Tyumen Teachers Institute. In 1936 I graduated from the Tyumen Teachers Institute and was sent as a geography teacher to the Isetsk District in Tyumen Province. I worked in this district until August 10, 1955. While working as a teacher, I continued my correspondence studies at Tyumen State Pedagogical Institute, which I graduated from in 1939. In 1955 I moved to Orenburg Province, due to family circumstances. At the present time I am working as a teacher at Pretoria Middle School."

Such a commonplace biography for that period. But it does not include any of his stories. We asked him, "Why are you alone? Why don't you correspond with anyone, why don't you see your relatives?"

"What for?" They abandoned me. I don't see them. I had an uncle who lived in Tiflis during 1920–21. I was there when the Whites were leaving. They abandoned me."

"Why did they do that?"

"What did they need me for—a cripple? It would have been dangerous for them to take me with them. They told me to go back to the ones who saved me. I stood on the dock in the port for a long time, and then I had to turn around and go back. What kind of relatives are they?"

We didn't ask him about that again. After his relatives abandoned him in 1921, he set out for the Oka River, where he knew his share of suffering and harassment. He worked as a shepherd, as a cook on a steamer, and as a furrier. During the civil war, he saved himself mainly by the extra something he earned in orphanages. It was very hard. Once he told me the following: "In 1924 I tried to make contact with my relatives abroad one last time and I went to Moscow for that. It was terribly cold, but I traveled on the roof of a railroad car. It was Lenin's funeral then, and people were coming from all over. When I reached Moscow I headed for Diplomaticheskaya Street to the embassy. It was my last attempt to get to Diplomaticheskaya Street where John was waiting for me." He reached the embassy, but a policeman chased him away. "Where do you think you're going?" he said. "John is waiting for me there." "What John! Get out of here!" He didn't make it. It was his last attempt, after which he set off on his travels again. Much later, reading Maurice Paleologue's book *Russia on the Eve of Revolution,* I learned that on February 2, 1924, the first foreign embassy was opened in Russia. It was the British Embassy, the first country to recognize Soviet Russia. That means he was on his way there. Evidently, he might have been awaited by the representative of England's military mission, some John, whom he might have known before—from the mission at military headquarters in Mogilev, for example. At that time the General Representative of the English military mission in Russia was John Hanbury-Williams.

Naturally, one wonders how such a sick boy could survive all this wandering around. First of all, he had been treated in Siberia and had doubtless been taught certain remedies and prescriptions for his condition. Second, you must not forget that the heir had been at the front for two years. He had been under bombardment with his father for three hours at a time nearly every day. He knew how fortifications were built, how to take cover under bombardment, even the techniques of hand-to-hand combat. Despite his illness, he was not a hothouse child.

I used to ask him how a homeless boy like him came by sufficient education to enter an institute. At the time he did not give me a convincing answer. He said he had "simply" entered the chemistry department of Sverdlovsk University and studied there. He had lived far outside town, in a dormitory. The town was being rebuilt, buildings repaired, and there was no glass in the windows. He himself had a single shirt, which he singed in the chemistry laboratory. This is why he abandoned his studies and later went to the Highway Institute, because all his life he had dreamed of building roads. But he didn't finish there either and transferred to the Teachers Institute, because there was a need for teachers.

He had occasion to travel a great deal all over Russia in his life—St. Petersburg, Shadrinsk, Tyumen, Orenburg, Chelyabinsk, Magnitogorsk, Nizhny Novgorod, Yaroslavl, Kostroma, Kaluga, Sukhumi, Yalta, Tbilisi, Batumi, Baku, Astrakhan, Vologda, and more. The geography of his life was a good deal broader than one might imagine, but in his autobiography he lists only Shadrinsk, the town of Grozny, the village of Aisengur, Tyumen, and the village of Pretoria in Orenburg Province.

During the war he was excused from military service because of his poor health, and he worked in Isetsk District as the head of the educational office. He was awarded a medal "For Labor during the Great Patriotic War." He came to the aid of children who had been evacuated from blockaded Leningrad, found housing for them in apartments, and provided them with the essentials. Not far away there were distribution camps through which many people passed, including former nobles. I know that at the time he had many contacts with various people, but unfortunately I know only a few by name.

He married late, at age forty-nine. Mama tells the story of how when she saw him for the first time she was astonished at the discrepancy between his intellectual face and intentionally simple clothing. He used to wear a traditional side-fastened shirt, a jacket, and lace-up boots—*shtiblety,* as he called them. They met in 1949, when he was teaching in the schools of Isetsk District, Tyumen Province. They married in 1952, and I was born in 1953. He lived quite a long time in Tyumen Province—seventeen years. (It's interesting that Maria Rasputina [Rasputin's daughter] lived not far from there.)

Oh, by the way. My father grieved for his sister all his life. He often played the bayan and sang "Soon I Shall Come Back to You, Dear Marusya." His favorite song was "At an Unnamed Height" from the movie *Silence.* Except that instead of "Only three of us remained," he would sing "Only two of us remained." He was constantly drawing some kind of landscape: a spruce, a dugout, a lake, a marshy bog.

When I was drafted and I told my father I was going to serve in the Urals, he asked me to check to see whether the Ipatiev house was still standing. I did in fact end up serving in Ekaterinburg, and at the first opportunity I went to see where the tsar's family had been executed. But the building was gone by then. It had been razed, evidently so that people would forget this crime. At the time, in 1979, I could not go to Shadrinsk. I went there especially in 1995, though, to do some research in the archives and obtain copies of documents. I recalled that, according to my father's story, he was brought to the outskirts of Shadrinsk, at No. 5 Lenin Street, which was next to a ravine. We got there and saw both the ravine and the unscathed wooden house. We began looking for people who had lived there at the time.

Vasily Filatov, summer 1984.

These were old people by now—seventy-eight, eighty, and ninety years old. No one remembered the shoemaker Filatov, and no one had seen either the cart or the guards. We went to the neighboring street, but there was no one there either. Later we did find some Filatovs, but despite the fact that this family numbered twenty-four in 1918, not one was left in Shadrinsk, and no one knew what had become of them. No one remembered the child who had been brought with the sickly left foot. This family lived at No. 50 Tyufyaevskaya Street (later renamed Soviet Street, and the address changed to 5). It turned out the building had been razed. Next to it stood a wooden house that was equally old, but this one, the stone one, had been razed. Nothing is simple.

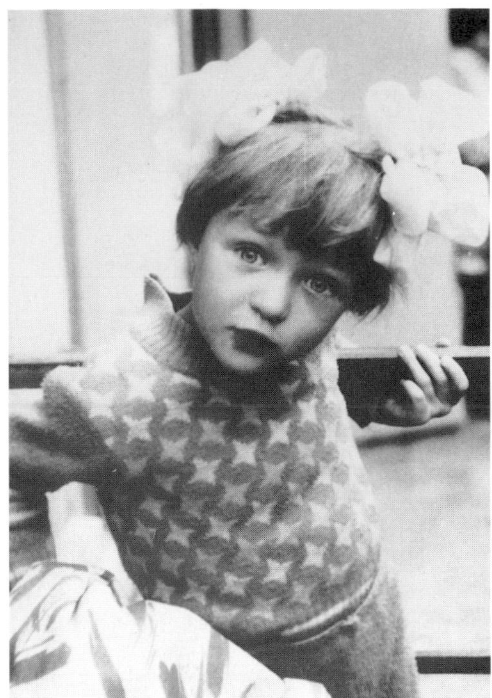

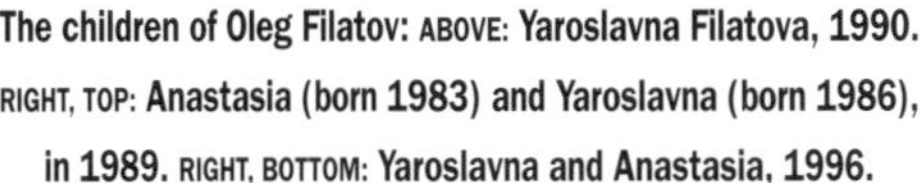

The children of Oleg Filatov: ABOVE: Yaroslavna Filatova, 1990. RIGHT, TOP: Anastasia (born 1983) and Yaroslavna (born 1986), in 1989. RIGHT, BOTTOM: Yaroslavna and Anastasia, 1996.

On April 4, 1994, together with my sister Olga Vasilievna, I had a meeting at city hall with the mayor's aide, A. G. Stebakov, and we told him the story of our father. He called the Russian General Prosecutor's Office and asked the Prosecutor-Detective Vladimir Nikolaevich Soloviev to look into our story. At the time they asked us two questions: "Where are the bank numbers?" and "Are you going to seek vengeance?" We were stunned. To the first we were unable to give not only an answer but even any comment. As for the second, how could we seek vengeance against the Russian people, who had known so much trouble and suffering?

Yes, it is a fantastic and not entirely untangled history. Most people's first reaction to it is "That can't be!" When children encounter something strange they resort to tears, but adults try to brush off and ignore what they don't understand. This is evidently why, despite a number of serious expert analyses conducted at our initiative and the substantial body of factual material that has been accumulated by various scholars, the official structures have still not begun to investigate this story, which is full of gaps, in earnest. There is not a single proof that this is not so. No one is interested in checking to see whether it is a true story. Maybe the problem is that this story does not suit everyone. This is one form of amnesia, one of the ways of forgetting. I am an Orthodox man and I am deeply convinced that you have to prove this only to nonbelievers. Naturally we simply believe our father, but even for us not everything in his life is completely clear because he was forced to hide in order to ward off any danger from us and the people who were helping him. Therefore we are attempting to uncover more and more facts in order to learn the full truth about this martyr, who lived a long life and who experienced and saw enough to last several lives. As far as the fantastic nature of his story, the rescue of innocent children from a horrible death was a miracle. The Lord was watching over them.

Oleg Filatov and his daughter Anastasia, 1987.

The fact that the Lord saved him and did not allow him to perish with the rest of his family is a miracle. He was given a long life, evidently, in order to live it alongside the entire country and to witness what the Bolsheviks did to Russia. In his last years he often asked: "Take me back to my home in St. Petersburg. I want to see the places I remember." But he could no longer walk. Recently my mama confessed that it was at his insistence that she sent me to Petersburg in 1983. Here, evidently, there was at least one miracle as well: Here I met my future wife, Anzhelika Petrovna. In 1982 she had been in Bulgaria, in Plovdiv, where to everyone's surprise she was blessed by the metropolitan. He suddenly appeared out of the monastery and picked her alone out of the group, blessed her, and even showed her his chambers. In 1982 she returned to Russia and soon afterward we met and married. My father recognized her immediately. It was to her that he first told the truth about himself, not hiding behind his usual allegories.

My father died from a stroke and heart attack. Evidently he had sensed death coming long before. Before his death he was only about 5 feet 4 inches, but they ordered a coffin for him that was 6 feet 5 inches long. The ailing, thin, broken man, who was missing two ribs and suffering from a disease that tormented him all his life, finally experienced release after death and stretched out to his full length.

Reminiscences of Anzhelika Petrovna Tămaş

I heard the family history for the first time in April, 1983. I had come then to meet my husband's parents. Oleg and I had gotten married on March 26 and he was in a hurry to share his joy with his mother and father.

After the feeble spring of a northern city, the Astrakhan sun seemed particularly bright. There were many fishermen out in boats on the Volga. This was the spring fishing season. The leaves were turning green, and human hearts, softened by the warmth, were ready to open up to communication.

On the morning of April 2, my husband and I set out on the Meteor hovercraft down to the Volga to the village of Ikrianoe, where his parents were living. His mother was busy with housework, but the father was not feeling well after doing work in the garden. The slightest scrape or blow caused serious pain. "Doctors can give me no relief," he said. "They prescribe bed rest for a day, and sometimes two or three."

Anzhelika Tămaş, the wife of Oleg Filatov.

He lay in bed and read, knowing full well what would come next in this disease, and the reason he knew—to tell that we must go back several decades. But more about that later.

All day on April 2, I talked enthusiastically about myself and my family, answering interested questions. At first the questions were general and then became precise and laconic. Direct questions demanded a direct answer.

Vasily Ksenofontovich listened attentively without interrupting. Then he asked if I remembered my ancestors. My answers satisfied him. He deemed me sufficiently prepared for his own story.

In his family, there was a very famous man—Metropolitan Filaret (Fyodor Nikitich was his worldly name). The lands belonging to him were in the middle Volga in the Kostroma Province. The peasants living on monastery and metropolitan lands and his relatives all had the surname Filatov, which sounds more Russian. Filaret (Philaret)—Filafet—Filat is the same name and means "lover of good deeds."

During the Time of Troubles [1602–12], Filaret was taken prisoner by the Poles, and upon his return to Russia he accepted the position of Patriarch. Vasily Ksenofontovich described Filaret as a man experienced in politics with an influence on state affairs.

"That is where our roots come from. You should know that," he liked to say. "Remember that."

The story was very interesting and naturally, I remembered.

He reminded his son, Oleg, often about Filaret, talked about the need to study languages, understand affairs of state, and know history very well so as not to make any mistakes.

Vasily Ksenofontovich asked if there were any people in my family who were in the church. I told him that my great-grandfather, Ivan Karmaleev, of bourgeois estate, had a house in Tver. The house was next to a church in a picturesque spot where the Tvertsy River falls into the Volga. On one bank of the Tvertsy was a convent, and on the other, a monastery.

The whole Karmaleev family was tied to the river. Hence the name. [Karmalak is a type of fishing pole used on the Volga.] In his youth, Ivan even hired out to haul barges on the river. And it took its toll on his old age. He developed water on the joints of his legs. He could not do active physical labor, but he worked as a church elder and bell ringer. He taught bell-ringing to his oldest son, Arseny, who eventually became the conductor of a military orchestra and also painted works on historical themes.

Vasily Ksenofontovich was interested in the fate of the rest of Ivan Karmaleev's children and life in Tver in those days. He told me that back in the fourteenth century the tsar sent to Tver for a bride (Princess Maria). He said that his family had kept genealogical notes, what they call a genealogical tree nowadays. I asked him if they still existed. "No, the revolution and wars washed it all away," he replied.

It was only after Vasily Ksenofontovich's death that the family began comparing all his stories and realized that Patriarch Filaret (Fyodor Nikitich Romanov, 1553–1633) was the father of the first Romanov tsar, Mikhail Fyodorovich.

My grandmother, Karmaleeva Alexandra Ivanovna, was born in Tver, April 18, 1898 and my grandfather Ostalopov Efrem Alexeyevich in 1896 in Torzhok.

Vasily Ksenofontovich stressed that Torzhok used to supply gold fabric for the imperial house. Here I told him that my grandmother had studied that craft when she worked in a salon.

After that he talked about Nicholas II, pointing out that there had been a mass execution. His story amazed me with the detailed descriptions of the events and the way he spoke of the dead as if they were his relatives. Talking about Alexei in the third person he gradually, and without noticing, switched to narration in the first person.

He described in great detail the rescue of the boy, naming his rescuers, the Strekotin brothers, and the later helper Mikhail Pavlovich Gladkikh.

My husband listened to him with me and asked his father directly, "You mean, you are Alexei?"

Vasily Ksenofontovich replied, "I've told you that already. You have to remember things the first time!"

Reminiscences of Olga Filatova

Vasily Filatov, 1984.

From 1955 to 1966, our family lived in the German settlement of Pretoria, which was founded by Tsaritsa Catherine II in Orenburg Province. The settlement was situated in a picturesque locale, amid steppes and hills covered with a chain of woods, lakes, and streams, where there were fish and game in abundance. In the spring, bright red poppies bloomed, as did white and dark blue crocuses and yellow tulips, and golden feather-grass covered the hills all the way to the distant horizon. We frequently picked huckleberries, strawberries, forget-me-nots, lily-of-the-valley, violets, and tulips, and that scent has remained with us for life, the smell of our childhood.

In Pretoria we had a four-room house with a veranda that the collective farm had given to our family. The outside doors of the house were always closed from the inside with a special Russian bolt, which made it impossible to open them from the outside. A shed was added on to the house, and in it we kept our livestock: a cow, chickens, and a hog. Early in the morning, Mama would milk the cow, and Father would drive her out to the herd. Once a week, Mama baked bread.

My father and his friends, Germans who were schoolteachers, often went out on the steppe to hunt or shoot off wolves and foxes. They also took fishing trips. I remember the names of these friends of his—Reimer, Beller, P. P. Martynov, Vankov, Bergen, G. P. Penner, Shietz. People had a great deal of love and respect for my father. He was sociable, witty, and resourceful. His manner was direct and unfettered, independent, despite his disability. No one ever offended him or called him a cripple, but if anyone like that did turn up, my father could wound him with a word that would make him regret his lack of tact. My father's speech was sprinkled with Russian folk sayings: "Our calf thinks he can catch a wolf," or "If you don't have a mind, then calamity can be awkward."

We children would go with him to the little river Gusikha or to the lakes to fish, making a campfire and cooking fish soup. Father was a pretty good swimmer. Mama spent all of her time taking care of the house. My father was a fairly good swimmer and would take a swim with us. In the spring we would go out catching gophers from their burrows. We would observe nature's awakening. My father was a geography teacher, and every day he measured the air temperature at the school's meteorology post. He would tell us about popular wisdom, about the days when you could tell what kind of spring, autumn, or winter it would be according to the weather. We observed the birds and animals in the forest and steppe.

Sometimes he wrote poetry. He would recite Fet, Pushkin, Tyutchev, Zhukovsky, or Lermontov from memory, depending on his mood. We attempted to come up with rhymes, too, and to write poems, and he would correct them, suggesting how we might make them sound better.

In everything we saw the personal example of our father and mother. The greatest holidays in our family were greeting the New Year and birthdays. We always prepared painstakingly for these family celebrations—sewing costumes, making masks and toys, straightening the house. Just before the New Year, we would decorate a tree, which was always large and tall—up to the ceiling—and give each other presents. In our family, everyone cared for everyone else, the older children helping the younger. Oleg looked after little Ira and Natasha.

My father was a balanced, calm, and modest but secretive man, steadfast in his affairs, assiduous. He was exceptionally consistent in everything he did. He felt that every matter needed to be done precisely, with meaning and purpose—and without haste. Better a little each day, but of good quality. His manner of speaking with people could change. With simple people he himself seemed to have come from simple people; with intellectuals he was on their level. People considered my father highly educated. He had no close friends; he kept all his acquaintances at a distance and was never completely candid, but only joked. There were Germans, Bashkirs, Kazakhs, Tatars, Russians, and Caucasians living in Pretoria. But both there and subsequently, wherever our family was living, we always enjoyed the respect of people of different nationalities.

He was very neat. All his belongings—books, texts, school items—had their place. He also had special tin and cardboard boxes in which he sorted his various fishing tackle, nuts, screws, springs, and so on, saying as he worked that anything might come in handy in a household. Indeed, we found he had all kinds of small items as soon as a need for them arose (for instance, springs for ballpoint pens, small shanks, razor blades). In our house we had all the carpentry tools, which my father used to repair shelves, stools, chairs, and doors himself. He also sharpened our kitchen knives himself to a fine edge.

My father was very fond of classical music: the mazurkas and waltzes nos. 6 and 7 of Chopin, Beethoven, Tchaikovsky. He himself played Russian waltzes on the piano—"A Tale of Old," "Amur Waves," and other compositions. He knew the marches of all the tsarist regiments. He also loved folk songs, the humorous ditties called *chastushki,* and Russian ballads. He took special pleasure in listening to Chaliapin. He himself had a pleasing tenor voice. He used to say that at one time he and his father sang in the church choir. Moreover, his father sang bass.

Later we lived in the south, in Astrakhan Province, in one of the settlements on the banks of the Volga. My parents kept an orchard that had sixty trees: various sorts of apricot, cherry, apple, plum, and peach. When the apricots were ripening in mid-July, a huge number of flies, horseflies, and wasps would swarm around the trees. They would fly into our house, too, and onto the veranda, despite the specially hung netting. My father had a very good reaction. He would trap a fly in flight or thread a large sewing needle and tack the fly to the wall. He did this very expertly, to our constant amazement.

When I was studying in the ninth class in secondary school, my father began preparing me for entrance to the History Department of Moscow University. He and I analyzed the *Iliad,* the *Tale of Igor's Campaign,* and other sources in detail. He drew up questions that combined historical, literary, philological, and culturological themes. As we analyzed each chapter, he and I would check the map to see why, for example, Igor followed precisely that route. What were his other choices, and what would have happened had he chosen one of those? We studied the poetic foot—the iamb and the trochee. My father told me then, too, about the lost library of Ivan the Terrible, where the original of the *Tale of Igor's Campaign* had been kept.

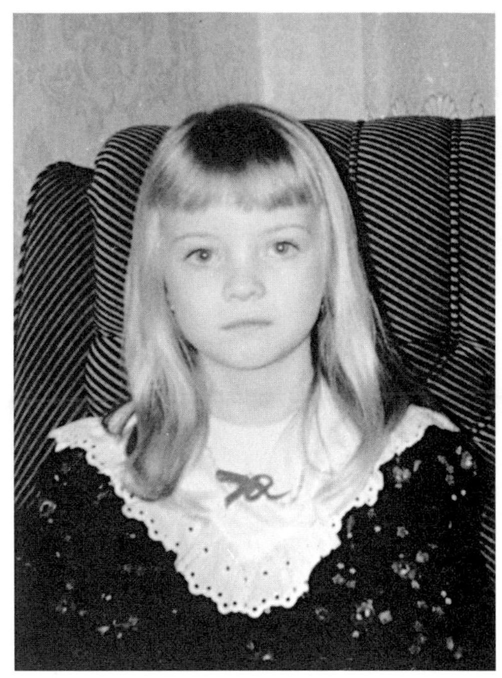

Olya, the daughter of Olga Filatova, 1995.

My father used to tell me about the Ipatiev house when I was a child. I remember his description of the house: brick, whitewashed on the top portion, with a half-basement and semicircular windows. The roof was covered with tin and painted green. The gates were brick and had little towers. The house was surrounded by a garden. The gate opened onto a swampy area and a path leading to the forest. My father used to tell me: "The boy, Aleshka he was called, often spoke with the guards when the family went out on walks. And even though he was sickly, the soldiers loved him."

■ Reminiscences of Nadezhda, Olga, and Irina Filatova ■

In 1918 after the execution in the Ipatiev house, Father told us that two people—Uncle Sasha and Uncle Andrei [the Strekotin Brothers]—with the help of the signalman, pulled him out of the mine shaft, bandaged him with some rags, and got him to the city of Shadrinsk, where they got him help. A third man, Uncle Misha [Mikhail Pavlovich Gladkikh], went with him to Tobolsk, to the village of Dubrovnoe, and later to Surgut, where he handed him over to the Chukchees [a Siberian tribe] for treatment and protection, where he spent the whole winter of 1919. Father recalled: "I was treated for loss of blood, I was weak. The Khanty-Mansy are northern people, and they kept making me eat fresh fish and fresh venison with blood, and they boiled eyes of animals for night blindness. The Khanty-Mansy treated themselves that way, and they used the treatments on me, and they also gave me herbs, dried and boiled up."

We have maps that show his marks of the route and the places he stayed. Then he returned to Shadrinsk, where he lived in the family of a shoemaker until 1922 on Lenin Street, 5. In 1922 he moved

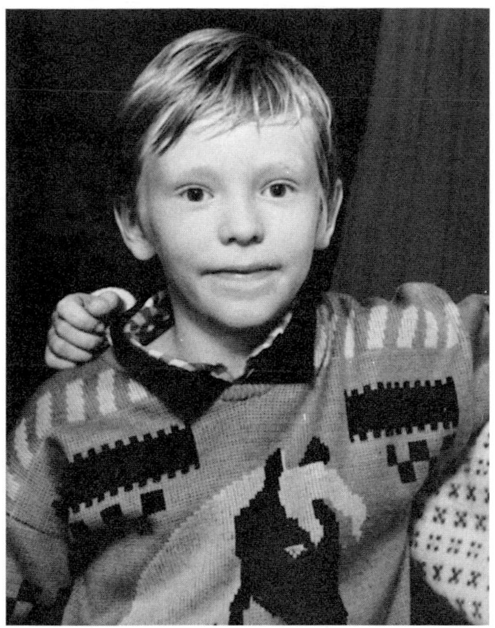

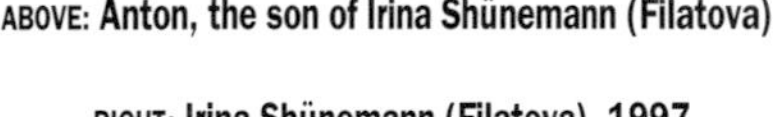

ABOVE: Anton, the son of Irina Shünemann (Filatova).

RIGHT: Irina Shünemann (Filatova), 1997

to the European part of Russia. Father recalled, "I had almost no family left by them." From Shadrinsk to Nizhny Novgorod, Father walked with a half-blind grandfather, and when he lost his eyesight completely, Father found him a place in a home for invalids and got himself a job with a family that raised pigs, but it was so difficult that he quit and returned to his grandfather, but he had died by then. Father recalled, "And that's when I was left completely alone, I wept bitterly, and then I moved in search of work up the Volga: the places where my ancestors had lived, and where our line began: Kostroma, Murom, Yaroslavl, Tula, Kaluga. There on the Uvod River, I lived with monks in the hut of Ivan III, there I hid in the summer, and in the winter I had to live in orphanages."

"In 1924 I was in Kaluga in a orphanage, from where I headed to Moscow," Father recalled. "It was very cold, the kids went to Lenin's funeral, but I stayed behind since I had no clothes and no shoes." Later, that summer, he was still in Moscow, "I reached that diplomatic street, where I was going to try my luck on last time, and I hit it and went straight up to the house, when some man came out and chased me away, a cripple."

After that Father found himself in the South and lived in the cities of Yalta, Batumi, Tiflis, Sukhumi, and Baku until 1928, where he worked in the oil fields. When he ended up without a job in Baku, he and his friends met a German engineer. Father told us, "We were sitting in an entryway, the German was coming up the stairs and he said, 'There'll be work soon in Magnitka, you should go there.' I went to Magnitogorsk [in the Urals]." It was hard there, they had to do the work by hand, the construction was only beginning, they slept under carts, and Father went back to Shadrinsk to the "uncles." Recalling that period, Father almost never said anything about any remaining living relatives, unless we insisted.

"He preferred remembering his rescuers, and when I said to him, how could you have been homeless when you had relatives?" relates Oleg, "he replied that after the Civil War he was in Tiflis and found some relatives at an old address. 'I had an uncle Konstantin, a very distant relative, but after all that had happened, when he abandoned us, I did not want to have anything to do with him, but need forced me. What did they need with me, a cripple, plus it was dangerous. He gave me some money for travel and said that I shouldn't bother them anymore. Go to the ones who saved you, we have a different life now.'"

According to some sources, Konstantin was shot in the South in the 1920s. So Father returned to the Urals, to Shadrinsk, and then the "uncles" sent him to study in Sverdlovsk. First he was in the chemistry department, but when he burned his last shirt during an experiment, he went to the Workers' School at the Road Transport Institute in Tyumen, then the institute was moved to Omsk, and after graduating from the Workers' School he entered the Tyumen Teachers Institute in 1934 and graduated in 1936 and was sent to the Isetsk District, Tyumen Province, to the village of Sloboda-Beshkil to work as a teacher, but at the same time he kept studying part time at the Pedagogical Institute in Tyumen in the geography department. In 1952 in the village of Krasnovo, Father married. In 1955 he moved to the village of Pretoria, Orenburg Province, Novosergievsk District, and lived there with the family until 1967, the period of the first "thaw."

Oleg recalls that "he began telling me as early as 1962–66 about St. Petersburg, telling me that history made the city, founded by Peter I, 'the home of the first Russian tsars and of the last one.'" In that period he personally took the whole family to St. Petersburg to see "memorable places," as he liked to put it. And whenever he went to the city to see our mother's relatives, the first thing he did was go to the city of Pushkin and every time he expressed his sadness over the loss of the "Amber Room."

Our youngest sister Nadezhda, who lived there after school, would get requests from Father—to find out what is at 5 Egorova Street, and so on. Father used to say that he had tried to get to St. Petersburg before the war, but it was very hard to get a job there in those days. When Father retired, we moved to Vologda Province, lived there for three years, and moved to Astrakhan Province, because Grandmother, Mother's mother, invited us to move to the warm climes of the south. Mama started persuading him—he was in shock and said, "I'll leave you, but I won't move, who knows what's there. Here Leningrad is nearby, the children will study there, the memorable places are nearby." But we moved nevertheless. We lived in the lower reaches of the Volga, we spent eighteen years there. And even though we had spent so much time on the Volga, Father always recalled the past and Leningrad. And we, his children, applied to schools in Leningrad and at our Father's bequest moved here permanently.

Reminiscences of Lydia Kuzminichna Filatova (Klimenkova)

Lydia Filatova (Klimenkova).

I was born in 1917 on March 3 in Orenburg, in the family of a railroad worker. My father was the son of a deacon of the Sorochinsk Church, Samara Province, Buzuluksk District. As a boy he sang in the church choir and planned to enroll in the church seminary, but the revolution interfered. His father, Nestor, went to Samara for advice on what to do with his only source of income. And so my father began working as a telegraph operator for the Orenburg railroad. Since he was very hard-working and honest, he quickly moved up the ladder: from telegraph operator to station master, supervisor, dispatcher. He studied all his life. In Moscow, at the Institute of Transport Engineering, in Leningrad, in courses to improve his qualifications. Always and everywhere he took books with him, and he read night and day. My mother (daughter of an Orenburg Cossack and deputy of the Third State Duma) took care of father, taught her four daughters to be housewives, to sew and embroider. My father was an example to me. His relations with family, children, people, his kindness, and tact awed me.

When he was station master of Sorochinsk (1933–34), where there was an enormous meat-packing plant where they made sausage, hams, etc., we always ate scraps, and Papa said that he did not take bribes and that those meat products were not for us. He was principled and just. He always fought for justice and he paid for it.

It was 1936 and we were living at Samarkand Station. Father was chief dispatcher of the analytic group. There was a conflict in the group, father refused to agree out of principle, and they said, "Give up your Party card and get out." That's what he did. In those days they kept denouncing people as "enemies of the people." And so Father became an enemy of the people. And our family of six was persecuted all over the country.

We were forced to leave our apartment and move into a room in a house that was in a pit from the earthquake. Papa went to look for work. He got a job as assistant to the station master of Aralskoe More Station. When I was finishing tenth grade in Kazalinsk, a denunciation came: "You have an enemy of the people working for you"—and father was fired. He started working at the double-track station of Kamyshla-bali (near Kazalinsk)—and he was fired again. The history teacher in class said, "We have children of enemies of the people in school." I cringed and a lump filled my throat; they had to give children a chance to finish school. We lived in a dormitory—Olga, Antonina, and I. Mother and little

Diana moved in with her brother, Gennady, in Chimkent. He rented a house from an Uzbek for the summer for our family. There was so much my father had to suffer for no reason. But the humiliation of my father and his family did not end there. Upon his arrival in Chimkent, Papa got a job as controller of passenger trains. We were given half a house, three rooms and a garden, on the edge of town, and the other half of the house was occupied by a big shot from the political section (he later shot himself). It was 1938. It was summer, we were settling in the house, we had moved all our things in a horse cart, and suddenly there was an earthquake.

There was such a strange rumble coming from below ground. The horse neighed and the dogs howled. But it lasted only a second. Mother said it was a bad omen. When we came to Samarkand we had been greeted by an earthquake, too. And what do you think happened? A short time later, in the fall, we were forced out of the house (as enemies of the people) into a dormitory room ten meters square [thirty square feet] with a stove, and besides the stove was a table and two beds. Father lived at his sister Natalya's house, at the station. She had her own house. Because of his health (Father had a bad heart) he could no longer work for the railroad. But he worked as a guard, at forty-eight! And so we lived, cramped but not beaten. In 1938, I enrolled in the Teachers Institute and graduated in 1940. We lived from hand to mouth. Mama took in sewing, Father had a small pension. My sister Antonina worked as a bookkeeper and Olga was still at the Teachers Institute and then married a pilot and moved to the Kuban region. After graduation from the institute I worked in the middle school in Chimkent, and we were all still living in that room. The war began, evacuees moved to the area, and in order to have bread rations, they let teachers work hours that were just enough for a salary that paid for bread. Our clothes were wearing out. We wore shoes and boots that had holes. It was spring of 1942; teachers and pupils went to weed cotton fields at the Pakhta Aral (Sea of Cotton) state farm. In the fall, we picked it. In 1943, I left for the front. I had a choice of which hospital to work in: 4559 or 1530, which was leaving earlier. Apparently, God led my decision, and I went with hospital 4559, which was the right choice. My parents went to the Kuban to be with Olga. Olga's husband was a pilot and he trained pilots for the front. On the way, at Gudermez Station, Father had an infection and he was put in the hospital. So Mother with her daughters Antonina and little Diana had to stay. They started crying, walked down the road, and sat down in the grass. A woman came along and asked, "Where are you from and where are you headed?" Mama told her the whole story. And the woman said, "Come to our village. We have many empty houses. They made the Chechens leave." My parents took a house on the edge of the village next to the woods and the spring water source. Antonina got work in the oil industry office and mother took up vegetable gardening. After the war, I came to visit them in Novogroznensk, but Father was gone. He had died in 1945 without seeing the victory he had been waiting for.

A new life began, with new hopes for a better future. I knew that Father was dead, buried by Mama and Antonina. It was winter and the roads were icy. The Russian cemetery was in Gudermez, ten miles away. They were given a truck; no one else came. My sister told me that the coffin, so huge, rolled around in the back of the truck, and she and Mother wept. Oh, God! The driver and the cemetery guard helped them bury him. They raised the cross. And now where the cemetery used to be is the

Second from the left: Vasily Filatov, circa 1947, Tyumen Province.

city of Gudermez. Damn all wars! They bring so much sorrow to people! There were so many families likes ours, who are still suffering from need.

So I went to the front. Our unit, with freight and medical personnel, moved through territory where the villages and cities had been burned and destroyed. Only chimneys were left. When we went through Voronezh—oh horror!—the station was on a hill, elevated, and the whole panorama of destruction was spread out below us. The chimneys were like candles!

Our train reached the small town of Romny, where the hospital was set up and we began taking in the wounded. There were a lot of people with self-inflicted wounds, and the special section was kept very busy.

The front was nearby. The hospital was supposed to move to Berdichev Station. They decided to send the medical personnel by truck and the equipment and service personnel by train. The trucks were bombed along the way, then bogged down in mud. There were a lot of wounded. The train was also bombed, the last car hit. We turned back to a school one-and-a-half miles from the station, and hospital 1530 was supposed to load into our echelon 4559. Just as they were finished, the station was bombed. The station master had concentrated military units, trains with fuel, and, most important, the hospital, with brilliant surgeons and doctors, all at the station. The brain surgeon was wounded. There was so much groaning, weeping, and sobbing! It was heartbreaking. The sound wave from the explosion knocked all the glass from the window. Amazingly the school building was not razed. So the school was filled up with the wounded. I remember an officer with a head wound who sang the popular war ballad, "The Night Is Dark," through his moans. In the morning trucks pulled up with wounded from the front. We did not sleep for four nights—not at all, we could barely stand. All December trucks brought in the wounded. Berdichev was constantly bombarded. Shrapnel rained on the roof.

By February, the flow of wounded slowed, but there were trucks with German war prisoners. Orderlies used twig brushes to beat the lice from them, and there was lots of cursing and swearing. And in the hospital yard there were trucks loaded with the frozen corpses of dead Germans. It was horrible and frightening to see all that. By spring, the front moved away and we headed in the direction of Zhitomir to free territory. I saw the end of the war in Zhitomir. There were shots in the night. Rockets sparkled and joyous voices shouted. Everyone rushed outside, crying, laughing, hugging. The war was over, our sorrow was over! What more could people want? Our Russian homeland! How lovely are your forests, fields and rivers, your land. So bountiful, so filled with the aromas of goodness and life. All we need is to live and be happy. Where has the happiness gone, the inspiration? Where?

Well, I went to see Mother in the Caucasus and got a teaching job there. Mother got malaria and started weakening. She was told to change climate. My sister had moved to Tyumen, and we followed. That's how I ended up in the village of Sloboda-Beshkil, Tyumen Province, in 1949. I worked in a seven-grade school. The school director was Nikolai Kornilovich Sheshukov, and the dean, my future husband, was Vasily Ksenofontovich Filatov. My first impression of the dean was horrible. The man was crippled, he swayed like a drunkard when he walked, dragging his left leg and swinging it forward, plus his wrinkled cotton suit, pink wrinkled shirt, and boots with turned-up toes. His pale face with regular features were animated by sorrowful, dark, and deep-set eyes. His voice was calm and even. When asked why he was crippled, he replied that he had been born that way. V .K. [Vasily Ksenofontovich] did a lot of public service, he was a deputy in the village council and a member of the lectorium under the Isetsk Regional Party Committee. He gave lectures in the village hall and to teachers on any topic. He had great erudition.

The school staff was not large: the director and I taught physics and mathematics and the dean, geography. Literature and Russian language were taught by A.Varaksin, the teachers of the primary grades were Bezhentseva, Sheshukova, and Varaksina. Ekaterina Masson taught German, and her husband was the superintendent at the school. During the war they had been sent from the Volga Region to Tyumen Province and they stayed on in the village. The teachers' lounge had a table, and the dean was always hunched over it, working on the schedule, reading and writing, he was always very tactful with the teachers: when he went over the lesson plans, he was never harshly critical. He was kindly. He was always careful not to hurt people at the pedagogical councils and never gave his personal opinion. He would say, "I am in complete agreement with Augusta Petrovna's statement and can add nothing" when it was obvious that a lot could and should be added. He was always friendly and smiling. The village was eighteen miles from Isetsk, the regional seat, twenty-five miles from Yalutorovsk, and forty miles from Tyumen, and rather big. The village had a hall seating around a hundred fifty people, where we held holiday festivities, read lectures, and put on shows. V. K. was well known in the collective farm's council. They all called him by a shortened form of his first name and patronymic, "Vasilich." During the war years he worked as a school inspector and deputy chief of the public school administration in Isetsk. He worked day and night and lived in the public school building. He found apartments and jobs

Far right (bottom row): Vasily Filatov; third from the right (top row): Lydia Klimenkova, 1951, in Sloboda-Beshkil.

for teachers evacuated there from other cities. So he knew everyone and they knew him. For his work, he received certificates and medals: "For Work Excellence" the medal "For Valorous Work in the Great Patriotic War 1941–1945" and the jubilee medal "Forty Years of Victory in the Great Patriotic War 1941–1945." During the war the mathematician Boris Vasilyevich Zhuravlev (from Leningrad) worked with him in the Isetsk school and his two daughters studied with him. V. K. always had good things to say about Zhuravlev. After the war they met in Leningrad in 1962, when we went there on vacation.

I worked in the village of Sloboda for three years. A lot of time went into preparation and grading homework. After classes the teachers and students helped harvest potatoes. The soil was soft, with lots of sand. All the teachers took an active part in amateur shows. There was a teachers' choir. We sang songs of the war years—"The Sun Is Behind the Mountain," "Sevastopol Waltz"—and folk songs—"Dubinushka" and "Holy Baikal." I played guitar and sang "Sormovskaya Lyric Song" and "Far, Far Away." Performers sang folk ditties, declaimed poetry and fables. V. K. read Chekhov stories: "The Chameleon," "Nasty Boy," and others. We put on Ostrovsky's play "A Profitable Place" and Ivan Franko's "Booth N 27." V. K. studied his parts assiduously every day. Rehearsals and performances brought the teachers closer together. We learned more about one another. We talked about our lives and our parents. V. K. said that his parents had died in the civil war, and everyone grew sad.

We were married in 1952. We were no longer teaching in Sloboda and had moved to Krasnovo, 10 miles from Isetsk. I was dean and mathematics teacher, and V. K. taught geography and history. We worked very hard. The man attracted me with his spirituality, his beautiful, deep, and sad eyes, which showed so much sorrow and longing. He knew how to listen, even when my voice rose as I went on about how he couldn't play chess all day or read . . . He said nothing. Parents of teachers who had

The Filatov family: Lydia, Oleg, and Vasily Filatov, 1955.

worked in Isetsk lived in Krasnovo. Everyone knew V. K. and respected him. We worked for three years in Krasnovo. Our son Oleg was born there. We were in seventh heaven with happiness, and years later our daughter Olga was born. A heavenly creature with blue eyes. The children were blond heavenly creatures, placid and healthy. And suddenly V. K. wanted to leave; he said he was tired of living there.

And so we ended up in Orenburg Province in the German village of Pretoria, where V. K. taught geography and history in grades 5–9. I taught mathematics and physics in grades 5–7. We were given housing, at first in two rooms just thirty steps from the school, and later a small, four-room house. We came to Pretoria in 1955. V. K. tired easily, his legs hurt a lot. He had headaches. He would come home from school and fall into bed with exhaustion. He never complained, he would sit down to play chess or read. V. K. often told the children casually, "Tsar Nicholas and the whole family were executed, only the boy survived." The children accepted that as a historical event.

He told me that his uncles guarded the tsar, were in his guard. He told about his orphaned childhood, how he had traveled all over Russia, had worked in Magnitogorsk, where it was very hard for him, that he had been in the Caucasus in the city of Baku, that he had finished a parish school in Shadrinsk and then was in an orphanage, after the death of his father and mother. Where are they buried? Where were their graves? He avoided answering and never told me. When he was asked, "Why are you so crippled?" he replied that he was born that way and the question was never repeated. He always suffered from headaches and I was constantly giving him back massages, there were indentations in the lower back and under the ribs, and his left leg just dangled, with a scar on the heel. I wondered to myself, "Lord, how much has this man suffered and how much will he have to suffer?"

The teachers from the Pretoria Secondary School at a New Year's party. Vasily Filatov is making a toast.

The school staff in Pretoria was large and most of the teachers were young—from Moscow, Saratov, Orenburg. They all had higher degrees. They were lively and energetic. We meshed into the staff without any problem. V. K. was a gregarious and cheerful person who quickly found common interests, joked, and was always tactful. The village was surrounded by hills and meadows, and there was a small river, the Gusikha. Within four miles were the villages of Kichkas, Sudbodarovka, and others. In Pretoria V. K. was active in public life: he gave lectures on international topics and was a deputy in the village council. We worked a lot. Especially me. I had small children, Oleg was two, Olga, six months, I taught twenty hours of math a week, and there was homework to check, plus my work as class mentor. The director didn't even want to hear about it. But I had to learn how to bake bread, which I did, and I learned how to sew everything, literally, including the children's coats. I taught myself to embroider.

In Pretoria in 1957, our hazel-eyed Irina was born, and in 1961 Nadezhda. I was so happy and rich. I had so much energy. And what joy there was in watching our children grow by leaps and bounds in the pure steppe air. Yes, I also want to write that I received honorable mentions not only for my amateur theatrics but also for my embroidery, which was exhibited in a crafts fair of the regional teachers. I taught girls in grades 5–7 to sew and embroider in the home economics classes. For International Women's Day, March 8, we exhibited our embroidery: the girls embroidered napkins, tablecloths, pillowcases, and towels. I received a lot of thanks from the parents.

We lived for eleven years in Pretoria. In that time, there were three different school directors. The first, Kocherga, was fired for negligence. During a terrible snowstorm when the sky and land were indistinguishable and you couldn't see more than a yard in front of you, two ninth grade girls decided to go home. They refused to wait for their parents. It was close to school and they left. It was a blizzard. The snow swirled and swirled. The girls lost their way and ended up in the steppe, where they died. Mountains of snow fell overnight. They searched for them all night with tractors and for another week after that, but they were not found until spring. A tractor came upon them during plowing. After that incident, they put a light and a bell on the roof.

The next director was Gurbenko Alexander Alexandrovich, and after him, Buchnev Nikolai Vasilyevich, who was fired after a conflict with a group of teachers who were unhappy with his actions. Intrigues started at the school, and with the help of the chief a tenth grade student, Kulakov Vladimir, was made school director, and Party secretary of the collective farm, A. Streltsov, was made dean. The latter never taught a single class and told the pupils, "I'm giving you a C just because you are a citizen of the USSR." Of course, there were worthy teachers who were outraged by such dealings.

V. K. and I moved to Vologda. To Volgo-Balt, Vyterogsky Region, in a workers' settlement called Bely Ruchei. We were there for three years, and by that time V. K. was no longer teaching. He spent most of his time at home, playing chess and reading. The whole family would head out into the woods to pick mushrooms and raspberries. We helped the children get the basics in history, Russian, and mathematics. The children always shared their successes and failures with us and we always found the right response in our hearts. There was always total understanding in the family. V. K. always behaved with dignity in the family. He never raised his voice at the children or me. In Bely Ruchei I was dean in a school with over one thousand students and spent all day at school, and then at home until midnight or 1 A.M., so often V. K. had to make a simple meal. The house was heated by stove. V. K. and I sawed logs, but he did the chopping, saying that it was a skill worth knowing. That it was an art. After he died, I chopped wood the way he taught me. Once when he was chopping wood a piece flew off and hit him hard in the leg. A terrible blue bruise formed, which we bandaged up, and he limped for a long time. If he accidentally cut his finger he would shout, "Where's the iodine? Where's the iodine!?"

There was constant rain, very little sun, and V. K. kept getting chilled and suffering from the influenza. In the winter there was a terrible epidemic, even I got it, because my heart was weakened by my difficult labor. I gave six mathematics lessons in the first and second shift, plus made up the schedule for the school (of course, V. K. was a great help), and I sat in on the classes of teachers in the primary school, grades 5–9. The teachers were marvelous, very hardworking. My hat is off to them. The school director was A. I. Lunichev, I was dean with V. P. Dunyshkina and others. We decided to go south. My mother lived in Astrakhan Oblast, and that's where we headed. We went to Leningrad by steamship through the Volgo-Balt Canal, and then by train to Astrakhan. In 1970, when we moved to Astrakhan, a cholera epidemic was rampaging there. From Astrakhan we got to Ikrianoe. We bought a house on the edge of the village made of bulrushes with land. We received our pensions.

Mother had many friends, and I began to take in sewing right away; in fact, I opened an illegal tailor shop for ladies, clothes and embroidery. The girls were in school and they helped by doing the hemming, finishing seams, and so on. Then the children moved away: Irina to the Moscow Textile Institute, Olga to the Academy of Art in Leningrad, Oleg to the Astrakhan Pedagogical Institute of Foreign Languages, Nadezhda to Leningrad to the Pedagogical Institute and to Astrakhan for the music school. And then V. K. helped me by sewing on beadwork, hemming, and other minor work. In the seventeen years we spent in Ikrianoe, we planted a garden with many apricots, several grape varieties, apple and cherry trees, strawberries, and vegetables. V. K. was so happy in the sunshine on the river, where he liked to fish. But despite this, his health continued to deteriorate, his heart problems increased, his back ached. He refused medical treatment. He was almost eighty. Throughout his life he took large white tablets of ginseng, ascorbic acid, and he loved meat and meat dishes. He had little boxes where he kept fishing hooks, screws, and nails. Whatever the occasion, birthday or holiday, he always calculated old style and new style calendars. That irritated me and I would say, "Everyone's already forgotten the old style calendar and accepted the new one, but you still recalculate!" Having lived thirty-six years with him, I learned that his whole family had died in 1921, and some simply abandoned him and he did not want to have anything to do with them now. Sometimes he said things that seemed strange to us. He always watched television greedily (especially in the perestroika years) and talked back to it: "They're driving at it, but they won't find or get anything. . . ." We simply shrugged.

And then on a moonless night a very tall man in a checked shirt slipped past the window. He entered the garden and hid in a corner behind the veranda. We started looking for him, V. K. came with us, but we didn't find him. He was hidden. He was in the corner, hunched over, he couldn't see, but he could hear our voices. V. K. did not go into the house, but took an ax and lay down on the bed in the garden and covered himself with a dark blanket. We thought the man had left. We all slept on the veranda, which had netting around it, but now we went into the house and began to fall asleep, except for me, I wasn't sleepy.

I heard something fall. I thought, what's that? We don't have a cat. And then I heard the metal creak of the lock. I got up and went into the hallway. I was just going to look out the window when I bumped into extended hands. I screamed, grabbed a stool, and threw it. The man opened the door and ran away. V. K. said that they had come for him; Olga thought he was after all of us. After that I couldn't sleep for many nights; the lights burned all night in the house.

We didn't turn off the lights for a week after that horrible night. I couldn't sleep and kept guard. Our daughters Irina and Olga went back to work very upset and worried. Vasily suffered, as usual, in silence. He sat down to play chess. I looked at him and thought, "Why did he say that they had come for him?" It was very hot, almost 40 degrees [104°F]. It was very stuffy in the house. But Vasily did not go outside. He did not react to my remarks. Oleg came to spend time with his wife, Anzhelika, and then our daughter Nadezhda came from Leningrad on vacation. Gradually, that horrible night slipped from memory. The children relaxed, picked fruit and berries, made jam, Vasily fished. Life was back on track. Vasily's health left a lot to be desired. He was constantly suffering from headaches, pains in his legs and back, and his hearing deteriorated rapidly. He would not listen to my persistent suggestions to go to a resort. He said there wasn't enough money for a trip and let me know that he was not going to discuss it. Period.

We never had time to be bored in the summer. There were thirty apricot trees, almost all were fruitful, there were grape vines running through the apricot trees, and the peach and plum trees were fruit-bearing too. Behind the house were two huge Vladimir cherry trees, where the starlings ate their fill and beneath which the grandchildren played and Grandfather Vasily rested.

The Filatov family: from left to right: Olga Klimenkova (Lydia Filatova's sister), Lydia, Oleg, Vasily, and Nadezhda, 1963.

The gardens demanded constant work. I loved those trees, those plants, those streams of water feeding the seedlings of life. When Nadezhda came to visit, she would say, "Mama, here I am and you keep running off to your trees." I sometimes thought that those trees, planted with such love, prolonged our lives. I just want to tell people: plant trees, have gardens, that is kindness and love, that is the joy of life, that is health!

On the weekends our children came to the garden, and those were our happiest minutes and hours. So many heartfelt conversations, jokes, and sincere laughter!

The years passed. Our house of rush and clay started to fall apart. The roof, covered with artificial rubber, began to leak. And we fell apart along with the house. But we did not give up. We were revived by the arrival of our children—with our grandchildren. Vasily became a grandfather and I a

The Filatov family. From left to right: Irina, Olga, Lydia, Nadezhda, Vasily, and Oleg, 1969.

grandmother. Grandpa read and told stories to our grandson, Anton. He treated him with great love and gentleness. And he sang lullabies to our granddaughter, Lyolya. In the winter, he worked on chess problems and listened to the radio. In the fall he chopped wood and stacked it the way they do in Siberia. He read a lot. His heart bothered him and he started taking pills and drops for his heart. The headaches almost never stopped. I constantly massaged his back, steamed his feet, rubbed various creams into his back. Grandpa spent hours lying down. On October 24 at noon he died from a brain hemorrhage. The man died in silence, he had lost the ability to speak, he suffered from headaches, and he could express his pain only through his eyes. It tore my heart apart. To this day I remember his suffering eyes, but I could do nothing to help. By the time the ambulance arrived he was dead. Anton [his grandson] and I were horrified. He was three, and he stopped talking, tears falling on his tiny hands. At that moment no one from the family was with us. Oh, God! What grief befell our family!!

Description of the State of Health of Vasily Filatov as Remembered by Members of His Family

Our father, Vasily Ksenofontovich Filatov, according to his documents was born December 22, 1907, in Shadrinsk. He died October 24, 1988 and is buried in Astrakhan Province. We, his children: Oleg Vasilyevich, born 1953; Olga Vasilyevna, born 1955; Irina Vasilyevna, born 1957; and Nadezhda Vasilyevna, born 1961; and his wife, Lydia Kuzminichna, born 1917, hereby record the following regarding the illness and suffering of our father.

According to our father, he survived the execution in the Ipatiev house in Ekaterinburg, was rescued by soldiers and workers, and was sent via Shadrinsk in the direction of present-day Surgut for treatment, where peoples of the North knew how to stop bleeding and heal blood loss, from which he constantly suffered at that time. How would we characterize his health?

1. In the North, Father said, he was given infusions of herbs, in particular plantain, and evergreens, fir, pine, angel moss, and he was forced to eat raw venison, fresh fish, bear meat, and bull's eyes. When he was asked why he had been treated by the Khanty-Mansy tribe, he usually replied that in the North they often suffered from gingivitis, which causes major blood loss, and the locals living there had learned to use natural methods to stop bleeding and heal the body.
2. Through his life Father drank bull's blood, and there was always hematogen and Kagor red wine at home. Father took E and C vitamins, especially ascorbic acid, glucerophosphate, and gluconate of calcium.
3. Accidental bumps on the legs, arms, and body made the bruised spot swell up quickly, turning first pale blue, then brown, and then yellow with capillaries that looked torn and dark blue. On days like that he took to his bed and lay in silence; it was eerie, as if he had died, not a moan, not a complaint, he issued no sounds. His face turned waxy, he grew feverish, his temperature jumping to 39°C [102°F]. Lighter injuries he got over by "forgetting himself" by playing chess. External cuts healed rather quickly. In his final years he prayed openly, not hiding his knowledge of prayers as he had in the past. He would sit down in the position of a coachman and ask, "Lord, how long will I suffer? Lord, when will I die?" and he asked our mother to take him to his homeland, in Petrograd. When he was in pain he read the prayers, "Our Father," "Holy Mother of God," and to St. Seraphim of Sarov.
4. Father knew breathing exercises, poured cold water over himself, and did yoga.
5. He remembered Grigory Rasputin and his sister, whom he visited in the village of Pokrovsky. Father said that Rasputin kept him from dying.
6. Father went to private persons for dental and denture work and always worried about finding "plasma."
7. When Father was sick, he never went to spas or hospitals, even if there was an opportunity to do so.
8. There was no medical conclusion from VTEK declaring him disabled.
9. His left leg was practically paralyzed; he wore a size 40 shoe on his left foot and a 42 on his right. Father tried to wear orthopedic or stiff footwear, especially boots or army shoes that laced up, or what he called "general's shoes" with elastic on the sides.
10. He loved solitude, peace, and quiet, especially being in the woods or on the river, hunting.
11. He was exempted from military service, as shown on his draft card.

Appendix

■ Birth certificate of V. K. Filatov ■

[No later than 2 December 1954]*

Original, filled-out printed form

*dated on the basis of the receipt of passport for V. K. Filatov stamped on the reverse of the original certificate

People's Commissariat of Internal Affairs of the USSR
Department of Acts of Civil Conditions
Certificate of Birth
AR N 3649415
Citizen Filatov Vasily Ksenofontovich
Born 22/XII 1907 Twenty-second of December one thousand nine hundred seven which is duly recorded in the register of acts of civil conditions on the births for 1907, "24" of the month of December.
Parents:
Father: Filatov Ksenofont Afanasyevich
Mother: Filatova Elena Pavlovna
Place of Birth: city: Shadrinsk, Chelyabinsk Province
Place of registration: Shadrinsk, Chelyabinsk Province
Head of Bureau [signature]

Olga, Irina, and Oleg Filatov looking at photographs and documents.

Appeal by O. V. Filatov to the International Court at The Hague

[no later than 12 September 1997]
Copy, computer printout

The Netherlands
International Court of The Hague
Het Internationale Gerechschof
Carnegeiplein 2 2517 KJ Den Haag Nederland
tel. +32 (70) 30 22323, fax +31 (70) 3649928

from Filatov Oleg Vasilievich, citizen of Russia

Appeal

I ask the high court to hear the question of the identity of my father, Filatov Vasily Ksenofontovich (born 22.12.1907, died 24.10.1988 in Russia) and the son of the last Russian Emperor, Alexei Nikolaevich Romanov (born 12.08.1904 in Russia, shot, but not killed the night of 16/17 July 1918 in the cellar of the engineer Ipatiev in Ekaterinburg).

The basis for this appeal to your court is the three-year study (9.09.1994 to 20.08.1997) done by Russian scholars into the person of Filatov Vasily Ksenofontovich and the person of Romanov Alexei Nikolaevich, which showed that they are one and the same person, who was not killed but remained alive. The research was based on historical materials, investigative materials of 1919 by investigator Sokolov V. N. into the circumstances of the death of the royal family, the work of scientists on the burial site in Ekaterinburg, accounts of family members of what Filatov Vasily Ksenofontovich told them about the rescue of tsarevich Alexei Nikolaevich Romanov by the brothers Strekotin, soldiers of the outdoor guard. However, all appeals by the scholars using the mass media and appeals of our family on 8.07.1994 to investigator Soloviov Vladimir Nikolaevich of the Procurator General's Office of the Russian Federation, who led the investigation into the circumstances of the death of the royal family and determined that two of the children of the last Russian emperor were not in the burial site, went unnoticed, since the investigators have a strict theory that all the members of the royal family died in one way or another, but the Filatov family version has not been disproved.

Therefore our family, in view of the research and wanting to know the truth about our father, are defending our rights and those of our father and are turning to your high court in the hope of an objective evaluation of the research. We also ask the high court to help our family and Russian scholars get access to the archives of the royal family, which are found abroad as well as in Russia and which may have important information—for instance, the diaries of Maria Feodorovna, mother of Nicholas II, the last Russian emperor—medical data about the family's health, and other historical materials, and also connect us to the research done by institutions in other countries, if the court decides that this present research is not enough to determine that Filatov Vasily Ksenofontovich and Romanov Alexei Nikolaevich are identical. It should be noted that all the research was done at the expense of the family and people who are not indifferent to the history of the royal family's death. However, the family does not have funds for more major research nor for expanded scholarly research.

We feel that this issue is of international character. Many relatives of the tsar's family came from other countries, but no one has asked where the body of Alexei Nikolaevich Romanov is when its absence from the Ekaterinburg burial site was discovered. There has never been a death certificate for Romanov Alexei Nikolaevich at any time in any place. An old legal rule says: if there is no body, there is no evidence of death, and therefore no murderers.

Eighty years after the death of the royal family, no one should interfere in this research. The family has also turned over the materials to the Synod of the Russian Orthodox Church. The work of the scholars and scientists continues, however there is no support from the state and that is the fault of indifferent bureaucrats. Many archives are keeping us from finding needed documents about the boy's fate.

We are appealing to you because the court may be able to help make a final discovery of the truth and the tragedy of the death of Russia's last emperor, Nicholas II.

We hope that acceptance by the court of this case will bring it to the attention of the Russian government and help re-establish the civil rights of our father.

With the deepest respect, the Filatov family:
daughter: Filatova Olga Vasilievna, residing in St. Petersburg, Russia;
daughter: Schünemann (nee Filatova) Irina Vasilievna, residing in Wolfsburg, Germany;
daughter: Härting (nee Filatova) Nadezhda Vasilievna, residing in Heppingen, Germany.
In the name of the family, son: Filatov Oleg Vasilievich, citizen of Russia.

Addenda:
1. Research and conclusions of Russian scholars.
2. Archival materials.
3. Biographical data.
4. Other materials.

Reply to O.V. Filatov's statement by the International Court at the Hague

12 September 1997

Dear Sir,
I acknowledge receipt of the documents concerning the "Investigation of the identity of Vasily Ksenofontovich Filatov, Russian citizen, and the son of the last Russian Emperor, Nicholas II."

I regret however to inform you that, by virtue of Article 34 of the Statute of the International Court of Justice, "only States may be parties in cases before the Court," and that only international organizations authorized within the meaning of Article 65 of the Statute may request advisory opinions of the Court.

It follows that neither the Court nor its Members may consider applications from private individuals or groups, provide them with legal advice, or assist them in their relations with the authorities of any country.

That being so, you will, I am sure, understand that no action can be taken on your letter.

[Signed:] Jean-Jacques Amaldez
Deputy Registrar
International Court of Justice
The Hague Netherlands

The International Court at The Hague. Arthur Witwein, Secretary of the International Court, and Oleg Filatov, September 12, 1997.

Response of the Shadrinsk City Soviet on the Request of the Road Building Workers' School about the Voting Rights of V. K. Filatov

26 February 1933, N 183

Original, typescript, stamped by Shadrinsk City Soviet

To the Road Building Workers' School

Regarding yours of 15/II-33 N 09 Shadrinsk City Soviet informs you that citizen Filatov V. K., son of a shoemaker, poor classes, is not in the Shadrinsk City Soviet list of people denied voting rights.

Executive Secretary of the City Soviet, Ivanov

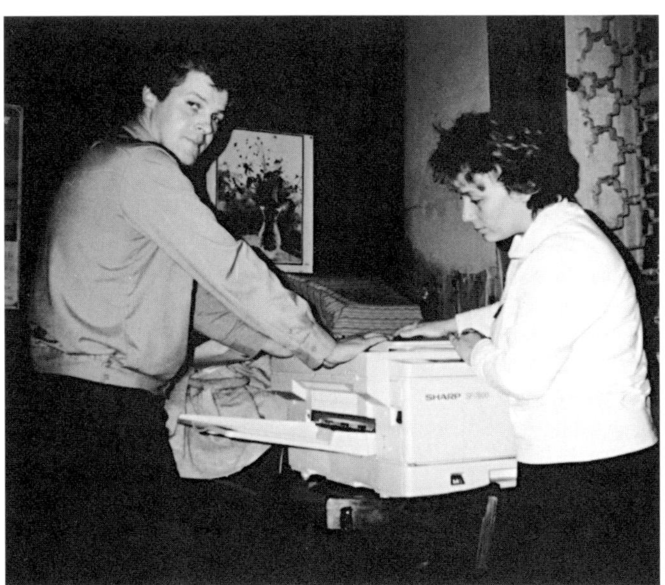

Police major Sergei Simonenko doing research in the Shadrinsk municipal archive, 1995.

Certificate of V. K. Filatov's Graduation from the Workers' School at the Urals Pedagogical Institute

30 June 1934, Tyumen, Urals Province, Lunacharsky St., N 2
original, filled-in printed form

Certificate

The holder of this, citizen Filatov Vasily Ksenofontovich, born in 1907, entered in 1930 the department of the day (evening) Tyumen Workers' School of the Urals Pedagogical Institute. During his time at the Workers' School, in the department indicated, Citizen Filatov Vasily Ksenofontovich received the following evaluations of academic preparedness in disciplines according the records of sessions, promotion and graduation tests:

List of disciplines	Grade
1. Mathematics	Satisfactory
2. Physics	Good
3. Chemistry	Good
4. Biology	Satisfactory
5. Russian	Good
6. Literature	Good
7. HistoryVery	Good
8. History of the Party	Good
9. Political Economy	Good
10. Economic Politics	Good
11. Physical Geography	Satisfactory
12. Economic Geography	Good
13. German	Good
14. Military affairs	Satisfactory
15. Physical Education	Satisfactory
16. Introduction to dialectical materialism	

On the basis of the above Citizen Filatov is considered a graduate of the Tyumen Pedagogical Workers' School.

Head of the Workers School [signature]
Head of Education [signature]
Secretary [signature]

■ Certificate of V. K. Filatov as Middle School Teacher ■

9 August 1938
Original, filled-in printed form

N 22909
Russian Socialist Federative Soviet Republic
People's Commissariat of Education RSFSR
Certificate
to title of middle school teacher

Filatov Vasily Ksenofontovich, graduated in 1936 from the teacher's institute in Tyumen and passed the required provisional stage of pedagogical work in school, is granted on the basis of the resolution of the Central Executive Committee and Soviet of People's Commissars of the Union SSR on the introduction of the personal titles for teachers of 10 April 1936.

title of middle school teacher
with the right to teach in the first seven grades of middle school.
9 August 1938
People's Commissar of Education RSFSR [signature]
N 22909
Seal of the People's Commissariat of Education RSFSR

■ Reference from the Isetsk Department of Public Education ■

17 July 1942, N 118
Original, manuscript, stamp and seal of the Isetsk Regional Department of Public Education

Reference
Given to Comrade Filatov Vasily Ksenofontovich to show that he in fact works as a teacher in the Isetsk school since 7/IX-1936.

Chief RONO [signature]

Diploma of V. K. Filatov upon Graduation from the Tyumen State Pedagogical Institute

16 December 1939
Original, filled-in printed form

Diploma
N 054485

Bearer, Filatov Vasily Ksenofontovich began in 1934 and graduated in 1939 from the complete course of the Tyumen State Pedagogical Institute with a specialty in Geography and by the decision of the State Examination Commission on 16 December 1939 he is given the qualification of instructor of geography in middle school.

Chairman of the State Examination Commission [signature]
Director
Secretary [signature]
Tyumen 1939
Registration N 125

Archive Reference from the State Archive Tyumen Province

20 December 1996, N F-47
Original, typescript, archive letterhead [to the "Living History of the Homeland" Foundation]

The documents of the archive fund of the Tyumen State Pedagogical Institute, the orders, and the personal file contain the following information on the scholarship of Filatov Vasily Ksenofontovich:

By Order N 63 of 2 July 1934 accepted in the first year of the Tyumen Teachers Institute as of 1 July 1934

From the reference signed by deputy director of the pedagogical institute on 17.07.1937, it follows that on 1 July 1936 Filatov V. K. graduated from Tyumen Teachers Institute with a specialty in geography.

On the orders of assistant director N 24/79 of 18.07.37, he was enrolled in the third year of the pedagogical institute's geography department in the part-time sector, as having graduated from the TPI teachers institute.

The order on graduation from the institute was not found, since documents for those years were not complete when turned over to the archive.

His personal file has an excerpt from the graduation report of 19 December 1939.

Basis: f. 765, op.2, d. 3, l. 50, d. 556, ll. 1, 2, 3, 7.
Director of the Provincial Archive [signature] G. I. Ivantsova
Chief of Desk [signature] V. N. Sedykh

Excerpt from the Report with the Diploma of V. K. Filatov upon Graduation from the Tyumen State Pedagogical Institute

19 December 1939
Original, typescript

Excerpt from report
(not valid without diploma)
Comrade Filatov Vasily Ksenofontovich during his time in the Part-Time Department of the Tyumen Pedagogical Institute passed the following disciplines:

1. History of the Party(B)	Excellent
2. Political Economy	Fair
3. Dialectical Materialism / Historical Materialism	Excellent
4. Leninism	Fair
5. History of the USSR	Excellent
6. World History	Excellent
7. Pedagogy	Fair
8. Psychology	Fair
9. History of Pedagogy	Good
10. General Land Science	Excellent
11. Astronomy	Excellent
12. Mineralogy and Petrography	Fair
13. Cartography with basic topography	Excellent
14. Physical geography of the USSR	Fair
15. Physical Geography of the world	Excellent
16. Methodology of physical geography	Fair
17. Economic geography of the USSR	Excellent
18. Economic Geography of Capitalist countries	Good
19. Methodology of Economic Geography	Good
20. Chemistry non-organic	Fair
21. Physics	Fair
22.Military Affairs	Fair

Besides which Comrade Filatov Vasily Ksenofontovich passed State examinations and received the grades:

1. Pedagogy	Good
2. Economic Geography USSR	Fair
3. Economic Geography World	Good
4. Physical Geography USSR	Fair
5. Physical Geography World	Fair

Director of the Pedagogical Institute [signature] Korolev
Deputy Director of the Institute for Part-Time Study [signature] Gulyaev
Secretary of the department [signature] Reshetnikova
Tyumen 19 / XII-1939

Reference from the Isetsk Regional Department of Public Education about the Work of V. K. Filatov

[...] September 1957
Original, typescript, stamp of the Isetsk Regional Department of Public Education
the date is not clear in the original

Reference:

Given by the Isetsk Regional Department of Public Education, Tyumen Province, to Filatov Vasily Ksenofontovich that he did in fact work as teacher in the schools of Isetsk Region:

1. from 22 August 1936 as teacher of geography in U.-Beshkil middle school until 28 August 1938. Order N 128 of 17/VIII-36.
2. from 28 August 1938 as teacher of geography of five grades in Isetsk middle school until 12 November 1940. Order N 355 of 28/VII-38.
3. from 12 November 1940 in regional ONO inspector of schools with salary of 450 rubles /month until 18 September 1941. Order N 461 of 14/IX-1941.
4. from 18 September 1941 temporary acting director of Isetsk Regional ONO until 26 December 1941, Order N 593 of 25/XII-41.

This reference is given to confirm seniority of work level.
Chief of Isetsk Regional ONO [signature] Sycheva

V. K. Filatov's Application to the Tyumen State Pedagogic Institute

18 August 1937
Photocopy of original (State Archive Tyumen Province, f. 765, op. 2, d. 556, l. 5)

Tyumen Pedagogical Institute
Part-Time Sector. Geography Department

from Filatov Vasily Ksenofontovich

Application

I request enrollment in the third geography year of part-time study. On 1 July 1936 I graduated from the Tyumen Teachers Institute with a specialty in geography. I enclose a report of my graduation from the Institute and I am asking that you send me a program and textbooks for the third year.

My address: Upper-Beshkil, junior middle school
Isetsk Region, Omsk Province
Filatov Vasily Ksenofontovich
18/VII-37 Filatov

Archival Reference from the Department of Public Education of the Administration of Isetsk Region

15 January 1997
Original, computer printout, stamp of the Department of Public Education

St. Petersburg
National Humanitarian Foundation
Living History of the Homeland

In reply to your query, we state that the Isetsk Regional Department of Public Education has the following documents that confirm the work seniority level of Filatov Vasily Ksenofontovich:

Order 128 of 17 August 1936
To appoint Filatov V. K. teacher of geography in Upper-Beshkil junior middle school.

Order 355 of 28 August 1938
To transfer Filatov V. K. to the Isetsk middle school.

Order 123 of 8 September 1940
To appoint Filatov V. K. director of the Isetsk junior middle school for adults as of 5 September 1940.

Order 189 of 12 November 1940
To transfer teacher of Isetsk school Filatov V. K. to work in RONO as senior inspector of schools.

Order 461 of 17 September 1941
In accordance with the director of RONO Lyashkov's recruitment into the Red Army, to make Filatov V. K. acting director of RONO.

Order 593 of 26 December 1941
To appoint Filatov V. K. teacher of Isetsk middle school.

Chief of education department [signature] V. E. Plotnikova

Excerpt from Order on Novosergievsk Department of Education

Order N 93 of 31 August 1955, p. 4*

*The excerpt was produced by the Education Department of the Novosergievsk Region Orenburg Province no earlier than 1995

Comrade Filatov Vasily Ksenofontovich, with a higher pedagogical education, is appointed teacher of geography of grades 5–10 in Pretoria middle school as of 1 September 1955. Pay travel expense from Moscow.

Basis: Order of Province Education Department N 134 of 29 August 1955
Chief RONO [signature]
Excerpt is accurate: [signature]

Reference from Department of Education Novosergievsk Region Orenburg Province

23 December 1966
Original, typescript, stamp of Novosergievsk Department of Education

Reference:

Given to Filatov Vasily Ksenofontovich that he did in fact work as a teacher of geography in grades 5–10 in Pretoria middle school from 01.09.1955.
(Basis Order RONO N93 p. 4 of 31.08.1955)

and worked in our region until 1. 07.1965
(Basis: salary receipts for 1955/65)

Chief of RONO: [signature] G. N. Emchenko
Correct: Secretary RONO [signature] A. Dedlovskaya

■ Certificate of Exemption from Military Service for V. K. Filatov ■

5 December 1942
Original, filled-in typographical form

Certificate N 973
(no time limit)
(keep with draft card)
On exemption from military service
This certificate is given
By the Isetsk R.V.K. [draft board] Omsk Province
to draftee born 1908
Filatov Vasily Ksenofontovich
soldier in the reserves
second category VUS N
born in Chelyabinsk
city of Shadrinsk
certifying that he was examined
on 5 December 1942
by the commission of the Isetsk R. V. K
Omsk Province
and certified unfit for military
service and to be removed from the draft registration
under paragraph 1 art 12 of the list of illnesses
of the order NKO USSR 1942 N 336
and is removed from the draft registration.
Subject to review
in No Time Limit
M. P.
Regional military
Commissar [signature]
5.XII.1942
Seal: Familiarized with the regulations of the new registration record
5.XII.42 [signature] Filatov
Seal: For draft registration on orders of the NKO
N 0315-43 appeared at the commission of the Isetsk RVK
Kurgan Province, 12 June 1943
Regional Draft Board [signature]
Postscript: 16 January 1945 the medical commission of the Isetsk
RVK found unfit under art 12, paragraph I, order 3 36-42
Regional Draft Board [signature]

Archival reference from the Archive of Military-Medical Documents of the Ministry of Defense of the Russian Federation

19 May 1997, N 7/1/1/1471
St. Petersburg
Original, typewritten, archives form

National Humanitarian Foundation
"Living History of the Homeland"

In accordance with the "instruction on Medical evidence, description of illnesses, regulations on determining fitness and table of distribution of certifying military contingents by class and unit," introduced by the order of the People's Commissar of Defense N 226 of 24 October 1942, paragraph I article 12 reads: "Chronic illness of muscular system of a neuropathic character (all forms of myopathy, myotonia, myoplegia, and so on) with a stable disruption of function are 'Unfit with exclusion from the register'."

Under paragraph I article 19, it reads: "Anemia, malignant anemia or bleeding Unfit with exclusion from the register."

Basis: f. 6198, op. 69772, d. 59, p. 23.
Chief of Section 7 [signature] V. Kulishenko

Reference from Ikriano Regional polyclinic

15 December 1975
Original, manuscript, seal of polyclinic

Reference:

Given to Filatov V. K. 1908 that he suffers from a strongly expressed curvature of the spine with secondary radiculitis of the chest and lower back, left-sided lower monoparesis, atherosclerosis of the aorta, and symptomatic hypertonia.

15 / XII 75 [signature]

Reference from Military Commissariat Isetsk Region Tyumen Oblast

8 April 1997, N 4/158
Original, typescript, military commissariat letterhead

Living History of the Homeland Foundation

No documents on the results of the pre-draft medical examination of Vasily Ksenofontovich Filatov have been preserved in the Isetsk military commissariat. We do not have samples of handwriting or photographs of Filatov V. K. The only thing we can report to you is the memories of his student, Honored Teacher of the Russian Federation Anatoli Lavrentievich Emelyanov:

Vasily Ksenofontovich Filatov worked as geography teacher in Isetsk middle school in the prewar years. His students included Myakishev Dmitri, Stakheev Albert, and others. Filatov V. K. had been brought up in an orphanage, had a higher education. As a teacher he knew the material well and conveyed it in an accessible and interesting manner. But he did not control discipline. The reason was this: he told his pupils how in his youth he led a free life and once with his comrades decided to cross the border into Turkey, and they were seen by border guards who shot at them. Filatov fell from the cliff and broke his leg. He was in the hospital, the left healed but was shorter and he limped. They called him "gimp in the hall." Filatov V. K. was not a bad man but he had a flaw: he liked to drink. At the start of the war he married a woman from Krasnovo and moved there. In 1942 an orphanage was founded in Krasnovo. Since there were not enough cadres he had to teach at the village school and the orphanage. In 1943 A. L. Emelyanov was drafted. A. L. Emelyanov does not know the rest of Filatov's life story.

Military Commissar Isetsk Region
Lt. Colonel [signature] Zaikin

Autobiography of V. K. Filatov

19 August 1937
Photocopy of original autobiography (State Archive of Tyumen Province, f. 765, op. 2, d. 556, l.6-6 ob)

Autobiography

I was born in 1908 in the city of Shadrinsk, Chelyabinsk Province, in a family of a shoemaker craftsman. In 1918 I graduated from the fourth grade of the parish school. I lived with my father until 1921. That year my father died and I was left alone, since I had no family. Although I had two uncles, they joined the Red Guards while my father was still alive and disappeared without a trace.

Between 1921 and 1930 I worked as an apprentice in shoe factories in various cities of the Union. In 1930 in the city of Shadrinsk I entered a road building workers' school and graduated (workers' school) in Tyumen in 1934. From 1934 to 1936 I studied at the pedagogical institute TPI, which I graduated as a geography specialist and was sent to work in the Isetsk region.

Now I am working at a middle school, village of Upper-Beshkil, Isetsk Region, Omsk Province.

10/VII/37
[signature]

Autobiography of V. K. Filatov

1967
Original, manuscript, autographed

Autobiography

I, Filatov Vasily Ksenofontovich, was born December 22 1907* in Shadrinsk, Kurgan Province. Before the revolution my father worked as a shoemaker for hire for various people. After the revolution in the shoe cooperative, an industrial artel, in Shadrinsk. During my father's life time I finished the city primary school and started at the Shadrinsk Polytehnicum, where children were taught various trades. I was unable to finish up there due to my father's death in 1921. I went through the famine that began in our district after a failed harvest, and as a result these circumstances forced me to abandon my studies in 1922 and find work. I had to leave my native region, to save myself from starvation. By that time I had almost no relatives left. From 1922 to 1928 I lived and worked in various towns in the European part of our country, including orphanages. In 1928 I began taking courses for elementary school teachers in Grozny, and in 1929 I was sent to work in the village of Aisengur, now Novogroznensk, where I worked for about three years. In 1930 I returned to study by correspondence at the workers' faculty of the Urals Pedagogical Institute in Tyumen. In 1932, I transferred to daytime classes, and after graduating from the workers' faculty in 1934, I continued my studies at the Tyumen Teachers Institute. In 1936 I graduated from the Tyumen Teachers Institute and was sent as a geography teacher to the Isetsk Region in Tyumen Province. I worked in this region until August 10, 1955. While working as a teacher, I continued my correspondence studies at Tyumen State Pedagogical Institute, which I graduated from in 1939. In 1955 I moved to Orenburg Province, due to family circumstances. At the present time I am working as a teacher at Pretoria Middle School of the Novo-Sergievsk Region.

Filatov

*Crossed out "Old Style"
Postscript: Work record shows general work for hire before entering Upper-Beshkil middle school to be 5 years (verbal information)
School: Workers' School 1/IX/32-34.
Pedagogical Institute 1/IX/34-36
From 36 to present teaching
Salary: grades 5-7, 808.50 rubles
grades 8-10, 841.50 rubles
1967.

Letter from experts V. Popov and A. Kovalyov to Professor W. Bonte, director of the Institute for Forensic Medicine, Heine University (Dusseldorf, Germany)

9 September 1994
St. Petersburg
Original, typescript, letterhead of the Department of Forensic Medicine, S. M. Kirov Military-Medical Academy

Esteemed Professor W. Bonte
The Military Medical Academy (St. Petersburg) has been approached by Mrs. Filatova Olga Vasilievna with a request to check through expert analysis her information that she, her sisters Irina, Nadezhda, and her brother, Oleg, are the children of the son of the last Russian Emperor, Nicholas Romanov, Tsarevich Alexei Nikolaevich Romanov, who according to her lived on after 1918 in Russia and died in 1988. A study of the materials she presented (biography, reminiscences of the father and the children, photographs) and the results of tests on the remains found in 1991 near Ekaterinburg, in our opinion, lead to the conclusion that there is weighty evidence for an objective expert test on those factors by specialist in forensic medicine and genetics.

If you have a scholarly interest in doing these tests, we will be happy to participate in a joint study.

Respectfully,
Professor V. Popov
Doctor A. Kovalev

Letter from Professor W. Bonte, Director of the Institute of Forensic Medicine, Heine University to O. V. Filatov

4 July 1995
Dusseldorf
Translation from the German into Russian from the original letter

Esteemed Mr. Filatov.
Hereby I send you a letter about our previous results of research in Russian, intended for Professor Popov and Doctor Kovalyov. I am entrusting and sending it to you for you to pass it on. I have already informed Mr. Kovalev in January which materials we need to move further. In the case that it is possible, we would like a sample of bone from the Ekaterinburg remains that is guaranteed in identification as skeletons of the members of the tsar's family. If there are other samples (for instance, Georgi Romanov), we would be interested in them, too. Moreover, for DNA extraction we need solid bone (compact), for instance, material from the middle part of limb. Around 10 grams is enough for a test. In the case that other bones are used, then it would be better to obtain 15 grams.

We want to analyze the extracted DNA with samples from your family. Only then in our opinion, can we protect ourselves from mistakes.

In hopes of fruitful cooperation,
With best regards,
Yours,
Professor, Doctor of Medicine
W. Bonte

Letter from Professor W. Bonte, Director of the Institute of Forensic Medicine, Heine University to O. V. Filatov

4 July 1995
Dusseldorf
Translation from the German into Russian from the original letter

Esteemed Mr. Filatov,
We have spoken many times about your family and the problem of descent from the last tsar. We have presented you with the first results of the analyses that require further re-testing. We are prepared for that, but in order for the following tests to be independent, we must receive other material to test. I have informed you of this in detail before.

At first I was interested in working in cooperation with the scientists in St. Petersburg. I would like to recommend that you quickly add other international working groups to this project. Out of consideration of objectivity and additional results, the working groups should exchange test and results and re-check on another's work. For St. Petersburg, I would suggest bringing in experts from Finland. Finnish colleagues, according to my data, are much better equipped in scientific technology.

I would be happy to see a working meeting between the various participants in the research in the near future. But my request is to coordinate a suitable date for the meeting as soon as possible.

Best regards,
Yours,
Professor, Doctor of Medecine
W. Bonte

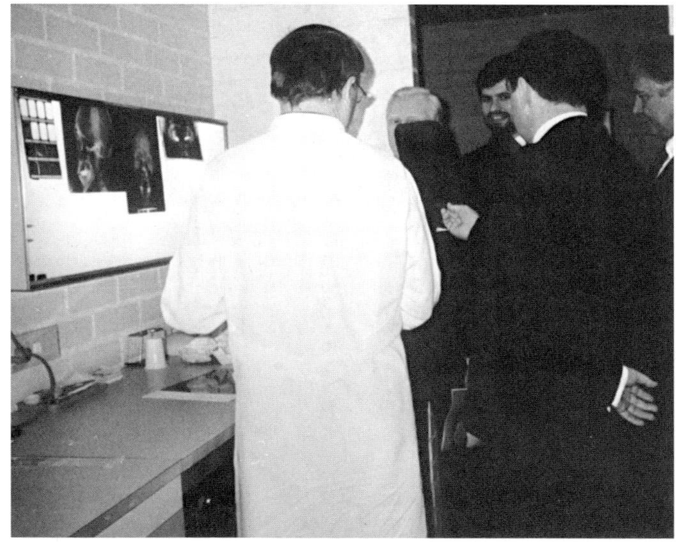

Medical research at the Radiology Department of Helsinki University, November 1995.

Letter from Professor A. Penttil, Head of the Department of Forensic Medicine, Helsinki University, to O. V. Filatov

3 January 1996
Helsinki
Letter sent by fax in Finnish and in Russian

The Department of Forensic Medicine of Helsinki University officially confirms that within the framework of the agreement between the Department and the St. Petersburg Academy of Sciences and Arts (relating to the possible relatedness between the last emperor of Russia, Tsar Nicholas II, his family and the Filatov family), the Department is undertaking forensic medical and forensic dental studies of Russian citizens Oleg Vasilyevich Filatov, Olga Vasilyevna Filatova, and Irina Vasilyevna Mozzheiko (Filatova).

The research includes a clinical examination of the mucous membrane, teeth, a study of the dental status through plaster models, X-ray studies of the jaw and skull (orthopanoramatomography, side projection of skull in cephalostat, RA projection of the skull in cephalostat), as well as DNA of the blood.

On the basis of the tests (the DNA test has not been done yet) the research group feels it necessary to test other living members of the family as well as the remains of Vasily Ksenofontovich Filatov.

On behalf of the research group,
Professor Antti Penttil
Head of the Department

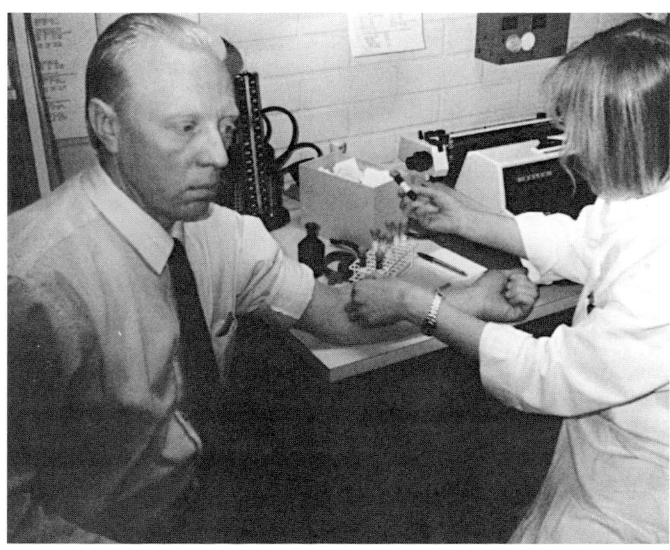

Oleg Filatov giving blood for DNA testing at Helsinki University, November 1995.

Certificate from the Republic Center on Treatment of Hemophilia of the Russian Scientific-Research Institute of Hematology and Transfusiology

24 October 1996, N 802

Original, typescript. Given in response to a request from the Living History of the Homeland Foundation

1. Transfusion therapy with modern blood medications has led to certain success in the treatment of hemophilia, which has led to a steady rise in longevity of hemophiliacs. In the 1940s the average age was 1.65 (Andressean 1943), in the 1960s it was 24 in the severe form and 36 in the light form (Fisher 1966), in the 1970s, forty plus (Z. D. Fedorova, L. P. Papayan 1977), and in the 1980–1990s, over 60 (data of the hemophilia center 1994).

2. Yes, there are hemophiliacs known to have fought in Great Patriotic War, however there has been no statistical work done on the data. The hemophilia center has no information on wounds in hemophiliacs during the war.

3. Yes, hemophiliacs over forty have been known to have children (patient P., born 1949, N i/b 236. Diagnosis: hemophilia A, severe, inhibitory form. First child born in 1992).

4. Oblique determination of whether the father had hemophilia can be made via analysis of the daughters' blood, however a more competent answer to the question can be obtained from geneticists.

5. The basic method of treatment of hemophiliac bleeding is replacement of the blood with blood containing antihemophilial factors. The technology of production of virus-inactiviated and highly purified preparations is constantly being improved in the world. However, intensive replacement therapy for hemophilia patients has led to a growth of various complications. So now methods are being developed using nonspecific activation of hemostasis. In 1960 Bouzdedux et al. used a preparation to increase hemocoagulation made from peanut shells. I. E. Akopov in 1965, 1977 had positive results using lagohilus infusions. A. A. Klement et al. in 1978 studied the qualities of another medicinal herb, ordinary marjoram, a water infusion of which had a hemostatic and sedative effect on hemophiliacs after tooth extraction. Z. S. Barkagan (1974), L. V. Egorova et al. (1982, 1984) successfully prescribed corticosteroid therapy for kidney bleeding. However, prevention and treatment of bleeding caused by injury to joints, stomach and intestinal bleeding, peritoneal bleeding require the use of replacement therapy with preparations with high contact of factor VIII or IX.

6. Hemophilia is the most widespread and severe hereditary hemorrhage diathesis. There are three types of hemophilia.

- Hemophilia A is caused by a deficit of factor VIII, and 85–93% of all cases fall in this group.
- Hemophilia B is caused by a deficit of factor IX, it is also known as Christmas factor, and 13% of all cases belong in this group.
- Hemophilia C is caused by a deficit of factor XI, and only 1–2 % of all cases fall in this group.

The frequency of all types of hemophilia in the population is 13–18 cases per 100,000 of the male population.

The illness is hereditary, passed through the recessive gene, and tied to the X chromosome. It is passed from the ill grandfather through the healthy daughter-carrier to her son. According to the rules of heredity all daughters of a hemophiliac will be a carrier, and all his sons will be healthy. Women–carriers have a 25% chance of having a hemophiliac son or a daughter-carrier and a 25% chance of healthy sons and daughters. Besides the hereditary forms of hemophilia there is illness caused by sporadic mutations that form 20–25% of all cases.

In hemophilia, the hemorrhage manifestations of the hematoma type are predominantly bleeding into the large joints, deep, subcutaneous, intramuscular and intermuscular hematomas, peritoneal hematomas, stomach and intestinal bleeding, hematurias, and lengthy and copious bleeding in traumas, surgical interventions, and tooth extractions.

Classification. The severity of hemorrhage manifestations correlates to the degree of deficit of factor VIII or IX. The Biggs classification is:

with a level of F VIII or IX of 0-1%—extremely severe form
1–2% —severe form
2–5% —medium severe
over 5%—light, but with the possibility of severe bleeding in trauma or surgical intervention.

Besides the Biggs classification, there is also the Wesbach, which takes the clinical picture into account (onset of hemorrhage manifestation, amount of hemorrhages per year, frequency of hospitalization), so that even with the same level of F VIII or IX various patients can have varying severity and frequency of clinical manifestations.

7. The address of the World Federation of Hemophilia is
1310 Greene Avenue, Suite 500
Montreal, Quebec Canada H3Z2 2B2
President: Brian O. Mahoney

Director of the Hemophilia Center [signature] T. A. Andreeva

Statement from the ZAGS Section [Registry Office] of the Central Region of St. Petersburg on the Registration of the Deaths of Romanov A.N. and Romanova M.N.

1 December 1997
Original typescript, form from the ZAGS section of the Administration of the Central Region of St. Petersburg

193144, St. Petersburg, Suvorovsky prospect 41
01.12.1997 N1/70–135
for N 202557 of 26.11.97

To Chairman of the Permanent Commission on Education and Culture
Romankov L.O.
in response to your request—202557
of 26.11.1997

The ZAGS Section [Registry Office] of the Central Region of St. Petersburg informs you that our ZAGS Section indeed has registered the deaths of Romanov Alexei Nikolaevich and Romanova Maria Nikolaevna. The basis for the registration were reports from the FSB [Federal Security Service] of the Russian Federation, Central Archives of Moscow N 10/A-4245 of 26.09.1997.

Chief of the ZAGS section [signature] V. P. Malysheva

Stamp of the Chancellery of the Legislation Assembly of St. Petersburg 05.12.97
202557 and the handwritten notation: To Filatov O.V. (strategy section)

Appeal by O. V. Filatov to Metropolitan Yuvenal of Krutitsk and Kolomna, Chairman of the Commission of the Holy Synod on the Canonization of Saints

23 October 1996
Original, typescript

Your Eminence!

I am submitting for examination by the commission of the Holy Synod on the canonization of saints, of which you are chairman, information on the fate and subsequent life of the son of the last Russian emperor Nicholas II, tsarevich Alexei Nikolaevich Romanov, who miraculously avoided death in the execution of the royal family in 1918 in Ekaterinburg, and who, according to our data, was our father, Filatov Vasily Ksenofontovich.

I believe that this information will help the commission of the Holy Synod decide the question correctly. At the present time I am working with the National Humanitarian Foundation "Living History of the Homeland" on checking the biographical data of my father. I am appending his biography.

Eight years have passed since the death of my father, Vasily Ksenofontovich Filatov. Father did not like talking about his past and did it only when he was in a certain mood. But even if he began, he would suddenly stop and it would be impossible to get any details from him. When we grew up, we discovered many contradictions in our father's life for which we could find no explanation at first. He was a geography teacher who had worked in village schools for thirty-eight years, but his education without a doubt exceeded the limits set by small-town schools and part-time pedagogical institute. Father knew English, German, Latin and Greek. He had an outstanding memory and was an excellent chess player, by correspondence and in blind games. He played all the keyboard instruments, saying that his family had been taught using a number system; he sang tenor; he recited Fet, Tutchev, Esenin, Pushkin, Lermontov, and Chekhov by heart. He performed in amateur theatricals, he painted in water color and oils, drew with pencil, embroidered, and was a good shot. As he had told us, by the age of fourteen he knew his catechism well and he knew prayers by heart.

We know that our grandfather was a shoemaker, and we could not understand how a shoemaker in the years of collapse and civil war could have given his son such an education. But sometimes Father forgot himself and he would speak about an entirely different family, "As a child I was very fair, my hair was curly, everyone loved and babied me, called me 'poo,' and my sisters were also fair-haired, kind and gentle, and when I was sick, my mother loved sitting with me, embroidering with a hoop."

Father was a very sick man. He limped with his left leg, which was almost dried out, significantly shorter than the right, with a scar from a jagged wound on the heel, and he had to use a metal plate under it. He said it was from a shard of a grenade. His arms and back were also scarred and his lower back was severely twisted. Father's blood coagulated poorly, the simplest cut created incredible suffering and it was very difficult to step the bleeding. When he spoke of his parents, he grumbled, "Why did they marry? They knew their children could be born crippled or sick." He avoided using doctors throughout his life, he took ascorbic acid and glucophosphate. In his final years he did breathing exercises and when the pain was bad he repeated "Our Father," the prayer of Xenia the Blessed, and asked St. Seraphim of Sarov to intercede on his behalf, and when it got very very bad, he would take to his bed and say, "Lord, when will I die, how long can I suffer like this? Lord, when will I die?"

Father often told us that we should know history the way it really was and kept returning to the tsar's family, the horrible tragedy in July 1918, which "was impossible to forget," and he insisted that "the family was shot, but the boy survived." At first we ascribed his stories to a knowledge of history, but later we realized that if there were any books and research on the topic, they were completely inaccessible in those days. Later, we decided that Father had all this information in his own memory. Once, hearing the incredible and terrifying details of the death of the royal family and the rescue of Alexei, we asked him straight out: "And you are that boy?" He did not reply, he rose and left the room.

Father told us that on the eve of the execution the guards gave Alexei a white handkerchief wrapped around a Nagan pistol. That night they led them to the cellar, seated them in chairs, and shot at them. The Romanovs wore corsets of diamonds, made in case they could escape. The bullets glanced off, the room began sparking, and the sight frightened the shooters. The tsar fell on top of the boy. It was decided to take them all to the woods and finish them off there. The boy was hit on the head and he regained consciousness when he fell from the truck into the mud. He was tied in a sack and he heard drunken arguing and the voice of one of the guards: "Leave him, he's dead anyway." It was dark and the boy managed to crawl away, get out of the sack, and hobble several dozen meters along the tracks. They found him, forced him with bayonets into a prospecting shaft, and threw a grenade inside.

Father told us about the rest using the first person narrative. The shaft was not deep and the wounded boy, who did not have a single unhurt spot on his body, was found by the woman who watched the signals and she sent for help. Two men, "Uncle Sasha" and "Uncle Andrei," pulled him out of the shaft and took him to Shadrinsk (Chelyabinsk Province). There, in the house of a shoemaker and his brothers, the boy was nursed, but he was an orphan and crippled. They hid him, gave him another name, and changed the year of his birth from 1904 to 1907.

Then, one of the bothers, "Uncle Misha," took our father to Surgut and arranged for him to live and be nursed by the local inhabitants. Father spent the winter of 1919 there. He recalled, "I was treated for loss of blood, I was weak. The northern people made me eat fresh fish, drink herbal infusions, and eat specially prepared raw meat." In 1919–1920 he was in the south, in Sukhumi, where the last ship to Europe, the *Georgy Pobedonosets,* was leaving. Stronger, father returned to Shadrinsk and lived with the shoemaker's family until 1922 and then, when "no family was left," he started moving around. He walked to Nizhny Novgorod and looked for work moving up the Volga. He lived in Moscow and then moved south—to Yalta, Batumi, Tiflis, and Baku, where he worked in the oil fields until 1928. Then he came back to his home ground—"home" was the city of his rescuers, Shadrinsk, the Urals, and Siberia.

In 1936 Father graduated from the Tyumen Institute and was sent to work in the Isetsk Region. By 1955 with Mother he moved to the village of Pretoria, Orenburg Province. After they retired, my parents moved (at Mother's wishes) south, near Astrakhan, where my father died.

With respect for Your Eminence,
23.10.96
[signature] O. V. Filatov

Appeal of V. V. Petrov to Metropolitan Yuvenal of Krutitsk and Kolomna, Chairman of the Commission on the Canonization of Saints

22 October 1996
Original, typescript

To Chairman of the Commission
on the Canonization of Saints
His Excellency
Metropolitan Yuvenal of
Krutitsk and Kolomna

Your Eminence!
I felt it was necessary to appeal to you with this letter for the following reasons. Since 1994 my father, Professor of the Law Department of St. Petersburg State University, doctor of medical sciences, Petrov Vadim Petrovich, and I, as forensics physicians and criminologists, have been studying the problem of the issue of direct relationship between Russian citizen Oleg Vasilievich Filatov with the royal Romanov dynasty. Unfortunately, my father, Professor Petrov V. P., passed away on 10 October 1996, before he could express his written opinion on this matter as he had intended. Our opinions on the possibility of the descent of Filatov O. V. from the Romanov family coincided fully. Therefore I am expressing our joint opinion which in brief can be reduced to the following.

1. There is grave doubt about the so-called Ekaterinburg remains as belonging to the members of the Romanov family and people of their entourage.
2. The remains of Tsarevich Alexei were never found. The possibility of burning a corpse of a fourteen-year-old boy without leaving a trace under the circumstances described in historical literature is infinitesimal from a forensics point of view.
3. The organs of ZAGS have never issued a death certificate for Romanov Alexei Nikolaevich, born 1904, and the time of his death has never been established officially.
4. Preliminary expert analysis of some features of Tsarevich Alexei Nikolaevich Romanov and Vasily Ksenofontovich Filatov, father of Oleg Vasilievich Filatov shows a coincidence or similarity, taking into account the gap in time between the fixation of those features.
5. A study of depictions of the Russian emperors, starting with Alexander II, shows a resemblance with Oleg Vasilievich Filatov.

Thus, on the basis of the above, including results of preliminary stages of complex research in the persons of Tsarevich Alexei and Vasily Ksenofontovich Filatov, we can assume that they are one and the same person. Of course, this question is extremely serious, and therefore it naturally requires additional expert analysis.

I am prepared to meet with Your Eminence at any time convenient to you and to answer any questions.

With profound and sincere respect
Senior Instructor of the Department of criminal process in criminology
of the Law Department of St. Petersburg State University
Candidate of Medical Science
(specialist in forensic medicine, working in it for 13 years)
[signature] V. V. Petrov
22 October 1996

Letter from Archpriest Vladimir Basmanov to Metropolitan Yuvenal of Krutitsk and Kolomna, Chairman of the Commission of the Holy Synod on the Canonization of Saints

9/22 October 1996
Original, manuscript

On the letterhead of the Latvian Orthodox Church,
Holy-Uspenski Church, Balvi, Latvian Republic

To His Eminence Yuvenal
Metropolitan of Krutitsk and Kolomna
Chairman of the Commission of the Holy Synod on the Canonization of Saints

From the Abbot of the Holy-Uspenski Church
Balvi, Blagochinny Madonsky District
Archpriest
Vladimir Basmanov

I, Archpriest Vladimir Basmanov, attest that Mr. Filatov Oleg Vasilievich and his entire family are well known to me as pious Orthodox Christians, who recognize all the Sacraments of our Church, regularly go to confession and take communion. I have performed the Sacrament of the Holy Unction for the whole family, his mother and sisters, and I have heard their confession many times.

On my visit to St. Petersburg we began by revering and praying at the city's holy places: the relics of the Blessed Prince Alexander Nevsky, the Righteous John of Kronstadt, and Xenia the Blessed. We would devote an entire day to this.

The issue on which they, i. e., the Filatov family, are appealing to Your Eminence has many positive factors.

First of all, why should their father, Filatov Vasily Ksenofontovich, tell them before his death about his royal ancestry and send his children down a false path?

Second, there are positive results from the research and analysis done on the relatedness of the Filatov family with the Romanovs.

Third, many of the stories Vasily Ksenofontovich told his children were confirmed by a trip to Shadrinsk by a group of five people (of which I was one).

Conclusive confirmation can be made by the exhumation of the body of Filatov Vasily Ksenofontovich, but that must be done either under the auspices of your Commission or other authorized representatives of the Moscow Patriarchate.

9/22 October 1996
in memoriam of Apostle James
[signature] V. Basmanov
Seal of the Abbot of the Uspenski parish,
Balvi, Latvian Orthodox Church

Archpriests Nikolai Golovkin and Vladimir Basmanov.

Report of Archpriest Nikolai Golovkin to Alexei, Patriarch of Moscow and All Russia

18.10.96
Original, computer printout

To His Beatitude Alexei, Patriarch of Moscow and All Russia
From the Abbot of the Church of Sts. Peter and Paul in Pargolovo
and chairman of the Committee for the Protection of Culture of the Peoples of Russia
Archpriest Nikolai Golovkin

Report:

Your Beatitude, I have been closely acquainted for over a year with Oleg Vasilievich Filatov, a profoundly Christian man, his family, mother and sisters. The Filatovs maintain that they are the children of Tsarevich Alexei Romanov.

As a priest, I have heard their confession many times and I am convinced of their sincerity and honesty. As chairman of the Committee for the Protection of the Culture of the Peoples of Russia, I am helping the Filatov family in getting scientific testing. In particular, the State Archives of the Russian Federation sent samples of the Tsarevich Alexei's handwriting to the Committee for comparison with the handwriting of Vasily Ksenofontovich Filatov. We visited Ekaterinburg and Shadrinsk, where we worked in the archives. We did preliminary studies of the photographs, and so on. On the basis of the above, as well as what Oleg Vasilievich Filatov has told me, I am convinced that this question must be further examined at a higher level.

Your Beatitude's humble servant
Archpriest Nikolai Golovkin
18.10.98 (signature)
Stamp: Archpriest Nikolai Golovkin

Materials of research on samples of handwriting of Alexei Nikolaevich Romanov and Vasily Ksenofontovich Filatov

1977
Original, computer printout
[see illustrations, pages 114–15]

Conclusion of Specialists

From November 4, 1996 through January 17, 1997, the specialists Leonard Nikolaevich Gavrilov and Vadim Vadimovich Petrov conducted research on handwriting.

Mr. Gavrilov received his higher education in law, specializing in crime detection. He has worked in this field for more than 45 years, mainly as an associate professor. He has a master's degree in legal science, specializing in the criminal process and crime detection.

Mr. Petrov received his higher education in law and medicine, specializing in forensic medicine and crime detection for 14 years. He is an experienced teacher of forensic medicine and crime detection. He has a master's degree in medical science, specializing in forensic medicine.

Oleg Vasilievich Filatov submitted for investigation:

1. Six letters (photocopies):
1.1. From December 15, 1916, beginning with the words: "Headquarters, December 15 . . ." and ending with: ". . . Faithfully yours, Alexei."
1.2. From February 12, 1917, beginning with the words: "Tsarkoe Selo . . ." and ending with: ". . . a big kiss from Your Alexei."
1.3. From March 13, 1917, beginning with the words: "Tsarkoe Selo, March 13, 1917 . . ." and ending with ". . . God keep you, Your Alexei."
1.4. From June 16, 1917, beginning with the words: "Tsarkoe Selo, June 16, 1917 . . ." and ending with ". . . a big kiss from Your Alexei."
1.5. From November 27, 1917, beginning with the words: "Tobolsk, November 27, 1917" and ending with "God [keep] you! And how's Pulka!!!"
1.6. From January 7, 1918, beginning with the words: "Tobolsk, January 7, 1918 . . ." and ending with: ". . . Your loving Alexei."

2. Five pages from a diary with notes, written by hand (photocopies):
2.1. Page 4, with the text: "Received Captain K. Kiker at my home today 12 Sibirskavo construction regiment . . ."
2.2. Page 5, beginning with the words: "Got up this morning . . ." and ending with: ". . . was in bed at ten o'clock."
2.3. Page 312, beginning with the words: "Didn't go to church . . ." and ending with: ". . . played and read."
2.4. Page 352, beginning with the words: "Arm has worms . . ." and ending with: ". . . Went to bed early."
2.5. Page 353, beginning with the words: "The day passed as usual . . ." and ending with: ". . . Went to bed early."

3. Handwriting samples of Vasily Ksenofontovich Filatov:
3.1. A handwritten copy of certificate No. 56 from August 7, 1948, in the name of Lydia Kuzminichna Klimenkova.
3.2. A handwritten autobiography, dated 1967.
3.3. A handwritten copy of certificate No. 52 from July 12, 1957.
3.4. A handwritten copy of an unnumbered certificate form August 7, 1967.
3.5. A sheet from a notebook, with handwritten text recording the temperatures for January and February 1966.
3.6. A handwritten text (notes) Nos. 4–5 on 2–5 pages in a workbook in the name of V. K. Filatov, issued on February 16, 1939.
3.7. A handwritten certificate in the name of Lydia Kuzminichna Filatova, concerning work from January 9, 1955 through December 1, 1966. (photocopy)
3.8. A sheet of paper from a notebook with handwritten notes, beginning with the words: "We congratulate you . . ." and ending with: ". . . going well." (photocopy)
3.9. Two sheets of paper from a notebook with handwritten notes from the year 1966. (photocopy)
3.10. Two sheets of paper with handwritten notes concerning solutions to chess problems. (photocopy)
3.11. Two sheets of paper with handwritten notes concerning hourly and weekly school commitments. (photocopy)
3.12. A sheet of paper with handwritten notes, beginning with the words: "Handed over to the State . . ." and ending with: ". . . Makarov, Sukha." (photocopy)
3.13. A letter dated August 31, 1985, beginning with the words: "Hello Natasha! . . ." and ending with ". . . at grandma Barishnikova's, in the hut."

The specialists are asked to determine whether the six letters (dated from December 15, 1916 through January 7, 1918) and notes on five pages submitted from a diary were written by Vasily Ksenofontovich Filatov.

INVESTIGATION
Photocopies of six letters, dated from December 15, 1916 through January 7, 1918, and photocopies of five pages from a diary with handwritten notes, are presented for investigation. The pages from the diary have been numbered 4, 5, 312, 352, 353 by a printer. The handwriting, which is put forth in the letters and notes from the diary, resembles school handwriting. This script is characterized by a small degree of skill, average tempo, a slant to the right, large and medium-sized letters, and small connections between letters. Most of the letters are written to an adequate degree of stability (stereotypical). On the fifth page of the diary the tempo of the first half of the notes is higher in comparison to the second half. The handwriting samples of Vasily Ksenofontovich Filatov are characterized by a higher and higher degree of skill, varying from an average to a fast tempo, a slant to the right, medium-sized letters, average coherence. A comparative analysis of the handwriting, exhibited in the six letters (dated from December 15, 1916 through January 7, 1918) and the notes from five pages of a diary in the script of V. K. Filatov, established a large number of concurrences between certain characters, among them the following variations:

The letter "a"
1. Form of motion upon execution of the initial part of the first element—oval, arched (1);
2. The point where motion begins—inside the oval, in its upper half (2);
3. Form of motion joining the elements of the letter—looped, angular (3).

The letter "b"
1. Form of motion on execution of the initial part of the letter—oval, arched (4,5);
2. Shape and direction of motion on execution of the second element—an arch curved to the left, turning into an angular motion in a straight line, practically horizontal (6).

The letter "v"
1. Form of motion on execution in connection with the following letters—looped, turning into an arch (7);
2. The point where motion begins—to the left, on level with the middle line of the second element (8).

The letter "g"
1. Form on execution of the initial and lower-case parts—angular (9, 10).

The letter "d"
1. Form of motion on execution of the initial part—oval (11);
2. Type of connection between elements—evenly spaced (12);
3. Motion comes to a stop to the right of the letter and on level with the line, or slightly higher (13);
4. Crossing motion comes to a stop in the lower part of the second element—on level with or below the line (14);
5. Structure of the letter as a whole—a variation of elements above and below the line (15).

The letter "D"
1. Form of motion on execution of joining the elements—looped (16);
2. Motion comes to a stop to the left of the first element (17);
3. Crossing motion comes to a stop upon execution of the final part, at the upper part of the first element (18).

The letter "e"
1. Motion begins from the left, in the middle of the line.

The letter "z"
1. Construction: the second element lacks closure to the left. This element is placed on the line and slightly lower (19);
2. Form of motion on connection of the elements is angular (20).

The letter "i"
1. Motion begins enthusiastically, that is, with a preliminary stroke (21);
2. Form of motion joining the elements is angular, rectilinear on return (22, 23).

The letter "k"
1. Direction of motion on execution of the second element—upwards (24).

The letters "l, m"
1. Form of motion on execution of the initial part of the first element is a fixed point or an angular motion, ending with more pressure than the following strokes (25, 26);
2. Form of motion joining the elements is angular, looped.

The letter "n"
1. Form of motion on execution of the second element—}arched, but closer to rectilinear (27);

The letter "o"
1. Motion ends at the top of the letter and in the middle of the line, inside and to the left of the oval (28).

The letter "P"
1. Executed enthusiastically, that is, with a preliminary stroke (29).

The letter "r"
1. Form of motion on execution of the second element—oval, angular, arched (30, 31).

The letter "s"
1. Form of motion on execution of the first part—with a point and oval (32);
2. Form of motion when following the letters "V" and "B"—looped, changing to straight (33).

The letter "t"
1. Form of motion joining the elements—angular (34);
2. The horizontal bar above the letter extends to the length of the letter.

The letter "u"
1. Form of motion on execution of the lowercase part of the first element—angular (35);
2. Executed enthusiastically, that is, with a preliminary stroke (36);
3. Crossing motion upon execution of the second element—below the line of text (37);
4. Horizontal motion of the lower part of the second element relative to that of the first element—shifted somewhat to the left (38).

The letter "x"
1. Form of motion on execution—arched (39).

The letters "ts" and "shch"
1. Form of motion on execution of the lower element, arched to the right.

The letter "ch"
1. Form of motion on execution of the first element—rectilinear or arched, becoming an arch to the left or rectilinear (40,41).

The letter "sh"
1. Relative length of the lower horizontal element—}equal to the width of the letter.

The letter "y"
1. Size of the looped part of the first element—small (42).

Along with the coinciding characteristics noted upon investigation of the letters, notes from a diary, and handwriting samples from V. K. Filatov, the following differences are revealed:
—degree of skill (A higher degree of skill in the handwriting samples of V. K. Filatov.)
—tempo of the letters (In the handwriting samples of V. K. Filatov, the tempo varies from average to fast, that is, for the most part, fast.)
—size of the letters (In the handwriting samples of V. K. Filatov, the letters are of average size, but in some sections of the six letters and five pages of a diary the letters are large.)
—connection between letters (In the handwriting samples of V. K. Filatov, the connection is average, but in the six letters and five pages of a diary the connection is smaller.)
—individual characters
Differences in individual characters:
The letter "B"
1. Structure: ordinary. In the handwriting samples of V. K. Filatov: simplified (1).

The letter "V"
1. Type of connection between the first and second elements—evenly spaced. In the handwriting samples of V. K. Filatov: unbroken (2).

The letter "ZH"
1. Structure of the letter is simple. In the handwriting samples of V. K. Filatov it is oversimplified by means of a straight motion.

The letter "I"
1. This letter is curved to the left. In the handwriting samples of V. K. Filatov it curves to the right (3).

The letter "P"
1. Structure of the letter is simple. In the handwriting samples of V. K. Filatov it is oversimplified (4).

The letter "ts"
1. Form of motion on execution of the lower element—looped. In the handwriting samples of V. K. Filatov it is arched (5).

The letter "ya"
1. Direction of motion on execution of the final part—from left to right. In the handwriting samples of V. K. Filatov, it is from right to left (6).

The number "2"
1. The initial part is curved to the left, but in the handwriting samples of V. K. Filatov it is curved to the right.

EVALUATION OF RESULTS

Evaluating the results of this comparative investigation allows us to arrive at the following opinion: The small number of differences discovered in the general and specific features of the records studied can be explained by the large interval of time that elapsed between the six letters and diary pages that were written in 1916–1918 and the letters and manuscripts written later by Vasily Filatov. The differences that were discovered in a few general features, and in a small number of specific features, in the handwriting samples are not sufficient grounds for concluding that the writing samples studied were executed by different people. In the process of an individual's personal development, the level of one's writing changes, the general features of one's handwriting change, and improve, and the specific features of one's handwriting can change as well. No inexplicable differences were discovered in the investigation between the executor of the diary and the six letters of 1916–1918 and Vasily Filatov's handwriting samples taken later. The differences in the general features and in a small number of specific features that were found during the course of the research can be fully attributed to the development of his writing (written speech) over the course of time.

The research has revealed similarities in the general and specific features of the handwriting. Each of the coinciding general and specific features taken alone is not unusual or rare. However, the discovery of such a large number of specific features coinciding in the handwriting samples studied as compared to the very small number of differences allows us to arrive at a very high degree of confidence in our conclusion that the writing samples studied (the six letters of 1916–1918, the five diary pages, and the handwriting samples from Vasily Filatov) were written by one and the same person.

CONCLUSION

Our research allows us to conclude that the writing samples we studied (the six letters of 1916–1918, the five diary pages, and the handwriting samples from Vasily Filatov) were written by one and the same person.

Specialists: L. N. Gavrilov [signature]
V. V. Petrov [signature]

Letter of A.V. Kovalyov, candidate for a doctor's degree of the Military-Medical Academy, to O.V. Filatov

June 6, 1996
Original, computer printout

On your request, I present to you an extract from my doctoral thesis on the subject of "Medical-jurisprudential identification through the structure of the chest and spine," which was submitted for defense to the Military–Medical Academy. (pp. 89, 90, 243)

The research fulfilled did not refute for certain the relationship in descent between the Filatov family and the members of the Romanov family. Owing to that fact, I consider it necessary to support and finance the continuation of investigations with employment of X-ray and genetic methods of mathematical analysis of obtained resutls.

Consideration of existing claims concerning the disappearance of the family members of Nicholas II; the Filatov family archives and research carried out have established grounds for a thorough scientific examination into the Filatov family's claim of their relationship to Alexei Romanov.

A.V. Kovalyov
Candidate for a doctor's degree from the Military–Medical Academy
Candidate [equivalent to a master's degree] of Medical Science

[Page 89]
Table 2.1.3.

Description of the state of the examined corpse material, researched under the resolutions of the department of the public prosecutor.

Description of the object's state	Number of objects
Expressed forms of late corpse phenomenon	2
Complete skeletoning of corpse	3
Damage to corpse by animals	2
Charring of corpse	5
Damage to face and brain of skeleton	4
Absence of the face of the skeleton	

III. The group of objects was researched in 1992–1995 on the basis of Ekaterinburg's regional Bureau of Medical–Jurisprudential commission of experts;

Departments of Medical–Jurisprudence, Surgery and Stomatology of the Military–Medical Academy and Orthopoedic Stomatology of the St. Petersburg Medical University named for I. P. Pavlov.

The research was executed within the realization of the jurisprudential-medical examinations into the affair of the death of members of the Romanov family in 1918–1920.

The purpose of the investigation was a working and practical approval of specific methods of chest and spine research for medical-jurisprudential identification.

The description and the number of objects researched are presented in table 2.1.4

[Page 90]
Table 2.1.4

Characteristics and the number of researched material touched upon in the expert's investigations of the affair of the death of the members of the Romanov family in 1918–1920.

Characteristics of objects researched	Number of objects
1. The remains of corpses found near Ekaterinburg	9
2. The remains of Grand Duke Georgy, son of Alexander, exhumed from the Cathedral of Saints Peter and Paul in St. Petersburg, in 1994	1
3. The Filatov family, living in St. Petersburg and Germany	4
4. Posthumous X-rays of the chest and spine	4
5. X-rays of the spines of living people	6

A special feature of this group was that it included not only the remains of corpses with the difference in time of nearly 76–96 years, but living persons, having claims to relationship to the Romanov family.

The characteristics of the state of the researched corpse material is presented in table 2.1.5.

[Page 243]

. . . The realization of 14 similar individual signs of the neck section of the spine structure were revealed, which can indicate the relationship of descent of the persons under investigation.

The results obtained are of great practical importance because they make it possible to ascertain independently or in aggregate with genetic analysis the relationship of descent of the persons.

For the present, this information is undoubtedly of propounding nature and should become the subject of independent scientific research.

Materials of the research on photo images of Alexei Nikolaevich Romanov and Vasily Ksenofontovich Filatov

1997
Original, computer printout

CONCLUSION OF SPECIALISTS

From February 24 through April 21, 1997, the specialists Leonard Nikolaevich Gavrilov and Vadim Vadimovich Petrov conducted research that requires specialized knowledge of crime detection and medicine.

Mr. Gavrilov received his higher education in law, specializing in crime detection, which he has worked in for more than 45 years, mainly as an associate professor. He has a master's degree in legal science, specializing in the criminal process and crime detection.

Mr. Petrov received his higher education in law and medicine, specializing in forensic medicine and crime detection for 14 years. He is an experienced teacher of forensic medicine and crime detection, and received his master's degree in medical science, specializing in forensic medicine.

Oleg Vasilievich Filatov submitted the following for investigation:

1. 17 black-and-white rectangular photographs, dimensions 13.1 x 8.9 cm to 24 x 18.2 cm, portraying a young person of the male gender, ages 1.5–2 years to 13–14 years. In the photographs, the young male is shown singly or among groups of different numbers of people. Several of the photographs are copies from the same negative. Some photographs show signs of having been retouched or enhanced in places.

2. 12 black-and-white rectangular photographs, dimensions 13 x 18.7 cm to 18.1 x 12.6 cm, portraying a man from a relatively young age to a mature middle age. In the photographs, the man is shown singly or among small groups of people. Several of the photographs are copies from the same negative.

3. 10 photocopies of photographs. The photocopies were done on standard rectangular sheets of paper, dimensions 29.7 x 20.9 cm. The photocopies portray a young person and a man.

4. 14 printouts of computer-enhanced photographs. The printouts were done on standard rectangular sheets of paper, dimensions 29.7 x 20.9 cm. The printouts portray the head and separate parts of the face of a young person and a man. Some photocopies are composed of various enlargements from the same image.

The specialists are asked to determine if these pictures of a young male and a man are all images of one and the same person.

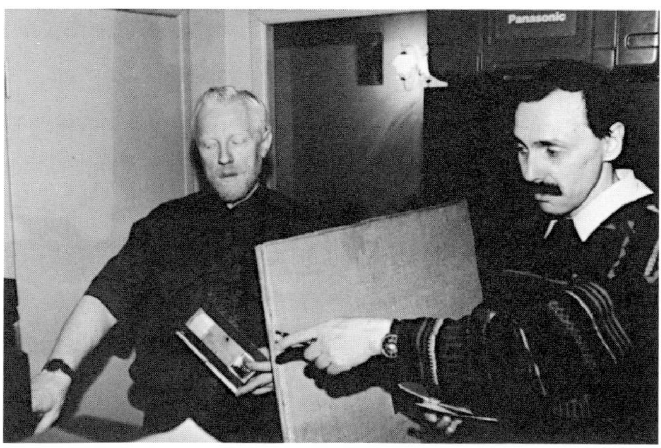

Oleg Filatov and Vadim Petrov researching the photographic depictions of Tsarevich Alexei and Vasily Filatov, 1997, St. Petersburg.

INVESTIGATION

The following items were presented for investigation: photographs, photocopies and printouts of photographs enhanced on a computer (for the purpose of increasing the contrast between details in the picture). In all, 53 items were submitted for investigation.

An investigation of the items presented was carried out in order to study the characteristics of the structure of the face and head of the young male and the adult male represented. This structure was studied in accordance with a system of the elements of a "verbal portrait." It was concluded that the photographs of the young male and the adult male share identical characteristics for the following features:

1. Head
Average size relative to torso.

2. Face
Average width. Contour of the full face appears oval, widening at the top.

3. Forehead
Average height, closer to tall. Wide width. (A wide forehead).

4. Eyebrows
Eyebrows of average length, width, and thickness. Contour is weakly arched, closer to straight. Interrelation of the eyebrows: far apart.

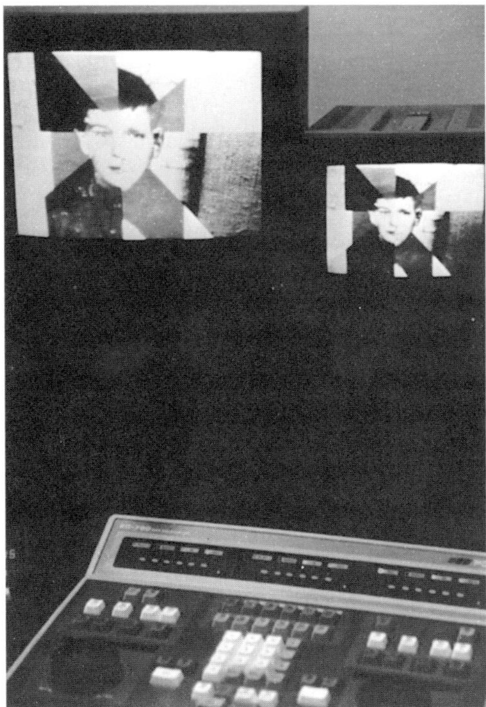

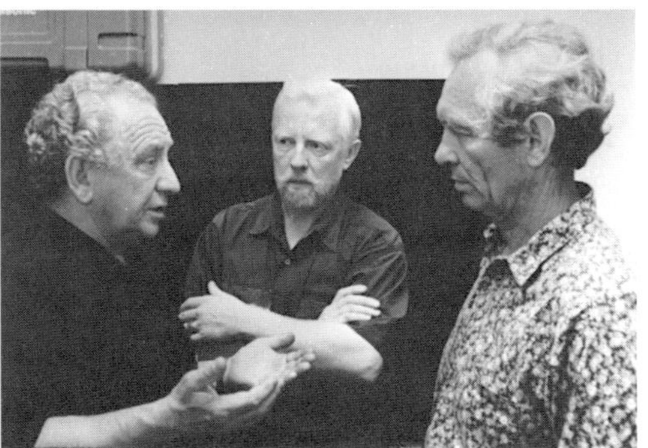

LEFT AND TOP RIGHT: Research of the photographic depictions of Tsarevich Alexei and Vasily Filatov, 1997, St. Petersburg.
BOTTOM RIGHT: Discussing the results of video analysis. From left to right: criminologist Leonard Gavrilov, Oleg Filatov, and television studio director Valery Polyakov, 1997, St. Petersburg.

5. Eyes
Average size, oval contour.

6. Nose
Average size, closer to large. Average width between nostrils. Contour is rather straight. The tip is of average width, bordering on large. Round tip.

7. Mouth
Average size. Corners of the mouth are higher than the horizontal line of the mouth.

8. Lips
Average thickness, closer to thin. Both lips protrude evenly. Contour of the red edge of the lip is arched, but closer to straight, with a slight bow-shape.

9. Chin
Average length. Protrudes forward slightly. Contour of the chin is round in full face.

An analysis of the characteristics of the structure of the head and face of the young male and adult male establishes their similarity by lack of clearly defined differences. The results of this analysis permit us to move on to a search and investigation of specific (individual) characteristics. For the study of these particular characteristics, materials were selected which showed the young male and the adult male in practically the same position. It was concluded that the young male and the adult male share the following distinctive features:

1. Contour of eyebrows
The contour of the left eyebrow is more broken than the contour of the right one. The left brow has a break in the middle.

2. Placement of irises in the eye
A weak expression of dissipated crossed-eyes. (Hidden cross-eyes.)

3. Contour of the face in the lower jaw
The left side is more round, while the right side has a distinct corner.

4. Cross-section of the eyes
A cross-section of the left eye is more level than a cross-section of the right eye. (The latter is more slanted. In particular, the outer corner of the right eye is lower than the inner corner of that eye.)

5. Inter-arrangement of the corners of the eyes
The inner corner of the right eye is higher than the inner corner of the left eye. The outer corner of the right eye is somewhat lower than the outer corner of the left eye.

6. Distance between the inner corners of the eyes
The distance between the inner corners of the eyes is somewhat greater than the distance between the borders of the nostrils of the nose.

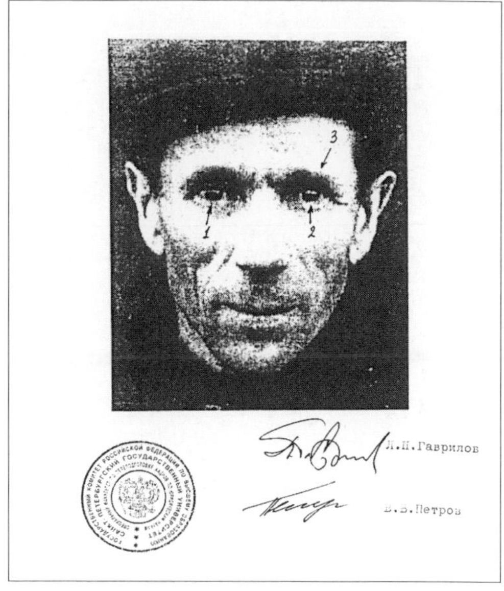

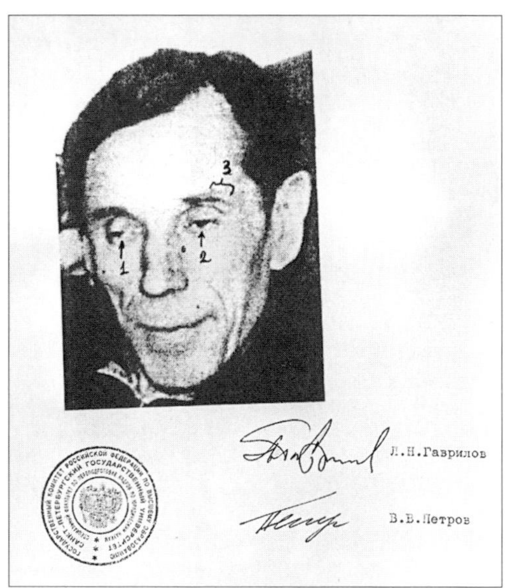

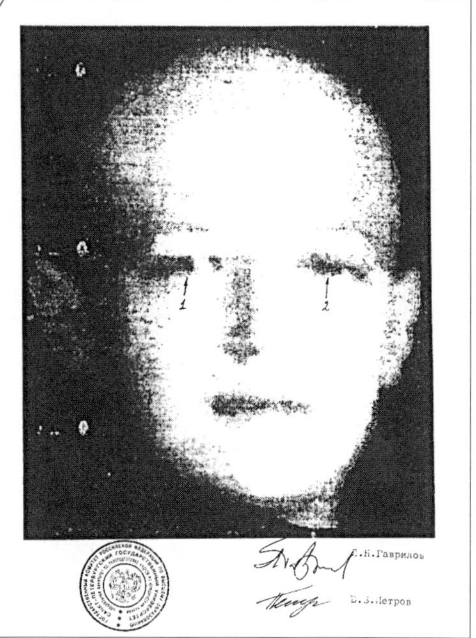

Photographic analysis comparing depictions of Alexei Romanov (upper left and lower right) and Vasily Filatov (upper right and lower left) with a superimposed layout showing identical distinctive features.

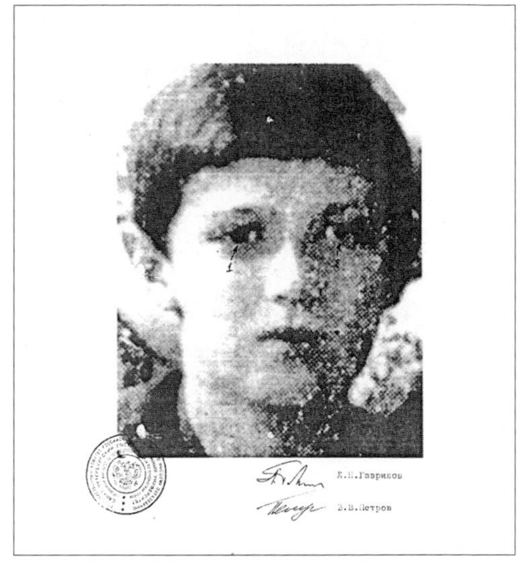

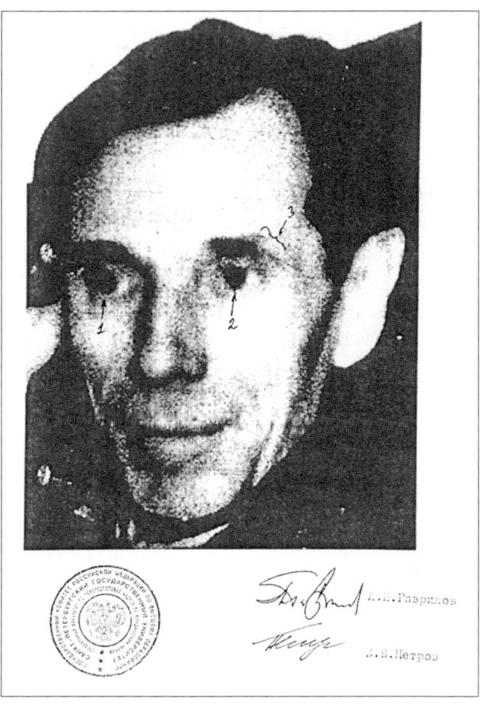

Photographic analysis comparing depictions of Alexei Romanov (upper right and lower left) and Vasily Filatov (upper left and lower right) with a superimposed layout showing identical distinctive features.

7. Distinctive features of the base of the nose
The base of the left half of the nose is on a slightly lower level than the base of the right half of the nose.

8. Corners of the mouth
Located practically on the same level.

9. Placement of the lower edges of the earlobes
The bottom of the left earlobe is lower than the bottom of the right earlobe.

10. Vertical contour of the bridge of the nose
The left contour is almost rectilinear; the right contour is in the form of a convex arch.

11. Outer opening of the nose
The left nostril is larger than the right one.

Upon a comparison of the entire correlation by means of an investigation of the examined characteristics of these two images, presented in columns three and four of table No. 2, it is established that they are identical and do not have any significant differences (explainable or unexplainable).

EVALUATION OF RESULTS
Evaluating the results of the comparative investigation allows us to arrive at the following opinion: An investigation of the portraits presented in the photographs revealed a large number of coinciding general and specific features in the structure of the heads and faces of the adolescent and the man. Also, despite the long interval between the time the photographs of the adolescent and the man were taken, we discovered no significant differences. The discovery of such a large number of coinciding general and specific features in the absence of significant differences allows us to conclude, with a high degree of certainty, that the photographs and printouts portray the same person at different times in his life.

CONCLUSION
Our research permits us to conclude, with a high degree of certainty, that the photographs and printouts portray the same person at different times in his life.

Specialists: L. N. Gavrilov [signature]
V. V. Petrov [signature]

ПРИЛОЖЕНИЕ №2

К заключению специалистов от 21 апреля 1997 года.

Часть представленных листов бумаги с ксерокопиями фотографий и принтерными распечатками изображений молодого человека и мужчины (листы 1-11).

На листах 8, 9, 10, 11 обозначены: цифрами 1 и 2 расходящееся косоглазие, цифрами 3 нарушение (перерыв) контура левой брови.

На листах 1, 2 ,7 обозначено цифрами 1 и 2 расходящееся косоглазие.

На листе 5 обозначено цифрой 3 нарушение (перерыв) контура левой брови.

Л.Н. Гаврилов

В.В. Петров

Addendum to the conclusion of specialists regarding the photographic analysis of Alexei Romanov and Vasily Filatov. On the preceding pages, the numerals 1 and 2 marked on the photographs indicate strabismic eyes; numeral 3 indicates the break in the contour of the left eyebrow.

Precipitation Table

Data on the Amount of Precipitation in the Ekaterinburg Region

1921

Precipitation in inches	Jan.	Feb.	Mar.	Apr.	May	June	July	Aug.	Sept.	Oct.	Nov.	Dec.
Water Evaporation (1887—1915)	.15	.29	.76	1.86	3.29	3.49	3.42	2.66	1.86	1.10	.37	.16
Average Amount of Precipitation (1836—1920)	.47	.39	.47	11.27	1.76	2.77	2.89	1.37	1.52	1.01	.90	.66
Greatest Monthly Precipitation (1836—1929)	1.91	1.33	1.40	2.54	1.76	6.83	8.31	7.80	4.91	3.94	3.51	1.21
Lowest Monthly Precipitation (1836—1920)	0	0	0	0	.16	.62	.43	.59	0	.04	.04	0

Endnotes

■ preface ■

1. Sokolov, "The report of the interrogation of N.A. Sokolov, court investigator of especially important affairs." Tsentr Khraneniia i Izucheniia Documentov Noveishei Istorii (The Russian Center of Preserving and Studying the Documents of Recent History), fond 588, inventory 3c, file 3, pp. 24–32.
2. From the letter of Markushevich to the editor of the review *Proletarskaia revolutsia,* Leningrad, November 15, 1929. Tsentr Khraneniia i Izucheniia Documentov Noveishei Istorii (The Russian Center of Preserving and Studying the Documents of Recent History), fond 588, inventory 3c, file 21, pp. 1–2.

■ chapter 1 ■

1. Gumilyov, *Poiski vymyshlennogo tsarstvo.*
2. Kasvinov, *Dvadsat' tri stupeni vniz; Padenie tsarskogo rezhima.*
3. Voeikov, p. 124.
4. Ibid.; Oldenburg.
5. Hanbury-Williams, *The Emperor Nicholas II as I Knew Him.*
6. Alexandrov, *The End of the Romanovs.*
7. Voeikov, p. 154.
8. Ibid., pp. 156–57.
9. Voeikov, pp. 158–59.
10. Grand Duke Kirill Vladimirovich, *Moia zhizn' na sluzhbe Rossii.*
11. Oldenburg, p. 632.
12. Oldenburg, p. 637; Platonov, *Ternovyi venets Rossii.*
13. Oldenburg, pp. 637–38.
14. Voeikov, p. 137.
15. Ibid., pp. 133–35.
16. Ibid., p. 135.
17. Ibid., p. 136.
18. Ibid.
19. Ibid., pp. 138, 139.
20. Shavelsky, pp. 289–90.
21. Voeikov, pp. 141–42.
22. Ibid., p. 144.
23. Ibid., p. 150.

■ chapter 2 ■

1. Voeikov, p. 192.
2. Miliukov, *Vospominaniia,* p. 301.
3. Alexandrov, pp. 377, 379.
4. Sorokin, pp. 112–17.
5. Voeikov, pp. 181–85.
6. Miliukov, p. 301; Sorokin, p. 105.
7. Sorokin, pp. 106–7.
8. Pankratov, "V Tobolske."

9. Alexandrov; Vilton; Sokolov, *Ubiistvo tsarskoi sem'i;* Mosolov.
10. Sokolov, *Popytka osvobozhdeniia tsarskoi sem'i.*
11. Kasvinov, pp. 403, 429.
12. Platonov, p. 371.
13. Kasvinov, p. 372.
14. Heuer.
15. Alexandrov, pp. 205, 211, 212.
16. Alekseev, p. 62.
17. Bykov, *Poslednie dni Romanovykh,* p. 80.
18. This is the opinion of Sokolov, *Ubiistvo tsarskoi sem'i,* pp. 44–45; Heuer; Alexandrov, p. 215; Pares; and Summers and Mangold.
19. Alekseev, pp. 52–82.
20. Ibid., pp. 53–63.
21. Ibid., p. 64.
22. Ibid., pp. 64–65.
23. Diterikhs, pt. 1, p. 46.
24. Dnevnik Nikolaia II, p. 574.

chapter 3

1. Platonov, pp. 391–92.
2. Ibid., p. 427.
3. Ibid., p. 426.
4. Diterikhs, pt. 1, pp. 56–58.
5. *Pis'ma sviatykh tsarstvennykh,* p. 342.
6. Primary information on the execution and burial of the tsar's family is contained in the descriptions, memoirs, and depositions of participants in the event: Yurovsky (Alekseev, pp. 108–16; Popov, pp. 31–38; 53; 54); Ermakov (Popov, pp. 38–41; Platonov, pp. 431–32); Mikhail Medvedev (Popov, pp. 41–46; Alekseev, pp. 119–31; Platonov, pp. 433–35); Nikulin (Popov, pp. 46–47; Alekseev, pp. 131–34); and Rodzinsky (Popov, pp. 47–48; Alekseev, pp. 134–38); as well as witnesses to the event: Sukhorukov (Alekseev, pp. 117–18); Strekotin (Platonov, pp. 429–31); and Netrebin (Platonov, pp. 425, 431); and participants in the investigation: Diterikhs (Diterikhs), Sokolov (Sokolov, *Ubiistvo tsarskoi sem'i*), and Vilton (Vilton). Most of the information extracted from archives in recent years has been concentrated in the works of Alekseev. (For the reader's convenience, the reminiscences of Yurovsky (1934) and Mikhail Medvedev (recorded by his son and turned into the archive in 1964), which we cite most often, are reprinted at the end of this chapter, pp. 65–76. Excerpts from these reminiscences are quoted in the text and not footnoted.)
7. *Pis'ma sviatykh tsarstvennykh,* pp. 331, 348; Popov, pp. 274, 275.
8. *Taina tsarskikh ostankov,* pp. 92–109; Sokolov, *Ubiistvo tsarskoi sem'i,* pp. 210–24; Popov, pp. 153–70.
9. Zhuk, pp. 38, 50–51.
10. Ibid., pp. 227–28.
11. Ibid., pp. 235–37.
12. Ibid., pp. 257–58.
13. *Taina tsarskikh ostankov,* p. 104.
14. Sokolov, *Ubiistvo tsarskoi sem'i,* p. 224.
15. Ibid., pp. 217, 224.
16. *Taina tsarskikh ostankov,* p. 104.
17. Sokolov, *Ubiistvo tsarskoi sem'i,* pp. 217–22.
18. *Taina tsarskikh ostankov,* p. 104.

19. Zhuk, p. 50.
20. Ibid., p. 38.
21. Ibid., p. 38.
22. Platonov, p. 454.
23. Ibid., p. 430; Smirnov, p. 33.
24. Platonov, p. 454.
25. *Pis'ma sviatykh tsarstvennykh,* p. 348.
26. Sokolov, *Ubiistvo tsarskoi sem'i,* p. 213.
27. Platonov; Diterikhs; Radzinsky, *Gospodi.*
28. *Taina tsarskikh ostankov*, p. 94.
29. Sokolov, *Ubiistvo tsarskoi sem'i,* p. 215.
30. *Taina tsarskikh ostankov,* pp. 95–97.
31. Platonov, p. 431.
32. *Pis'ma sviatykh tsarstvennykh,* p. 353.
33. Alekseev, pp. 111–12.
34. *Pis'ma sviatykh tsarstvennykh,* p. 353.
35. Sokolov, *Ubiistvo tsarskoi sem'i,* pp. 273–93; Radzinsky, *Gospodi,* pp. 437, 447.
36. The Yurovsky Note (Zapiska Yurovskogo) was written in 1920, the Yurovsky's reminiscences (Alekseev, pp. 108–16) in 1934.
37. Alekseev, p. 128.
38. Popov, p. 34; The Yurovsky Note.
39. The Ermakov Note.
40. Alekseev, p. 114.
41. Buranov and Khrustalev, *Ubiitsy tsaria,* p. 340.
42. Froianov, *Oktiabr'semnadtsatogo (gladia iz nastoiashchego).*
43. Alekseev, p. 104.
44. Ibid., p. 105.
45. Ibid., pp. 105–6.

■ chapter 4 ■

1. Diterikhs, pt. 1, p. 79.
2. Paganutstsi, pp. 86–87.
3. Diterikhs, pt. 1, p. 106.
4. Ibid., pt. 1, p. 109.
5. Ibid., pt. 1, pp. 109–14.
6. Ibid., pt. 1, p. 113.
7. Kasvinov, p. 502.
8. Diterikhs, pt. 1, p. 114.
9. Bogoslovskaia, "Poslednii russkii tsar'."
10. Diterikhs, pt. 1, pp. 168, 170, 173.
11. Ibid., pt. 1, p. 170.
12. Sokolov, *Ubiistvo tsarskoi sem'i,* pp. 210–24.
13. *Taina tsarskikh ostankov*, pp. 104–8.
14. Sokolov, *Ubiistvo tsarskoi sem'i,* pp. 279–94.
15. Ibid., p. 213.
16. Ibid., p. 272.
17. Ibid., p. 282.
18. Ibid., pp. 273, 279, 283, 289, 293.
19. Ibid., pp. 271, 272.

20. Ibid., pp. 255, 256.
21. Ibid., p. 256.
22. Ibid., p. 271.
23. Summers and Mangold.
24. Smetanina.
25. Summers and Mangold.
26. Ferro.
27. *Ubiistvo tsarskoi.*
28. *Ventsenosnye velikomucheniki.*
29. Diterikhs, *Ubiitsvo tsarkoi sem'i.*
30. Bykov, "Poslednie dni poslednego tsaria."
31. Bykov, *Poslednie dni Romanovykh.*
32. Summers and Mangold, pp. 175–81.
33. Alekseev, p. 32.
34. Bykov, "Poslednie dni poslednego tsaria," p. 305.
35. Bykov, *Poslednie dni Romanovykh,* p. 87.
36. Ibid., p. 95.
37. Alekseev, pp. 108–15.
38. Ibid., p. 136.
39. Ibid., pp. 117, 118.
40. Diterikhs, pt. 1, pp. 217–18.
41. Ibid., pt. 1, p. 182.
42. Ibid.
43. Paganutstsi, p. 94.
44. *Taina tsarskikh ostankov,* pp. 15–18.
45. Popov, p. 79.
46. *Taina tsarskikh ostankov*, pp. 17, 18; Pis'mo glavnogo sudebno-meditsinskogo.
47. Ibid., pp. 57–65.
48. *Taina tsarskikh ostankov.*
49. Popov.
50. Stepanov, *vagon absurda.*
51. *Taina tsarskikh ostankov*, pp. 111, 112.
52. Popov, p. 220.
53. Ibid., pp. 219, 220.
54. Ibid., p. 152–53.
55. A stamp on this document reads "KGB Archives. Without right of publication." It is not known from which KGB archives this document was obtained.
56. Popov, pp. 119, 120.
57. Ibid.
58. Diterikhs, pt. 1, pp. 41–44.
59. Bykov, *Poslednie dni Romanovykh,* p. 89.
60. Diterikhs, pt. 1, pp. 246, 248, 368.
61 Smirnov, pp. 35–38.
62. Popov, pp. 122, 123.
63. Ibid., pp. 135, 136.
64. Alekseev, pp. 102–3.
65. Massie, *Romanovy*, p. 139.
66. Popov, pp. 175, 176.
67. Ibid., pp. 178, 179.

68. *Taina tsarskikh ostankov*, p. 13.
69. Massie, *Romanovy*, pp. 255, 256.
70. Ibid., pp. 275, 276.
71. Ibid., pp. 211–23.
72. Popov, pp. 65–66.
73. Gryannik.
74. Popov, pp. 145–51.
75. Ibid., pp. 195–98; 77; 78; 79.
76. Cmetanina.
77. Ibid.
78. "Otechestvennye samozvantsy."

chapter 5

1. Andrei Valentinovich Kovalyov is a lieutenant colonel in the medical corps. A doctor of medicine (his dissertation was on "The Identification of an Individual according to the Characteristics of the Rib Cage Structure and the Spine"), from 1992 to 1994 he was a member of the scientific commission of the General Prosecutor's Office studying the remains discovered in the area of the Koptyaki road outside Ekaterinburg as well as the remains of Grand Duke Georgy Alexandrovich Romanov, which were exhumed from the Cathedral of Sts. Peter and Paul in St. Petersburg.
2. Vyacheslav Leonidovich Popov, a colonel in the medical corps, doctor of medicine, and professor, was the chief forensic medical expert of the military district from 1969 to 1974, and from 1992 to 1994 he was also a member of the scientific commission of the General Prosecutor's Office studying the remains discovered in the area of the Koptyaki road outside Ekaterinburg as well as the remains of Grand Duke Georgy Alexandrovich Romanov.
3. Kovalyov.
4. Popov, pp. 194–95.
5. Vadim Petrovich Petrov, a lieutenant colonel in the medical corps, a doctor of medicine (the topic of his dissertation was "Forensic Medical Expert Analysis in Establishing the Identity of a Deceased Individual"), and a professor, is a recognized specialist on identifying intelligence agents and partisans who died in World War II and the author of numerous methodologies for determining identity from photographs and for restoring a face from a skull.
6. Vadim Vadimovich Petrov, a candidate of medicine (his dissertation topic was "The Horizontal Diameter of the Iris and the Asymmetry of the Head in Forensic Medical Identification from the Skull and Photographs Taken in Life"), is a member of the St. Petersburg International Board of Attorneys.
7. Leonard Nikolaevich Gavrilov, a retired colonel, legal scholar, senior lecturer, and acting Leningrad criminal prosecutor, was director of the Criminology Laboratory at St. Petersburg University Law School.
8. Pankratov, p. 28.
9. Alekseev; Pankratov, pp. 422–23.
10. Radzinsky, *Nikolai II*.

chapter 6

1. Romanov; Massie, *Romanovy*, p. 415.
2. Massie, *Romanovy*, pp. 400–401.
3. Pavlovich.

pozvonochnika (rentgenologicheskoe i sudebno-meditsinskoe issledovaniia). 14.00.19—luchevaia diagnostika, luchevaia terapiia, 14.00.24—suedbnaia meditsina" [Identification of an Individual on the Basis of the Characteristics of the Structure of the Rib Cage and Spine (Radiological and Forensic Medical Research). 14.00.19—x-ray diagnosis and therapy, 14.00.24—forensic medicine]. Abstract of a dissertation in support of the degree of doctor of medical sciences. St. Petersburg, 1997, pp. 18–19.

Latyshev, A. K. "Lenin v rasstrele ne uchastvoval" [Lenin Had No Part in the Execution]. *Rodina,* 1993, No. 8, pp. 68–73.

Lukomsky, A. S. *Iz vospominanii* [From My Reminiscences]. Archive of the Russian Revolution, vol. 2. Berlin; Moscow, 1991.

Massie, R. *Nicholas and Alexandra: An Intimate Account of the Last of the Romanovs and the Fall of Imperial Russia.* New York, 1967. Translated from the English in *Roman-gazeta,* 1995, No. 2 (1248), 87 pages.

Massie, Robert K. *Romanovy. Posledniaia glava* [The Romanovs: The Final Chapter]. Translated from the English by T. Bushueva and I. Sokolova. Smolensk, 1996. 448 pages.

Miliukov, P. N. *Istoriia vtoroi russkoi revoliutsii* [The History of the Second Russian Revolution]. Vol. 1. Pt. 1. Sofia, 1921–1924.

Miliukov, P. N. *Vospominaniia* [Reminiscences]. Vol. 2. Moscow, 1990, 449 pages.

Mints, I., and A. Kakurin. "Grazhdanskaia voina v Rossii, 1918–1921" [The Civil War in Russia, 1918–1921]. In *Bol'shaia sovetskaia entsiklopediia* [The Great Soviet Encyclopedia], vol. 18. 1930. pp. 687–723.

Mosolov, A. A. *Pri dvore poslednego imperatora. Zapiski nachal'nika kantseliarii ministra dvora* [In the Court of the Last Emperor: Notes of the Head of the Chancellery of the Minister of the Court]. St. Petersburg, 1992, 265 pages.

Muranov, A., and V. Zviagintsev. *Dos'e na marshala. Iz istorii zakrytykh sudebnykh protsessov* [Dossier on a Marshal: From the History of the Closed Trials]. St. Petersburg, 1996.

Murzin, A. "O chem rasskazal pered smert'iu tsareubiitsa Petr Ermakov" [The Story the Regicide Peter Ermakov Told before His Death], *Komsomol'skaia pravda,* November 25, 1987, No. 217, pp. 1, 4.

Nazarov, G. "Avantiura Yakovleva" [Yakovlev's Escapade]. In *Vosprositel'nye znaki and mogilami* [Question Marks over the Graves]. Moscow, 1996, 304 pages, pp. 20–31.

"Obrashchenie uchastnikov nauchnoi konferentsii—Po tsarskomy delu" [Appeal of the Participants of the Scientific conference On the Tsar's Case]. *Sovetskaia Rossiia.* January 9, 1998, No.3 (11592), p. 3.

Oldenburg, S. S. *Tsarstvovanie imperatora Nikolaia II* [The Reign of Emperor Nicholas II]. Foreword by Iu. K. Meier. St. Petersburg, 1991. 672 pages.

"Otechestvennye samozvantsy" [Native Pretenders to the Throne]. *Itogi,* March 11, 1997, No. 10, p. 53.

Padenie tsarskogo rezhima. Stenograficheskie otchety doprosov i pokazanii, dannykh v 1917 g. v Chrezvychainoi sledstvennoi komissii Vremennogo pravitel'stva [The Fall of the Tsarist Regime: Transcripts of the Interrogations and Depositions Made in 1917 to the Extraordinary Investigative Commission of the Provisional Government]. Vols. 1–7. Leningrad and Moscow, 1924–1927, pp. 190, 197 (deposition of S. S. Khabalov at the March 22, 1917, session).

Paganutstsi, P. *Pravda ob ubiistve tsarskoi sem'i: Istoriko-kriticheskii ocherk* [The Truth about the Murder of the Tsar's Family: A Critical Historical Sketch]. Jordanville, N.Y., 1981, p. 138.

Paléologue, Maurice. *Tsarskaia Rossiia nakanune revoliutsii* [Tsarist Russia on the Eve of Revolution]. Translated from the French by D. Protopopov and F. Ge. Moscow, 1991, 494 pages.

Pankratov, V. S. *S tsarem v Tobol'ske: iz vospominanii* [With the Tsar in Tobolsk: From Reminiscences]. Moscow, 1990, 64 pages.

Pankratov, V. S. "V Tobolske" [In Tobolsk]. *Byloe,* 1924, No. 6, pp. 195–220.
Pares, B. *The Fate of the Russian Monarchy*. London, 1938.
Pavlovich, A. "Opium dlia naroda" [Opium for the People], *Novyi Peterburg,* October 3, 1997.
Perepiska Nikolaia i Aleksandry Romanovykh [Correspondence between Nicholas Romanov and Alexandra Romanova]. Foreword by M. P. Pokrovsky. 1914–1917. Vols. 1–5. Moscow and Leningrad, 1923–1927.
Pis'ma sviatykh tsarstvennykh muchenikov iz zatocheniia [Letters of the Holy Tsarist Martyrs from Their Imprisonment]. Collection under the editorship of E. E. Alfer'ev. Sviato-Preobrazhensky Valaamsky Monastery, 1996, 472 pages.
Pis'mo glavnogo sudebno-meditsinskogo eksperta Minzdrava RF ot 28.04.1992 g. [Letter of the Chief Forensic Specialist in the Russian Ministry of Health, April 28, 1992]. Archive of the Administration of the Government of Sverdlovsk Province.
Platonov, O. A. *Ternovyi venets Rossii. Zagovor tsareubiits* [Russia's Crown of Thorns: The Regicides' Conspiracy]. Moscow, 1996, 528 pages.
Popov, V. L. *Gde Vy. Vashe Velichestvo?* [Where Are You, Your Excellency?]. St. Petersburg, 1996. 305 pages.
Prishchev, V. I., and A. N. Aleksandrov. *Rassledovanie tsareubiistva: sekretnye dokumenty* [Investigation into the Regicide: Secret Documents]. Moscow, 1993, 336 pages.
Purishkevich, V. M. *Dnevnik* [Diary]. Moscow, 1990.
Rabochii kalendar' [Workers' Calendar]. 1924. Ekaterinburg, 1923. On the reverse of the page for July 21–23.
Radzinsky, E. S. *Gospodi . . . spasi i usmiri Rossiiu. Nikolai II: zhizn' i smert'* [Lord, Save and Pacify Russia. Nicholas II: Life and Death]. Moscow, 1996. 480 pages.
Radzinsky, E. S. *Nikolai II: zhizn' i smert'* [Nicholas II: His Life and Death]. Moscow, 1997, 512 pages.
Rodzianko, M. V. *Krushenie imperii* [The Collapse of an Empire]. Archive of the Russian Revolution, vol. 17. Berlin, 1923.
Romanov, Nikolai, Prince. "Ia ne gotov seichas obsuzhdat' problemu vosstanovlenie monarkhii v Rossii" [I'm Not Prepared Right Now to Discuss the Restoration of the Monarchy in Russia]. *Smena,* March 14, 1997, No. 56–57.
Ros, Nikolai "'Zapiska Iurovskogo' ili 'Zapiska Pokrovskogo'?" ["Yurovsky's Note" or "Pokrovsky's Note"?]. *Russkaia mysl',* 1997, April 10–16, No. 4168, p. 16.
Rossiia pered vtorym prishestviem [Russia before the Second Coming]. Moscow, 1995.
Russian Federation State Archive, f. 601, op. 2, ed. khr. 35, ll. 31–34.
Russkaia pravoslavnaia tserkov' i kommunisticheskoe gosudarstvo, 1917–1941 [The Russian Orthodox Church and the Communist State, 1917–1941].
Semenov, Iu. *S. Dvadtsatoe dekabria* [The Twentieth of December]. Serial screenplay, part 3.
Shaposhnikova, E. *Russkaia gazeta,* March 25, 1994.
Shavel'sky, Georgy. *Vospominaniia poslednego protopresvitera russkoi armii i flota* [Memoirs of the Last Archpresbyter of the Russian Army and Navy]. Vols. 1–2. Moscow, 1996, 415 pages.
Shirokorad, A. "'Krugom izmena, i trusost', i obman . . .'" [All Around Betrayal, Cowardice, and Deceit]. In *Voprositel'nye znaki nad mogilami* [Question Marks over the Graves]. Moscow, 1996, 304 pages.
Shul'gin, V. V. *Dni* [Days]. Moscow, 1989.
Smetanina, S. "Briussel'skaia mogila russkogo tsaria" [The Brussels Grave of the Russian Tsar]. *Kommersant deili,* February 10, 1998, No. 21, p. 2.
Smirnov, V. "Posledniaia taina tsarskoi sem'i" [The Last Secret of the Tsar's Family]. In *Voprositel'nye znaki nad mogilami* [Question Marks over the Graves]. Moscow, 1996, 304 pages.

Sokolov, K. *Popytka osvobozhdeniia tsarskoi sem'i.* Archive of the Russian Revolution, vol. 17. Berlin, 1921, pp. 280–93.

Sokolov, N. A. *Ubiistvo tsarskoi sem'i* [The Murder of the Tsar's Family]. Berlin, 1925.

Soloviev, V. N., and A. P. Sebentsov. Interview. *Obshchaia gazeta,* August 26, 1994.

Sorokin, P. A. *Dolgii put'. Avtobiograficheskii roman* [Long Journey: An Autobiographical Novel]. Syktyvkar, 1991, 304 pages.

Stepanov, A. "Vagon absurda. Voina ambitsii iz-za ostankov tsarskoi sem'i pozorit Rossiiu" [A Truckload of the Absurd: The War of Ambitions over the Remains of the Tsar's Family Will Bring Shame on Russia]. *Novye Izvestiia,* No. 17, November 27, 1997, pp. 1–2.

Sukhomlinov, V. A. *Vospominaniia* [Reminiscences]. Berlin, 1924.

Summers, A., and T. Mangold. *The File of the Tsar.* London, 1987.

Taina tsarskikh ostankov. Materialy nauchnoi konferentsii "Posledniaia stranitsa istorii tsarskoi sem'i: itogi izucheniia Ekaterinburgskoi tragedii" [Mystery of the Tsarist Remains: Materials from the Scientific Conference "The Final Page in the History of the Tsar's Family: Results from the Study of the Ekaterinburg Tragedy"]. Ekaterinburg, 1994. 145 pages.

Talberg, N. D. *Sviataia Rus'* [Holy Russia]. Paris, 1929.

Trewin, J. *House of Special Purpose.* New York, 1982.

Ubiistvo tsarskoi sem'i i ee svity. Ofitsial'nye dokumenty [The Murder of the Tsar's Family and Their Suite: Official Documents]. Constantinople, 1920.

USSR–Germany. 1939. *Dokumenty i materialy o sovetsko-germanskikh otnosheniiakh s aprelia po oktiabr' 1939 g* [Documents and Materials on Soviet–German Relations from April to October 1939]. Iu. Fel'shtinsky, comp. Vilnius, 1989. 128 pages.

USSR–Germany. 1939–1941. *Dokumenty i materialy o sovetsko-germanskikh otnosheniiakh s sentiabria 1939 po iiul' 1941 g* [Documents and Materials on Soviet–German Relations from September 1939 to July 1941]. Iu. Fel'shtinsky, comp. Vilnius, 1989. 192 pages.

Ventsenosnye velikomucheniki. Ubiistvo Nikolaia Romanova i ego sem'i [Thorn-bearing Great Martyrs: The Murder of Nicholas Romanov and His Family]. Compiled from original documents from the investigation files. Harbin, 1920.

Vertinsky, A. N. *Dorogoi dlinnoiu . . .* [Down a Long Road]. Moscow, 1990, 576 pages.

Vestnik dumskikh zhurnalistov, 1917, No. 4, p. 7.

Vilton, R. *Poslednie dni Romanovykh* [The Last Days of the Romanovs]. Translated from the English by Prince A. M. Volkonsky. Berlin, 1923.

Vitte, S.Iu. *Vospominaniia* [Reminiscences]. Vol. 2. Moscow, 1960.

Voeikov, V. I. *S tsarem i bez tsaria. Vospominaniia poslednego dvortsovogo komendanta gosudaria imperatora Nikolaia II* [With and without the Tsar: Reminiscences of the Last Commandant of the Court of the Sovereign Emperor Nicholas II]. Moscow, 1994. 272 pages.

Voitovich, N. "Segodnia kazhdyi delaet vybor. Interv'iu s imperatorom Nikolaem III" [Today Everyone Makes His Choice: Interview with Emperor Nicholas III]. *Kaleidoskop,* 1997, January–February, No. 5 (236), p. 7.

Yakovlev, V. V. (Miachin, K.). "Poslednii reis Romanovykh" [The Romanovs' Final Journey]. *Vospominaniia* (Urals), 1988, No. 8.

Yurovsky Note. *See* Zapiska Yurovsogo.

Zapiska Ermakova [The Ermakov Note]. Center for Documentation on Public Organizations in Sverdlovsk Province, inv. book Nos. 340, 2059, reprinted in Popov, pp. 38–41, and also in Alekseev and Kaeta, "Ot aresta, ch. 2," p. 5.

Zapiska Yurovskogo, 1920 [The Yurovsky Note, 1920]. Russian Federation State Archive, f. 601, op. 2, ll. 31–34.

Zhuk, A. B. *Revol'very i pistolety* [Revolvers and Pistols]. 2nd corrected, revised, and supplemented edition. Moscow, 1990. 432 pages.

index

Note: Page numbers in italics refer to illustrations.